Tigris River

River

yrna

ANATOLIA

phon

Miletus

RHODES

DITERR

E

The Etheredges

# FROM THE SILENT EARTH

*Introduction by*
*Sir Maurice Bowra*

*Photographs by*
*Alison Frantz*

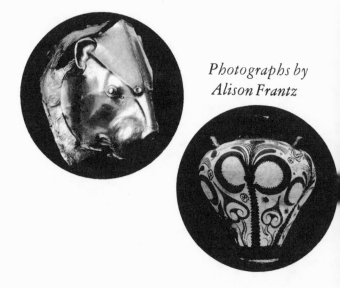

JOSEPH ALSOP DISCARDED

# FROM THE SILENT EARTH

*A Report on the Greek Bronze Age*

*Harper & Row, Publishers • New York • Evanston • London*

**GREENWOOD PRESS, PUBLISHERS**
WESTPORT, CONNECTICUT

Library of Congress Cataloging in Publication Data

Alsop, Joseph, 1910-
  From the silent earth.

    Reprint. Originally published: 1st ed. New York :
  Harper & Row, 1964.
    Bibliography: p.
    Includes index.
    1. Bronze age--Greece.  2. Civilization, Mycenaean.
  I. Title.
  DF220.A43  1981            938'.01            81-4122
  ISBN 0-313-23014-5 (lib. bdg.)                AACR2

This is a reprint of the First Edition, 1964.

Reprinted with the permission of Harper & Row Publishers, Inc.

Reprinted in 1981 by Greenwood Press
A division of Congressional Information Service, Inc.
88 Post Road West, Westport, Connecticut 06881

Printed in the United States of America

10 9 8 7 6 5 4 3 2 1

FOR SUSAN MARY

# INTRODUCTION

History is too serious a matter to be left exclusively to professional historians. Without them, of course, it would not exist, and theirs is the hard way to success in it. They look for new realms of discovery, establish new facts, sort out false theories from true, and provide a solid core of knowledge from which radiate in all directions the many varieties of historical writing which are so marked and welcome a feature of modern culture. Yet historians are hampered by the conditions and the obligations of their own task. They cannot but be cautious and, since much evidence is inadequate and often contradictory, they do not always find it easy to come to final decisions. To the outside world they seem to be too often attacking one another in controversy which is not the less enjoyable because it is acrimonious. They are liable to get stuck in certain problems which they cannot solve and will not relinquish, with the result that they fail to look beyond them to wider and more promising issues. In the last resort they are accused of being intelligible only to one another, either because they assume in their readers a wealth of technical information which only specialists possess or because they write in a technical jargon which has little relation to common speech and cannot be mastered without more time and trouble than most men have at their disposal. For these reasons they need interpreters if their work is to make an impact on other circles than their own, and the best interpreters are those whose interest is not confined to a single field but ranges over several fields with an enlightened curiosity. Such middlemen can do much more than translate the ideas of scholars into an easier language. They can amplify and illustrate and assess in wide terms what the scholars give them, and this is well worth doing; for without it the mass of educated men might find themselves starved in their civilized desire to know about the past. As learning inevitably becomes more and more specialized, the need for interpretation at a high and, in the best sense, popular level becomes an increasingly urgent need.

With admirable courage Mr. Joseph Alsop has chosen to write a book on a difficult and much-disputed subject, which demands for its specialist treatment a very high degree of technical knowledge from both philologists and archaeologists, to say nothing of historians. The unveiling of the lost world of Mycenaean Greece, of which the existence was not suspected until Heinrich Schliemann made his momentous excavations at Mycenae in 1874-1876, has in recent years entered a new and thrilling phase with the discovery in 1939 at Pylos of the palace of Nestor with its remarkable stock of inscribed clay tablets. When these were deciphered by Michael Ventris and proved, in the face of nearly all opinion, including that of Ventris himself, to contain an archaic form of Greek, the darkness had indeed been pierced, but, if many old doubts were shown to be worthless, many new questions arose and clamored to be answered. It was this combination of events which caught Mr. Alsop's imagination and so inflamed his curiosity that he felt impelled at all costs to master the subject and understand it for himself. The best, perhaps the only adequate, response to such a need is to write a book, and this Mr. Alsop has done for the best of all possible reasons. His book is a tribute to the commanding urgency which these questions have for him, to the demon which they have awakened and which he cannot but obey. It is partly a personal record, a straightforward account of a visit to Pylos with its discoverer, Professor C. W. Blegen, and this visit sets the scene for the speculations which follow. Professional scholars are usually shy of revealing their impulses and inspirations in this candid way, but Mr. Alsop has chosen wisely. Just because his book is at heart a personal document, it catches our interest from the start as it might not do nearly so easily if it were written in a distant and disembodied spirit. It is the story of a passionate devotion which refuses to be satisfied until it knows all that can be known about its beloved. But it is also the story of a triumphant feat of scholarship conducted by a great scholar. If the book has a hero, it is Professor Blegen, the most modest and most disinterested of men, whose judicious, wise, and yet imaginative and adventurous spirit has passed into these pages.

Mr. Alsop modestly claims that he is only a "political reporter," but hopes that his experience of politics will help him to understand this faraway world of heroic Greece. In this he is entirely justified. Comparison and analogy may at times be untrustworthy instruments of scholarship. They may try to prove too much and end by proving nothing. But in judicious hands they can do something that almost nothing else can; they can show how events which we find it hard to understand can be explained in this or that way, that strange and seemingly unique circumstances have illuminating parallels in other times and other climes, that though history does not repeat itself, it can often be most easily grasped if we compare one situation with another. The professional historian can hardly be expected to be at home over a wide tract of time or space or to extract enlightening analogies from outside his own field, but this lack may impoverish his contribution to learning and at times blind him to the truth or leave him undecided even when it stares him in the face. Moreover, analogies often give to remote events an immediacy and relevance and help us to understand them better by fitting them to something in our minds. Mr. Alsop does indeed make admirable use of his experience in political reporting, largely because he is much more than a political reporter. In his own profession part of his distinction comes from his being a well-trained and well-read historian, deeply concerned with the major movements of history and intimately acquainted not only with the United States and Europe but also with China both past and present. This enables him to examine the new Mycenaean discoveries with a fresh mind and to suggest, however tentatively, solutions which are very much his own and worthy of our close attention. He lacks the obstructing prepossessions and distorting loyalties of professional scholars and is not afraid of allowing his independent imagination to work freely on his material. He makes many apologies for speaking as an amateur, but not only is he much better informed than he allows us to think, but he has the great advantage of being uncommitted to any set of theories or any school of scholarship. He takes this lost world as he finds it, and applies his passionate curiosity to it.

The advantages of Mr. Alsop's independence are most clearly marked when he deals with topics which have excited and still excite anger and abuse among scholars. Why they should lose their tempers because someone disagrees with them is a dark chapter of morbid psychology, but *odium philologicum* undeniably exists and plays its baleful part even in Mycenaean studies. Mr. Alsop is aware of its slightly absurd side and at times displays a mild irritation with those pundits who are unable to treat each other with common courtesy. He even ventures into their battlefields, and more than once proves how useful his intervention can be. It has long been a matter for debate whether the splendid works of art found by Schliemann at Mycenae are the work of proto-Greeks or of Minoans from Crete. Schliemann held the first view, Arthur Evans the second, and for a time anyone who reverted to the earlier view was anathema. Now that we know that the Mycenaeans spoke Greek and must have been Greeks, the scale has again been tipped against the Minoans. Mr. Alsop, using his experienced eye for visible things, shows that the art of Knossos is essentially the same as that of Mycenae and pointedly asks how, at this stage of our knowledge, anyone can say with real assurance that "this art is Minoan" or "this art is Mycenaean." Instead, he proposes the compromise phrase, Greco-Minoan. But he also suggests the possibility that this compromise phrase may represent an historical reality—a true Greco-Minoan synthesis resulting from a Greek conquest of Knossos at a date early enough to explain the close similarities between the finest objects found in Crete and on the Greek mainland, and therefore a date much earlier than has been commonly supposed. On this hypothesis, two hundred years of history will have to be rewritten. Again, on the more generally accepted dating the records from Knossos are two hundred years earlier than those from Pylos, and yet the two sets are extraordinarily similar in almost every respect. How can we account for this? One way is to bring down the Knossos records to 1200, but this is regarded in some quarters as heresy, if not as blasphemy against Evans, who must have got his chronology sadly wrong. Another way is to accept the two dates as Evans gave them, and Mr. Alsop admits that after all this is possible. There *are* parallels to scripts remaining unchanged for long periods, and this explanation might be right.

As for the third solution of this knotty problem which Mr. Alsop puts forward as entirely possible, it may not in the end turn out to be correct; and he sensibly does not pretend to prove its correctness, merely saying that the record appears to contain no logical objections to this alternative solution, and asking, therefore, that it be inquired into. It is at least worthy of serious consideration, and inquiry is, therefore, in order. Chronologies depend on very delicate calculations, and it is easy to get them wrong. In the meanwhile an open mind on the matter will do more good than harm.

These are technical questions to which increased knowledge may in due course provide answers, but Mr. Alsop's insight ranges beyond such matters and is most happily at home in matters of wider interest. The collapse of the Mycenaean civilization was indeed an enormous catastrophe, from which it took the Greek peoples some five hundred years to recover. Even writing disappeared, and the Greeks remained illiterate until the arrival of the new alphabet about 750 B.C. The burnt ruins of Pylos and other cities pay their testimony to the speed and completeness of the general destruction. We are probably right to attribute this to the arrival of the Dorians from the northwest. We postulate that they triumphed because they used iron weapons against Mycenaean bronze. This is all easy enough, but Mr. Alsop has important comments to make on it. We must ask why the men of Pylos did not use iron weapons, of which they must have known, instead of bronze, and he points to the all too familiar conservatism of military men and draws an apt parallel from the cavalry with which the Poles, being a nation of horsemen, hoped to defeat the German tanks in 1939. But he probes deeper and asks why iron, which had not yet been strengthened into steel, was so effective against bronze. It would surely have buckled in use, and its mere existence explains very little. The answer is simply that iron, being much easier to obtain than bronze, enabled the Dorians to maintain a far larger force in battle than the Mycenaeans. This leads to the whole question of the number of men engaged in these high events, and the conclusion is that, by our standards, it was tiny. The small scale of the Mycenaean fortresses indicates that ancient wars were fought by a *corps d'élite*, as Homer indicates, and the whole population of Mycenaean Greece was probably smaller than that of modern Athens. The Greek losses at Troy were no doubt small indeed in comparison with the vast holocausts of our own time, but they were enough to weaken the Mycenaean world beyond any point of recovery. Even the Mycenaean conquest of Crete, which seems never to have been complete, may have been accomplished by a handful of determined and ruthless men, who had learned soldiering in some tougher school than the peaceful, mercantile Minoans and found no difficulty in defeating and dominating them.

The chapter of history which has so finely caught Mr. Alsop's imagination is perhaps still in its beginnings. We cannot forecast what unforeseen discoveries will be made by archaeologists or what progress will reward those grave and determined scholars who labor at the further interpretation of the Mycenaean records. Recent years have been generous with finds even in Greece, which has long been a fruitful field for excavation. Asia Minor still presents huge areas which have not been examined, and something may still come from the Aegean Islands, from Cyprus, or from Syria. Any new discovery may blow accepted theories sky-high and call for a new start and much reassessment of common opinions. Mr. Alsop is well aware that his theories are tentative, and that is part of their attraction for him. He has been so enthralled by what has been found that he feels a need to associate himself with other workers in this field and to make his own contribution to them. It is a world in which amateurs have played a distinguished part. Schliemann himself was a retired merchant, driven by a passion to prove that Homer told the truth; Michael Ventris was not a professional scholar but a gifted architect, who worked on the Mycenaean tablets in his spare time. Even Sir Arthur Evans, whose daemonic spirit still broods over Aegean excavations, did not begin his work at Knossos until he was over fifty years old. Mr. Alsop need not be shy of venturing into fields where other amateurs have ventured with triumphant success. He has consulted the best authorities, visited the important sites, thought deeply and carefully about what could have happened, and applied to it his own large knowledge of history. His book is meant for those who, like himself, lack the technical equipment to deal intimately with such matters, and they

xiii

will be delighted to find so sympathetic and so lively a guide. Nor should professionals dismiss what he says as below their notice. They will find their minds loosened and their interest exhilarated, if only because they must try to disprove some of his theses. There are many kinds of history, and one of the best is that which is born from a passionate concern for the past and an impelling desire to understand it. This is what Mr. Alsop has given us.

C. M. BOWRA

## PREFATORY NOTE

By its very oddity, this book requires a brief author's foreword. As a political reporter in Washington, my experience by now reaches back into prehistory, or at any rate what seems like prehistory from the perspective of the Johnson administration. But the middle years of Franklin Delano Roosevelt's New Deal are still considerably less remote than the Greek Bronze Age, so it may be reasonably inquired why the devil I am writing about it.

The answer is that this historical essay is the result, in a quite direct way, of two journeys. The first journey was a voyage of the mind. It began more years ago than I any longer care to count, when I started reading all the archaeological literature I could get my hands on. I am no expert; I am certainly not a Greek scholar; and I cannot give the meaning of a single character of the Mycenaean Greek script. But I have at least read just about everything concerning Crete and early Greece that has been published in my lifetime in the two languages I know, English and French; and I go on reading the new books, monographs and learned articles as they appear. As for the second journey, it was a trip to Pylos taken with the great American field archaeologist, C. W. Blegen. Concerning the second journey, enough has been said in this essay for those who care to read further.

The two journeys combined to produce such an unexpected result, for a rather simple reason. They convinced me that there was a gap worth filling and needing to be filled. The gap exists because, in all the learned disciplines, specialists now write more and more for other specialists. In fact, scholars more and more tend to communicate in private languages. This disease (for so I regard it) is not very far advanced among the archaeologists; yet it takes years and even decades of practice to learn to thread one's way with reasonable assurance through the mentions of pottery periods, the technical descriptions of different kinds of finds, the time references given in terms of "Late Helladic IIIB" instead of simple years B.C., and so on and on. In sum, the two journeys I have described convinced me that the remarkable story of the Greek Bronze Age, and the curious drama of that story's gradual recovery from the silent earth, were well worth putting into a book which would present none of the customary thorny difficulties to an intelligent, historically minded reader.

This original rather limited aim was then somewhat amplified, as the work progressed. It is impossible to write about a complex subject—or at least I cannot write about a complex subject—without carefully re-examining all the details and the probable relationships between the details. This re-examination convinced me that key parts of the archaeological record were demonstrably open to *political* interpretations that have not hitherto been suggested. I wish to emphasize the word political, for I have not ventured to judge the archaeological record itself, and with very minor exceptions, I have tried not to choose sides in the disputes about the record. I have merely ventured to apply to the record my own long, specialized experience as a political analyst. I hope that the reader—even the specialist reader—will be interested by the fairly unforeseen results of this attempt at political analysis. For these results, I claim no sort of finality. I merely suggest that they ought to be tested, along with the results of the more usual and, one must add, more expert approaches to the archaeological record. Within my own special field, I have dared to go thus far on my own.

A warning should be added to the foregoing. There are good practical reasons for what I have called the "Late Helladic IIIB" system of historical writing. All dates in the Bronze Age are conjectural within limits. What is not conjectural, or at least is much less conjectural, is the sequence of development, mainly revealed by changing styles in pottery. The experts use pottery periods because this does not involve them in a calculation of years B. C. which might be challenged by later facts. Dates thus given mean, quite simply, "the stage of development when pots were being made in the styles we have all decided to call Late Helladic IIIB"—which is obviously safer. Yet after decades of reading the literature I still find myself checked by the need to make hasty mental calculations every time a date is given in this manner. So I shall risk the use of years B.C. for all dates. Meanwhile, I have done all in my power to ensure that within the limits imposed by the nature of my project, this essay is as fully accurate, not only as to facts but also as to nuances and interpretation, as hard work can make it. The manuscript has indeed been read and minutely criticized by some of the greatest specialists in the field it covers, by whose friendship I have been honored. But I must take sole responsibility for everything herein; so I shall say no more, except to offer my respectful gratitude to Professor C. W. Blegen, who is this book's inspirer in a very real sense, and to acknowledge the generous help of Professor Sterling Dow, Professor Emmett L. Bennett, Jr., Dr. Emily Townsend Vermeule, Professor John L. Caskey, and Sir Maurice Bowra, whose introduction is a high honor. I must also acknowledge the great kindness shown me in the course of my work by Dr. John Kondis, Dr. Stylianos Alexiou, Professor Henri van Effenterre, Dr. Doro Levi, Professor James W. Graham, Dr. Truong Buu Lam, Dr. Li Chi, Dr. Hsu Cho-yun, Ambassador Edwin Reischauer, Professor Mitsusada Inouye, and Father Richard Rutt. On behalf of my colleague, Miss Alison Frantz, I should like to express special gratitude for the facilities extended by the great museums over which they preside, to Dr. Christos Karouzas, Dr. Nicholas Verdelis, Dr. Alexiou, and Dr. K. Davaras. And finally I must present my thanks and apologies to my wife, Susan Mary Jay Alsop, and my secretary, Miss Evelyn Puffenberger, whose patience and counsel were both continuously, even desperately needed throughout the period when this book was being written.

JOSEPH ALSOP

## CHRONOLOGICAL NOTE:

After problems of cult, the most contentious archaeological questions are those concerning chronology. For excellent reasons elsewhere explained, the professional students of the Bronze Age customarily use pottery periods to indicate chronology. For those who are interested, it may be noted that in the case of Crete, the Early Minoan Period extends from 2800 to 2000 B.C.; the Middle Minoan Period from 2000 to 1550 B.C.; and the Late Minoan Period from 1550 to 1100 B.C. This parallels the division of the Greek Story into the Early Helladic Period from somewhere between 3000 and 2500 to 1900 B.C.; the Middle Helladic Period from 1900 to 1580 B.C.; and the Late Helladic Period from 1580 to 1100 B.C. Unfortunately, "Late Helladic IIIb" means very little to the intelligent non-specialist reader. I have therefore dated events in simple years B.C. I must again emphasize, however, that this is a risky simplification; hence all dates must be regarded as no better than approximate, and in the early periods, before about 1400 B.C., as very crudely approximate.

That is not the end of the matter, either. In order to avoid burdening the text with endless ifs-and-buts about chronology, I have regularly used the dates that are now most generally accepted, even although these are currently being widely challenged and also contain certain internal inconsistencies. One such inconsistency arises from the fact that the dating system used for Mycenae by Professor George Mylonas differs slightly from the dating system used for Troy and Pylos by Professor C. W. Blegen. For this reason, Blegen's date for the fall of Troy, 1260 B.C., is ten years earlier than Mylonas' date for the Treasury of Atreus and the construction of the second Cyclopean walls at Mycenae. This order of events seems pretty doubtful, but as I am certainly not qualified to sit in judgment on Blegen and Mylonas, I have given their dates without further comment.

As to the above-noted challenges to the generally accepted dates, they are directed both to the beginning and the end of the chronology. In his fine dig at Lerna, Professor John Caskey of the University of Cincinnati found that the destruction level usually taken to indicate the arrival of the first Greek-speakers was considerably earlier than 1900 B.C.—the date of the accepted chronology. This led him to review the data from other major sites, with special emphasis on the Argolid. On the basis of this review, he has made a persuasive argument for pushing back the date of this destruction level for key parts of Greece, and hence, presumably, pushing back the date of the Greek-speakers' arrival in Greece, to 2100 B.C. Then too, many other proposed dates of events, notably including Professor Blegen's date for the fall of Troy, are in the main based on Arne Furumark's pottery sequence-dates. Among these, one of the most important is Furumark's terminal date for Late Helladic IIIb pottery, which is 1230 B.C. Near Eastern discoveries have lately led the English scholar, F. H. Stubbings, and some others to the conclusion that Furumark's terminus for LH IIIb is too early by about half a century. If this conclusion stands further testing, a whole series of other dates, including those of Mylonas for Mycenae as well as Blegen's dates for the fall of Troy and the destruction of Pylos, may have to be changed accordingly. These changes, if eventually agreed upon, will no doubt alter the detailed historical outline in quite important respects; for example, such changes can perhaps put the Trojan war *after* the first attack on Egypt of the "peoples of the sea," and they can hardly fail to place the Dorian invasion in a new chronological perspective.

But there is a crucial difference between the detailed historical outline and the basic outline. To illustrate, we may have to revise our picture of the detailed circumstances in which the Greeks prepared their expedition against Troy; but it is highly unlikely that the basic fact of the expedition itself will be successfully called into question. I have addressed myself exclusively to the problems that the basic historical outline poses. I do not think the aspect of these central problems will be radically transformed, even if all the date changes mentioned above are finally accepted by the scholarly consensus. Hence this brief note must serve as final warning to the reader about these disputed chronological points, which are so important to the specialists in the subject. J.A.

In Greece the past is omnipresent, and in all its epochs. Standing on the hill of Epano Englianos, you look down over slopes gray green with olive groves, to the blue waters of the Bay of Navarino. In 1827, the destruction of the Turkish fleet in Navarino Bay decided the hard fight for the independence of modern Greece. Beyond lies rocky Sphacteria. On this barren islet, in the seventh year of the Peloponnesian War, the Athenians forced the dreaded heavy infantry of Sparta to lay down their arms for the first time in men's memories. Thucydides tells us that this surrender of Spartan hoplites, who were trained to fight to victory or death, "surprised the Hellenes more than anything that happened" in the first great war among Western nations.

Yet these places with their historic stories are less ghost haunted, less redolent of the long, various past than the dusty little hill of Epano Englianos. The hill was only known as far as the next village, until just the other day, for the excellence of the olives from the trees that clothed its summit. But here the dean of American archaeologists, Professor Carl W. Blegen, has now uncovered the remains of a splendid, frescoed palace of the Greek Bronze Age. Here, if Blegen is correct, was the capital of Homer's "sandy Pylos." Here old Nestor, King of Pylos and the Polonius of the

1

*The Bay of Navarino from the road to Epano Englianos.*

*Iliad,* directed the muster of his ninety ships to go to Troy—the largest contingent in the *Iliad* ship list after the hundred ships of the Greek war leader, King Agamemnon of Mycenae "rich in gold." And here, a couple of generations or so after Troy had fallen, sudden disaster struck; and the palace of Nestor was burned to the ground; and oblivion descended on the hilltop, to endure for just a little more than three thousand years.

I went to Pylos not long ago with Professor Blegen, to see the remains of the palace. It seemed to rise before my eyes, and become peopled again, and resume the bustle of a powerful seat of government, as he quietly explained the meaning of what he had found. His discovery of the ruined foundations, where he and I poked happily about, was in fact only the first stage in a linked sequence of discoveries. Among the ruins, so to say, the Pylos of more than three thousand years ago was also found, and with such completeness that Professor Blegen talked about Nestor's kingdom as I might talk about Washington, D.C. And this resurrected Pylos of King Nestor in turn revealed the truth about the first great phase of Greek civilization, and hence, of course, about the earliest high period of our own Western civilization—if that is the right word for the culture of the jukebox-H-bomb

2

age. The truth that was thus revealed, it must be added, had its mildly ironical aspect. Pylos mainly proved that Greek civilization had always been Greek. But since a considerable majority of scholars and historians had believed the precise opposite for more than a century, the proofs that were found at Pylos came as something of a shock.

The irreverent pleasure of seeing the experts confounded, as they were by Pylos, is one of the many reasons for being an archaeological buff, which I am. In the rather short time since the landscape of the remote past began to be uncovered by the field archaeologists' spades, the experts have been confounded with remarkable regularity. The reason is always the same. Modern historians, who pride themselves on being scientific, have all the scientists' suspicion of the unproven and the traditional; and this is often a mistake. Thus the ancient tradition of China's Shang dynasty, during which Chinese society first took recognizable form, was never doubted from the lifetime of Confucius until the nineteenth century. Then science-minded Western historians sternly dismissed the Shang rulers as mere creatures of legend. Whereupon the last Shang capital was unearthed at An-yang, on the Yellow River; and the same royal names preserved in the traditional king lists were found inscribed on oracle bones by the Shang kings' official scapulomancers. In the same fashion, no one ever questioned the Rig-Veda's description of the Aryan conquest of India, when Nehru's Indo-European forebears poured down through the Himalayan passes to sack the walled cities "of the black men," until science-minded Western historians condemned the whole account as mere mythical moonshine. Whereupon the unknown pre-Aryan civilization of the Indus River Valley was unearthed at Mohenjo-Daro and Harappa; and these great cities of the forgotten past were found to have perished in just the way the Vedic bards described. In these two cases, the truth was re-established by a single swift stroke of discovery. The drama that culminated at Pylos was comparable, but it was also vastly richer both in triumphs and in ironies, and it took more than eighty years to unfold. Furthermore, the climactic Pylos chapter is hardly understandable without some understanding of this story's earlier chapters; so I shall try to summarize them briefly, hurrying as best I can over the more familiar ground.

The opening chapter's leading actor, the old German, Heinrich Schliemann, chose Homer as his private hero when he was still a boy in a poor Mecklenburg parsonage. Even as a boy, Schliemann was already indignant because, as the late Professor A. J. B. Wace once wrote, "practically no one [then] believed that the world of Homer had any real basis in fact." In Schliemann's boyhood, in the second quarter of the nineteenth century, devout persons still regarded the entire Old Testament as literally truthful, and were convinced of the accuracy of Archbishop Usher's chronology of world history, which set 4004 B.C. as the date of the creation. But the more remote past which every fairly well-educated man can now see with his mind's eye—the past of the great early civilizations of the Eastern Mediterranean and the Tigris-Euphrates Valley—was not suspected even by scholars. J.-F. Champollion had found the key to the Egyptian hieroglyphic

4

script in 1821, but many decades were still to elapse before Egyptian history began to be half-understood; and the history of Egypt was the first part of the landscape of the remote past to be explored in detail. As for the past's later-discovered provinces, like the Mesopotamian civilizations that began with Sumeria, the early Chinese and Indus Valley cultures already mentioned, the Hittite and other Anatolian cultures, the numerous and wonderfully rich pre-Columbian civilizations, the strange states that began to arise in Indonesia and Southeast Asia in the early centuries of the Christian era—all these and many more were quite unknown, and even unimagined unless there were conspicuous surviving monuments, as in the pre-Columbian case. Furthermore, some monuments that ought to have been conspicuous enough had never received scholarly attention. King Mongkut, the King of Siam of the musical comedy, had a model of Angkor Wat constructed in the grounds of one of his Bangkok temples, for instance; but the French "discovery" of Angkor occurred decades later. Other monuments, again, were not perceived for what they were. The great mound of Mohenjo-Daro, for one, was half destroyed in the Victorian era by British-Indian railway builders who mined the ruins for bricks. It was not until the early 1920's that more scientific digging began at this site, and at Harappa as well, at the order of a more enlightened British-Indian government. By the same token, ancient texts that now help to illuminate the remote past were either waiting to be discovered—by far the largest category—or such texts, although known, were regarded as wholly unhistorical. In the latter group, the Homeric epics were pre-eminent. Far more than today, the *Iliad* and *Odyssey* were part of the common heritage of all educated men and women; but almost all the most eminent Greek scholars were convinced that there was no history in Homer. Here was another irony. In the Middle Ages, when Greek was all but lost in the West, Agamemnon and Menelaus, Nestor, Achilles, Priam and Hector, were none the less accepted as true histori-

5

cal figures by everyone who had read history. But in the early nineteenth century, a period of the most flourishing Greek scholarship, Homer's heroes were widely held to be as mythical as the heroes of Ossian.

This was the state of affairs against which the boy Schliemann rebelled. He was not a scholar, either in his boyhood or later; but he was a good linguist—in his lifetime he mastered nine modern languages as well as Greek. When he read Homer, he became obsessed with the idea that Homer's story was true history as well as great poetry, and he wished to prove it. Nowadays, no doubt, he would have become an apprentice archaeologist; but archaeology as we know it had not even been invented. Schliemann ranks as one of the fathers of a new science precisely because the goal he adopted in his boyhood was then so entirely original. His goal was simply to prove the accuracy of Homer by digging up the buried remains of the Homeric past. Being a prudent Mecklenburger, he foresaw that the kind of digging he had in mind would be very expensive; so he set out

*Gold costume ornaments in the shape of octopi from the grave circle Schliemann found at Mycenae.*

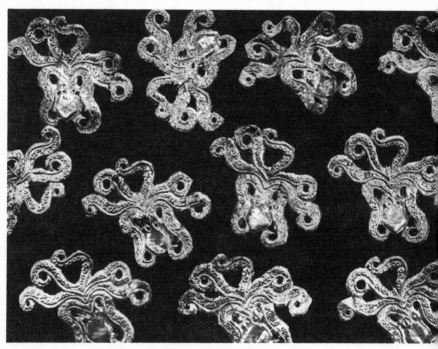

to make a fortune. Aided by the Crimean War, from which he made large profits, he acquired the needed fortune as a merchant in Russia, whereupon he promptly reverted to the pursuit of his boyhood aim. He began to dig at Troy in 1870; and he subsequently excavated Mycenae, Tiryns and Orchomenus and prospected Ithaca. The gold and electrum "Treasure of Priam," which he found at Troy, made a world-wide sensation considerably surpassing the later excitement about the tomb of Tutankhamen. The treasure-trove he found at Mycenae, in the royal grave circle within the citadel, was also the greatest single hoard of gold and silver, bronze and ivory, and other precious things that was ever discovered anywhere before Tutankhamen's tomb was opened; and the hoard included a golden death-mask which Schliemann promptly christened "the mask of Agamemnon."

Poor Schliemann! He had enormous luck, he won enormous fame, and he believed—for a while—that he had fully justified Homer by bringing to light the last mementoes of the two most powerful kings

*The "mask of Agamemnon."*

*Grave circle inside the citadel of Mycenae, discovered by Schliemann.*

of the *Iliad*. Yet he was wrong about his Priam, although he never knew it. The Troy-mound guards (or threatens) two major trade routes, from the Black Sea into the Aegean and from Europe into Asia Minor. In addition, the Troad has good land. The experts do not fully agree, even today, about the sources of Troy's wealth; but the remains show that this was a good site for a rich city. Here on the Hellespont nine cities therefore succeeded one another, from neolithic times until the early Byzantine period—from 3000 B.C. to A.D. 400 to be precise—for the site, being very profitable, was much fought over and never abandoned, except for a few hundred years in the deeply troubled times that came to the Eastern Mediterranean about a century and a half after Priam's city fell. Schliemann, however, had no notion of any of this. After being disappointed by the results of his first, relatively superficial earth-moving, he drove a deep trench straight through the whole mound, and therefore straight through close to three and a half millennia of history. The gold head ornaments and necklaces, the gold and electrum cups and vases and the bronze buckets of his "treasure of Priam" came from close to the bottom of the trench, from the second Troy. The second Troy is now known to have flourished from 2600 to 2300 B.C.; and this city of the treasure Schliemann found, was therefore more than a thousand years earlier than Priam's Troy which the Greeks destroyed.

As for Schliemann's Agamemnon, the wearer of the golden death-mask found at Mycenae was not the Greeks' war leader against Troy; but he at least belonged to the same line of kings. The royal grave circle inside the citadel, where Schliemann dug, is only one of several groups of Mycenaean royal tombs, and it was closed and perhaps covered over several centuries before Agamemnon came to the throne of the Lion-Kings. But in this case, after making a near-hit, Schliemann was bullied into repudiating his own greatest discovery. The tall diadems and heavy collars and gold masks and gold-and-silver-inlaid daggers and other objects in the Mycenae treasure-trove were splendid in themselves; but Schliemann's supreme discovery was not this splendid treasure. His supreme discovery was, rather, the previously unimagined Mycenaean civilization which had produced the treasure. The revelation that this high civilization had flourished in Greece in the Bronze Age, during the second millennium B.C., came as a nasty shock to the leading nineteenth-century Greek scholars. They had been teaching that the Greeks only began to emerge from barbarism during the iron age, some time after 1000 B.C.—a whole millennium later than the Bronze Age, in fact. The Phoenicians were also credited with bringing civilization to iron age Greece, because the Greeks of the early classical period developed the still-surviving Greek alphabet from the Semitic alphabet used in Tyre and Sidon. The experts therefore ganged up on Schliemann; there is no other way to put it.

Mycenae, the experts kept asserting in tones of vast authority, could not possibly be Greek. Schliemann, being so largely self-taught, held professional scholarship in awe. Hence he was finally hectored into agreeing that the Cyclopean fortress of Mycenae, now proven to be "rich in gold" just as Homer said, was nothing more nor less than a trading post planted in a savage land by the wealthy Phoenicians, the alleged civilizers of Greece. At this distance in time, it is hard to believe that anyone at all can have credited this extraordinary theory. Common-sensible eyes should have noted that the great walls of Mycenae were very unlike the stockade of a trading post; and there was the further difficulty that the almost equally strong-built citadel of Tiryns had been found by Schliemann down on the plain, only a few miles away from Mycenae up among the crags. It is still a puzzle how two such fortress-capitals can have co-existed with so small a distance between them. Nowadays, some scholars consequently argue that Tiryns was a Mycenaean dependency, being used as a winter palace, or to guard the port; although other scholars just as obstinately hold that Tiryns was the independent capital of Diomede, as

11

Homer said. How, then, can anyone have supposed that Phoenician traders could have needed, or have been able, to erect these two vast, almost neighboring piles of masonry, using single stones weighing many tons apiece, for the sole purpose of commerce with the barbarous Greeks? Yet this was the supposition, forced on Schliemann and almost everyone else by the reigning experts, and also accepted by Schliemann's very able lieutenant, Wilhelm Dörpfeld. The episode only goes to show what strait-jackets experts are capable of putting onto the hard facts, for the sole purpose of justifying their own preconceived notions. By this transference of the credit for the first flowering of Greece to the merchants of Tyre and Sidon, the new-found Mycenaean civilization was, in effect, quietly caused to disappear again. It was a fine feat of scholarly legerdemain, while it lasted.

In the next round of this odd contest between rediscovered truth and man-made error, the lead was taken by an Englishman of large means, immense learning and strong if somewhat tyrannical character. Sir Arthur Evans, to give him his later title, was one of the few scholars of the time who never heeded the nonsense about Phoenicians at Mycenae. It was clear to Evans from the outset that Mycenae must have been the capital of a powerful and wealthy state. But he was much troubled by Schliemann's failure to find any traces of writing, for he astutely reasoned that the Mycenaean rulers must have needed to keep records of some sort, if only for their tax rolls. Certain seals of Mediterranean origin inscribed with puzzling hieroglyphics were then turning up on the Athens antique market; Evans collected these, and in 1893 read a paper to the Hellenic Society announcing the discovery of a new Aegean script. At the same time, the seals caused him to follow the trail to Crete. In 1899, after surmounting many obstacles, he began to excavate the hill of Knossos. There he soon uncovered the huge palace of Minos—the Labyrinth of the story of Theseus, where they worshiped the Earth Mother, venerated as a cult

12

symbol *Labrys,* the sacred double ax, and loved to watch a strange, dance-like kind of bull baiting.

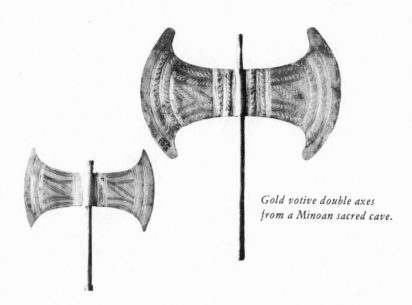

*Gold votive double axes
from a Minoan sacred cave.*

Besides wonderfully gay, life-celebrating frescoes, and remains of superb metalwork and stonework, and much magnificent pottery, and many other marvels including the world's first flush toilet, Evans found at Knossos precisely what he had set out to find. There was writing in plenty—not only the early, purely hieroglyphic form Evans had first noted on those seals; but also a different and later script which Evans called "Linear A"; and a still later, again different and very richly represented script, which he called "Linear B." Here was still another wholly unsuspected high civilization, enchanting, intensely creative, considerably earlier than the civilization found by Schliemann at Mycenae, and once again confirmatory of ancient stories long held to be legendary by all the experts.

In the sketch of earlier Greek history with which Thucydides introduced his incomparable account of the Peloponnesian War, there is a passage on "thalassocracies"—empires based on sea power, like the Athenian Empire that was overthrown by Sparta and her allies. The first thalassocracy, says Thucydides, was established by Minos, King of Crete, who was "the first person to organize a navy." This Minos of Thucydides, who is portrayed as a great Aegean ruler, planter of colonies and putter down of piracy, seemed to accord very ill indeed with the Minos of mythology, husband of Pasiphae, father of deserted Ariadne and still more wretched Phaedra, keeper of the Minotaur that Theseus killed. Thucydides was therefore held to have been foolishly credulous, until he was justified by the excavations of Sir Arthur Evans. Evans' Knossos was quite evidently the palace-capital of a great Cretan sea power, needing no walls because protected by its ships. Minos the man, meanwhile, was also depersonalized, so to say, by the discovery of Knossos. Minos, it was decided, was simply the customary title of every ruler of Knossos, as Pharaoh was in Egypt; and so the Minos of Thucydides and the Theseus legend was transformed from one king into a long line of kings, certainly comprising several dynasties.

Beginning with Sir Arthur Evans' first dramatic discoveries at Knossos, Aegean archaeology rapidly became intensely Knosso-centric; and so it remained for more than four decades. There are several reasons why this happened. To begin with, the Minoan civilization, as Evans called it after King Minos, was quite astonishingly rich and creative. In its high period, the palace at Knossos was an enormous structure—a great warren of grandiose halls and wide courts and luxurious private apartments and storage chambers, large and small, for wine and oil and grain and precious things. Simply in size, Knossos far surpassed Mycenae or any other main-land center as long as its prosperity endured; and Knossos was far from being alone in Crete. Almost at the same moment when Evans began to dig at Knossos, an Italian expedition started to uncover the palace of

14

The throne room at Knossos, restored by Evans.

*Gold ornaments from
Haghia Triada and
Knossos, c. 1500 B.C.*

Phaistos, in the fertile Messara plain, which may have been an even more important center than Knossos itself in the first phase of the Minoan story. As time went on, moreover, Mallia, Haghia Triada and other palaces and centers were added to Knossos and Phaistos; traces of roads were found linking to Knossos all the other major Cretan sites; and rich town houses were discovered clustering around the Knossos palace and some of the others. There were no serious fortifications anywhere; but there were important harbor works. Knossos alone had a major port at Amnisos and two more nearby harbors. All the evidence in fact pointed to a highly organized, refined and productive society, dependent on sea power for its defense and on sea-borne commerce for its prosperity.

Another reason for the long prevailing Knosso-centrism of Aegean scholarship was, quite simply, the sheer charm of so many of the things discovered in Crete. Here, at last, was a civilization of the dawn-

16

*Linear A tablet from
Haghia Triada and
Linear B tablet
from Knossos.
The tablets are
3 and 6 inches high.*

time which was not just strange, and impressive and seminal. Here was a beginning-civilization with everything from plumbing to pretty women in near-Parisian flounces and corsets, to make a twentieth-century scholar feel luxuriously at home. Yet the main reason for the long triumph of Knosso-centrism was, quite simply, chronology. Even on the basis of the recently shortened chronology, the Minoan story is a very long one, reaching backwards into the early third millennium before Christ, with the Cretan Bronze Age beginning perhaps as early as 2800 B.C. and certainly by 2500 B.C. As Knossos long predated Mycenae, and was so much more imposing, it was natural to conceive of Knossos as the very navel of the Aegean Bronze Age World.

The excavation of Knossos and the rediscovery of the glorious Minoan civilization, quite naturally earned for Sir Arthur Evans a unique position among Mediterranean archaeologists. His word was law for

17

almost everyone, from his first excavation of the palace of Minos until long after his death, at the age of ninety, in 1941. It cannot be said, however, that Evans always used his awe-inspiring authority with complete wisdom. He was overly possessive about his finds, for one thing. The clay tablets bearing the Linear B script composed by far the largest archive discovered at Knossos. No less than fifty different deposits of Linear B tablets were found; and most of these tablets were unearthed very early, in Evans' first years of digging. But as he uncovered more and more of the huge palace, Evans became more and more absorbed by the new wonders he was continually finding. As a result, although he quickly published his hieroglyphic and Linear A inscriptions, he never got around to publishing more than a handful of the Linear B tablets. Yet he would not allow anyone else to publish them either, and he became majestically angry when a Finnish scholar, Professor Johannes Sundwall, bootlegged copies of a beggarly thirty of the many hundreds of tablets. For half a century, in fact, the learned world had to put up with the frustration of knowing that these epoch-making Linear B tablets existed, while being altogether unable to get at the bulk of them.

Then too, besides hoarding his clay tablets, Evans rapidly succumbed to what can only be called Minoan imperialism. The origin of the Minoans remains in darkness to this day. Evans was only sure they had not been Greeks. Evans further thought that men of this mysterious Minoan race had never ceased to rule at Knossos until the terrible and final catastrophe which overtook the palace of Minos, in or about 1400 B.C. as he believed. Thinking that Knossos had always been Minoan, and seeing his superb palace as the undoubted navel of the early Mediterranean world, Evans therefore took to downgrading the Greeks. He began calling the civilization Schliemann had found at Mycenae "Minoan" rather than Mycenaean. This was, Evans said, no more than "the mainland branch of the Minoan culture"; and he further claimed that most of the finest things

18

found on the mainland were either imports from Crete or the handiwork of imported Minoan craftsmen. Until the destruction of the palace of Minos, Evans even maintained, Knossos had ruled over Mycenae, Tiryns and the other contemporary fortress-palaces in Greece; and their Greek populations had been one of the subject races of an Aegean empire sustained by the naval power of the Minoan kings of Crete. It was the old Phoenician trading post theory with a new Minoan-imperial twist. There is some substance, in fact, to the attack on Evans by L. R. Palmer, Professor of Comparative Philology at Oxford. At Knossos, says Palmer, "the spirit of the place entered into Evans; he seemed to put on the (bull) mask of the priest king and seat himself on the gypsum throne."

In Evans' lifetime, however, those who hinted that there might be a mistake somewhere got the shortest possible shrift. In particular, the full force of Evans' wrath was felt by a younger English archaeologist, the same Professor A. J. B. Wace already quoted on the view of Homer in Schliemann's youth. In 1920, Wace resumed the excavation of Mycenae with results almost as fruitful as Schliemann's. To Wace, and to the Greek, Chrestos Tsountas, who dug after Schliemann and before Wace, we largely owe the reconstruction of the history of the Lion Kingdom. The Mycenaean story began about 1900 B.C. or a little earlier. The first Greek-speaking peoples then emerged from the mists of Eur-Asia; and pushed into Greece with improved bronze weapons and (as is generally believed) with horses; and subjugated the previous inhabitants, who possessed no horses. As can be seen, therefore, there was at least a 500-year overlap between the beginning of the Mycenaean story and the destruction of Knossos, for which Evans gave the date of 1400 B.C. The question between Evans and Wace concerned what happened in this half millennium.

Wace concluded, to begin with, that Mycenae had always been politically independent; and thus he rejected the notion of a mainland empire of the kings of Crete, in which Sir Arthur Evans so strongly be-

19

*The palace of Knossos,
looking south.*

lieved. Wace of course admitted that the Cretans, who achieved civilization so much earlier, must have strongly influenced the Mycenaean beginnings, after the first Greek-speakers invaded and occupied Greece. But in his excavations at Mycenae, and in his careful studies of the earlier finds of Schliemann and Tsountas, Wace saw nothing to persuade him that Mycenae got everything worth having from Crete. In his opinion, all of the Mycenaean pottery and much of the bronzework and goldwork had a distinctive, native style. He claimed, therefore, that they were not Minoan, as Evans was now calling them, but truly Mycenaean as Schliemann had first called them. Nor did Wace stop there. He offered evidence that Mycenae, from about the middle of the second millennium B.C., had become more powerful and more commercially successful than Evans' Knossos. For example, a count of finds of imported pottery in Egypt was jointly made by Wace and

Blegen; and this count showed more pots in the Mycenaean style than pots from Knossos—which in turn indicated that Mycenae was Egypt's more important trading partner. Finally, Wace even dared to suggest that Greeks from Mycenae or one of the other mainland centers had actually conquered Knossos itself, and had ruled there for a while on the immemorial throne of Minos. This, Wace said, had happened during the glittering latest period of Knossos, the period of the "palace style" of which Evans was especially proud, between 1450 and 1400 B.C.

The Wace theory included a subsequent rebellion of the native Cretans, to explain the final burning of the Knossos palace in 1400 B.C. It will be familiar to readers of the first of Mary Renault's Theseus novels, *The King Must Die.* The theory's impact on Sir Arthur Evans may be imagined. His Linear B tablets were still unpublished, and the last volumes

21

of his majestic *Palace of Minos at Knossos* had not yet gone to press; but Evans took time off from his own discoveries to write a short book on the *Shaft Graves and Bee-Hive Tombs of Mycenae*. In this strange little volume he rather patronizingly sought to prove that Wace had completely reversed his Mycenaean chronology. In addition, it seems probable that Wace's heresy helped to prevent his reappointment as director of the British School at Athens. To be sure, he was not due for reappointment, since he had already served more than one term. But the success of his excavations at Mycenae would normally have led to his case being treated as rather special. Unfortunately, the opinions he had formed during those excavations were extremely unpopular, with Sir Arthur Evans above all. At any rate, he was not reappointed, and he had to interrupt his digging which had been sponsored by the British School.

The interruption of Wace's Mycenae excavations might have caused more general indignation if he had not been generally regarded as sadly heretical, and one must add, if he had not also gone on to make a brilliant career in other posts. The majority opinion was voiced in 1939, in J. D. S. Pendlebury's *Archaeology of Crete*. "In its relations with mainland Greece and the islands, the influence of Crete [was] overwhelming," wrote Pendlebury of the period when Mycenaean civilization was reaching its first peak. It was, he said, "impossible to avoid the conclusion" that all of the "rest of the Aegean" was "dominated politically" by Knossos, but he admitted that after the Minoan "conquest . . . as in [British] India, the native princes [of Greece] must have been allowed to continue ruling as vassals." As for the "mainland influence on the Knossian Palace Style" which Wace had discerned, Pendlebury said in a note, "I would regard [it] as resembling rather the Germanization of Palace circles in England after Queen Victoria's marriage." Such, then, was the state of the problem at the moment of the crucial intervention of my companion and leader on the journey to Pylos, Professor Blegen. From the murk that existed before

22

Schliemann, the archaeologists' spades had brought into the light palaces and shrines and tombs, jewelry and goldwork and carvings in ivory and vessels of bronze and silver and alabaster, a finished ceramic art and frescoes of a haunting loveliness, bronze weapons of every sort, three main kinds of writing, and many other things besides. But the writing was still undeciphered. The language or languages concealed behind the signs still remained to be identified. The key to the mystery remained to be supplied; and this was done by the American, Blegen.

Blegen today, in his seventies, is a markedly gentle, quiet-spoken man, whose exquisite manners belong to an earlier American era. He must have been just as gently polite as a young man, for he always managed to remain on friendly terms with Sir Arthur Evans—which was no mean feat, since Blegen was one of the few who openly sympathized with the outcast Wace. Blegen began his classical studies with his father, who was professor of Greek and Latin at a small Midwestern Lutheran college. He early acquired, and still retains, something of Schliemann's confidence in the historical reliability of Homer. He came out to Greece and began his career in field archaeology as a very young man, before the First World War. He made the first major installment of his towering reputation by a meticulously scientific re-excavation of the much-dug Troy-mound, whose real history had been sadly confused by Schliemann's untrained spadework, and not completely disentangled by the more careful further excavations of Schliemann's lieutenant Dörpfeld. In the late thirties Blegen's dig at Troy was finished. Being free again, he then began the prospecting for a new excavating site that resulted in the rediscovery of Pylos, the second Greek city of the Homeric age as indicated by the *Iliad* ship list.

Blegen's rediscovery of Pylos was different in character from Schliemann's excavation of Mycenae; for Mycenae had never ceased to be called Mycenae, and the great Lion Gate had never been lost to the sight of

23

men. In the classical age, to be sure, the Greeks were already somewhat puzzled because the most powerful capital of Homeric Greece had declined to a small country town, able to contribute only 74 men to the host that beat the Persians at Plataea.* But even when the town dwindled to a village, and even when the village was abandoned and the citadel was all but buried in the earth, the name Mycenae always clung to the place of the Lion Gate, high among the crags above the Argive plain. The location of Nestor's Pylos, in contrast, had been wholly forgotten even before the texts of the Homeric epics were standardized by order of the Athenian tyrant, Peisistratus, in the sixth century B.C. Where Pylos might have been was angrily debated by the Alexandrian Homer-experts of the Hellenistic period. The argument generated a surviving Greek epigram with the first line, "There is a Pylos before a Pylos, and there is another besides." At Athens, too, the Pylos mystery was so widely known that Aristophanes used it as a gag in one of his comedies; and Strabo, the Greek geographer of the Roman period, also wrestled with the problem at considerable length. Even today, scholars are still bandying back and forth quotations from old Nestor's cheerfully garrulous accounts of the glorious cattle raids of his youth, and other bits and pieces from the *Iliad* and *Odyssey* bearing on the location of Pylos; for a small minority of experts remains unconvinced that the palace found by Professor Blegen really belonged to Nestor.

"Let the future give the answer," Blegen replied tranquilly,

* *This stoutness in the cause of Greek independence in part caused the extinction of Mycenae's independence. Argos had held aloof from the resistance to the Persians, and the men of Argos were far from pleased to see the name of little Mycenae inscribed, along with Athens and Sparta and the rest, in the list of the saviors of Greece on the gilt bronze serpent-tripod the victors dedicated at Delphi, on which the name of Argos was so conspicuously absent. This was a major factor behind the Argives' successful surprise attack on the Mycenaeans. After this Mycenae, though still inhabited, was ruled from Argos. The serpent-tripod, incidentally, can still be seen at Istanbul, where it was probably taken by Constantine the Great when he founded his new capital of the Roman Empire.*

when I asked him about these doubters. "All I know is that I have found the capital of a rich kingdom, which is just about where Nestor's capital must have been. If someone else, later on, finds another, even finer palace in the same general area, then I'll be ready to agree that I've misplaced Nestor's Pylos."

The general area Professor Blegen here referred to is Messenia, in the Southwestern Peloponnese, which was the former kingdom of Nestor. After the First World War, several tholos-tombs—the beehive-shaped stone vaults, like the so-called Treasury of Atreus, in which Greek royalties of the late Bronze Age were so often buried—began to be spotted in Messenia. Where there had been royal burials, Blegen common-sensibly reasoned, there was bound to be a royal capital somewhere in the neighborhood. In 1938 and 1939, therefore, he spent some time spying out the most promising region on foot, making the first reconnaissance with his distinguished Greek working partner of that time, Constantine Kourouniotes. It must have been rough work. The Messenian countryside, though gloriously fertile, smiling and green even in the dry summer season, is a rough tumble of steep-sided hills divided by deep gorges; and the hilltops were the places where Blegen had to look. He had little to guide him except his own instinct and some observations already made by an archaeologically inclined village worthy, Charalambos Christopoulos, who felt so deeply about Greek history that he was once discovered weeping uncontrollably because he had suddenly remembered how Alexander the Great died young. In the olive grove on the summit of Epano Englianos, in the immediate neighborhood of indications of two tholos-tombs, Blegen was attracted by concrete-like masses protruding from the ground. His expert eye identified these outcrops as Bronze Age ruins of stone and adobe brick walls, fused together in a tremendous fire. The decision was made to dig at this site, which is just off the road from modern Pylos to the big hill village of Chora. He and Mrs. Blegen, who also is an archaeologist,

26

again obtained the financial support of Professor and Mrs. William T. Semple of the University of Cincinnati, the enlightened sponsors of the great dig at Troy. The Blegens organized an excavating team, and on April 4, 1939, they opened their trial trenches. The trenches were primarily laid out to avoid the olive trees, whose value was rising daily in the eyes of their owner. It was sheer luck, therefore, that the very first trench ran straight through the main archive room of a buried palace, almost immedi-

*A restored tholos tomb on the hill of Epano Englianos, which predates the building of the palace.*

*Linear B tablets
as they were found in
the archive room
(1939 photograph by
Carl W. Blegen).*

ately revealing a deposit of hundreds of clay tablets inscribed in the same
Linear B script that Evans had found at Knossos.

"They were the first Linear B tablets ever found on the Greek
mainland and the first too, since Evans' finds at Knossos, most of which
were nearly forty years earlier—so you can imagine how we felt," Professor
Blegen told me, and his eyes shone at the memory. "It was the time of the
spring rains. The ground was very damp, and the tablets were soggy and
horribly delicate. W. A. McDonald, who was with us that year, and I
spent day after day on our hands and knees, getting out the tablets one
by one. When we dried them on wire screens, they became almost as hard
as pottery; but still, each tablet had to be cleaned, inch by inch, with tooth-
picks. We didn't dare use acid then as we do now. It was a chore, I can
tell you—and we enjoyed every minute of it."

28

From the moment he saw the first tablets lying on the floor of the trench, Professor Blegen never doubted that he had at last located the much-disputed capital of King Nestor. He staked out his claim the same year, in his first report on the Pylos excavations. In this report, in the cautious, old-fashioned prose he reserves for such purposes, Professor Blegen also hinted that an archaeological-historical revolution was probably in the making. The discovery of the tablets at Pylos, he remarked rather stiffly, would "necessitate some revision of current theories [namely, the Evans theories] regarding the state of culture in the late Mycenaean world." To this he added a mild dig at a Scandinavian scholar, Professor Martin Nilsson, whose "picture [of the Mycenaean Greeks] as a body of illiterate adventurers who imposed their domination by a series of Viking raids" was "out of focus" with the "orderly methods of administration, so illuminatingly revealed by the tablets from our palace archives."

Unlike Evans, Blegen decided to publish his tablets with the least possible delay; yet a considerable delay was unavoidable, because the work at Pylos was harshly interrupted by the Second World War. Throughout the war years, the first batch of 600 tablets lay in the vaults of the Bank of Greece; and no work could be done except from photographs. When peace came, Blegen at once entrusted the tablets themselves to his student, Professor Emmett L. Bennett, Jr., the American who is now the leading authority on the subject. Bennett brought out his carefully edited edition of *The Pylos Tablets* in 1951. Only twelve years, including seven empty war years, had thus elapsed from first discovery to final publication, whereas a full fifty years went by, as we have seen, from the discovery of the main Knossos archive until Sir Arthur Evans' chosen successor, Sir John Myres, finally published his 1952 edition of the Linear B tablets from the palace at Knossos. Myres' work was far from dependable because of his great age; but it is more important to note that Bennett's work appeared a year earlier. For this quite simple reason, the tablets Professor

Blegen found at Pylos became the key that finally unlocked the mystery.

The man who found out how to use the key, and thus performed the most elegant and unexpected feat of recent scholarship, was a young English architect, Michael Ventris. Although only a spare-time classicist, Ventris had an unparalleled gift for languages, a deep knowledge of the Mediterranean past, and a remarkably orderly, visually retentive and penetrating mind. At a lecture for schoolboys given by Sir Arthur Evans, he first heard about the undeciphered scripts that had been used at Knossos. He was then only thirteen, but he immediately dedicated himself to deciphering these scripts—which had then been one of the chief riddles of the learned world for more than three decades. At eighteen, he had a paper on the subject accepted by the august *American Journal of Archaeology,* whose editors might well have been a bit shocked to learn the real age of their erudite new contributor. In the war, Ventris served as a bomber-navigator; and after the war, he was in active practice as an architect, with a family to take care of as well. Yet he succeeded in his self-imposed task in 1952, when he was barely thirty, and only one year after the publication of *The Pylos Tablets* at last gave him the mass of raw material he needed to break the code. With this help from Pylos, Ventris proved that Evans' Linear B script was a system of syllabic signs that had been used to write an exceedingly archaic form of Greek.

More than one book has already been written to explain how Ventris did it. For our purposes, a briefer account will serve. To begin at the beginning, the last thing Ventris expected was what he finally discovered. He himself believed that the Linear B hen-tracks concealed an early form of Etruscan—a gloomy choice, since the Italian documents in Etruscan, being written in a modified version of the Greek alphabet, began to be deciphered almost as soon as they began to be discovered; yet they remain unreadable to this day because the Etruscan language itself is still unknown. In 1949, moreover, Ventris sent a questionnaire to all the

*Linear B tablet from Knossos, 9 inches long.*

acknowledged grandees of Aegean learning, and collected their answers in a privately circulated paper called "The Languages of the Minoan and Mycenean Civilizations." G. Pugliese Carratelli and E. Peruzzi of Florence, E. Grumach, Fritz Schachermeyr of Vienna, and the others who answered Ventris offered widely varying diagnoses, but none of their proposed solutions of the Linear B problem was the solution that finally proved to be correct. On any journey, it is obviously far harder to reach your destination if you set off in a wholly wrong direction; and Ventris in effect did precisely that, with the encouragement of all the scholars he most respected. On the other hand, it should be noted that Ventris was considerably aided on his lonely journey by the work already done by others on the Linear B tablets.

The first, and perhaps the most important, of these precursors was Sir Arthur Evans himself. He had quickly realized that most if not all of the Linear B tablets were "business records, such as accounts and inventories." He had worked out the system of number-signs, which run from 1 to 10,000; and he had identified a good many of the ideograms, for weapons, animals and the like, which the script also contains. Certain other signs had also been tentatively read, like that for wine which was

31

spotted by the tablet bootlegger, Professor Sundwall; and Professor Bennett had made valuable suggestions. In fact, without Bennett's careful list of all the Linear B signs in *The Pylos Tablets,* Ventris' task would probably have been impossible. A most significant and original contribution had also been made by another American scholar, the late Miss Alice Kober, who had noticed that certain groups of signs regularly recurred in the same order, although with differing terminations. It was clear from the limited number of signs in Linear B that the script must be syllabic. Some signs were ideograms—actual pictures of the things represented—and other signs were numerals. But as this was clearly a syllabic script, each of the great majority of signs represented a single syllable or sound—as if the word "syllable" were written with four signs, *si-la-bu-le.* The recurring sign groups with differing endings therefore implied recurring series of identical syllables with changing endings; and this persuaded Miss Kober that the language of Linear B must have been inflected. In an inflected language, of course, the ends of words change according to their number or case, while the root remains the same, as in the Latin *Agricola* a farmer, *Agricolae* of a farmer, *Agricolam* a farmer in the accusative case, and so on. From these beginnings, Ventris then went forward by methods closely resembling those of the wartime code-breakers (although it is pure legend that breaking enemy codes was his wartime assignment). Without attempting to guess the sounds or meanings, he first analyzed the Linear B signs from every possible angle of approach—according to their frequency of occurrence, according to their occurrence in the declension-like formations pointed out by Miss Kober, and so on and on.

The essence of Ventris' work was the search for a pattern, or rather for patterns, among the signs; and for this he constructed tables of the signs, which he called "grids." In these grids he lined up horizontally or vertically the syllables he thought had the same consonant or vowel. He reduced the sign groups of frequent occurrence to rather well-defined

32

categories. And he formed an idea about just how the Linear B language was inflected—all this was done before he had successfully translated a single word or sign of Linear B. At each stage of his analysis, he kept other scholars interested in the subject abreast of his own progress, by circulating what he called "Work Notes." The turning point of his long effort appears in Work Note 20, dated 1 June, 1952, which was headed by the question: "Are the Knossos and Pylos tablets written in Greek?" The work note was based upon the supposition that sign groups which Ventris had placed in his Category 3 were in reality place names. He said of these sign-groups:

"They are . . . not personal names, and yet figure as the subjects of very varied lists of commodities, often recurring in fixed order . . . About a dozen [of these sign groups] . . . are found in a disproportionately large number of entries. From the analogy of the contemporary accounts from Ras Shamra/Ugarit . . . which should be our most valuable aids, I think it is likely that the Category 3 sign-groups correspond to the *towns and corporations of Ugarit.*'"

Here Ventris was referring to the cuneiform records uncovered by French excavators in the Syrian palace of Ras Shamra. In these records of receipts of taxes in kind, labor services performed, and the like, the towns of origin are regularly noted. On this analogy, he made the guess that a Category 3 sign-group in the tablets from Knossos referred to the harbor town of Amnisos, and he gave the group's four signs the values of *A-Mi-Ni-So*. If that guess was correct, he had the terminal syllable of Knossos; and he therefore read as *Ko-No-So* another three-sign group in Category 3 with the *So* terminal sign. From the starting point of these supposed sign values, he went on to find additional Greek words in his text. Yet he concluded his Work Note 20 with the warning that in the end "this line of decipherment" would probably "dissipate itself in absurdities." None the less, he continued along the same line, and before a month had

33

passed he had become convinced he had solved the long-standing riddle of Linear B. As it happened, he was asked by the BBC to deliver a Third Program lecture on Sir John Myres' edition of Knossos Linear B tablets, then just published at long last. He took the opportunity to announce:

"During the last few weeks, I have come to the conclusion that the Knossos and Pylos tablets must, after all, be written in Greek—a difficult and archaic Greek, seeing that it is five hundred years older than Homer and written in a rather abbreviated form, but Greek nevertheless."

One of those who heard this broadcast was the distinguished young English philologist, Dr. John Chadwick. Greatly stirred, he went off to call on Sir John Myres, a fellow don but at Oxford. Being Evans' scholarly heir, Myres was skeptical about Ventris' conclusion; but he gave Chadwick some of Ventris' Work Notes, which had been regularly sent to him. Using the Ventris grid of signs, Chadwick tackled the tablets on his own. Somewhat to his surprise, he quickly found a number of Greek words which Ventris had not deciphered. He wrote to Ventris, who at once proposed partnership; and thenceforward Ventris and Chadwick worked in tandem. They jointly signed both the preliminary paper that formally announced the great discovery to the world of scholarship in the autumn of 1952, and the big, authoritative book, *Documents in Mycenaean Greek,* which was published in 1956. Just as *The Pylos Tablets* gave Ventris the essential mass of raw material and a vitally needed dependable list of all Linear B signs, so Chadwick brought to the partnership the philological knowledge that was required for a sure analysis. Philology's techniques had to be employed, since reading Linear B Greek for the first time was like reading Chaucer's English for the first time. Yet Ventris alone accomplished the initial decipherment, as Chadwick is the first to admit; and even today, when a whole, dry-as-dust scholarly industry is carrying on where Ventris left off, it is hard not to feel there was something magical in this young man's solitary feat. Certainly it seemed magical at the time, precisely because it was so totally unexpected, and not least by Ventris himself. As for the established scholars in the field, their viewpoint can be judged, not only from their answers to Ventris' questionnaire in 1949, but also from their earlier comments on Professor Blegen's Pylos tablets when the existence of the Pylos archive was first revealed. One eminent authority suggested that the rude Greek King of Pylos must have hired Minoan scribes to handle his correspondence and accounts, much as illiterate medieval barons employed the church's clerks. Mere "loot" from a wild Greek pirate raid on the civilized shores of Crete, was the verdict on the Pylos tablets of another leading scholar, who rather lamely explained that the pirates must have been attracted to these dingy clay tablets adorned only with lines of hen-scratches, because they were supposed to be magical objects. Before Ventris, in fact, all but a tiny minority saw the Mediterranean past exclusively in terms of the Civilized-Minoan/Savage-Greek contrast that stemmed from Sir Arthur Evans' Minoan imperialism. Such was the picture that Ventris half turned upside down.

Ventris' feat did not of course diminish the great achievement of the discoverer of Knossos. The earlier, hieroglyphic and Linear A scripts that Evans found at Knossos remain undeciphered to this day, but it seems as certain as anything can be that they are not Greek. Hence the race that founded Knossos and ruled there for centuries was not a Greek race, just as Evans said. Furthermore, as we have seen, these still mysterious Minoans were already attaining a high civilization before the first emergence on the stage of history of the first true Greeks. As the man who rescued the superbly creative Minoans from the darkness of the past, Evans will always be remembered as a giant of archaeology. Ventris' feat very clearly proved, however, that Evans had been quite wrong and Wace had been largely right in the dispute that perhaps cost Wace his post at Athens. Once Linear B was shown to be Greek, it necessarily followed that Greeks must

*A three-handled "palace style" vase found on the eastern coast of the Greek mainland.*

have conquered Knossos, and must have ruled there in the period when the Knossos records were kept in Linear B.

As Wace had suspected, this almost certainly included, at a minimum, the glittering period of the "palace style," which Evans loved. In consequence, many of the finest Evans finds were abruptly transmuted. They ceased to be the latest, ripest fruits of the Minoan genius, and became instead the earliest masterworks of Greek art. In the same fashion, the Mycenaean civilization, which almost everyone except Wace had regarded as Minoan, was instead established as the Greek first-flowering. When Ventris announced his decipherment, the crash of long-established theories, the abrupt explosion of closely reasoned learned arguments, could be heard around the world. Normally, scholars are even less eager than most people to admit that they have been dead wrong. Yet Ventris' proofs were so elegantly watertight that most scholars accepted them soon after the first proofs of the decipherment were published at the end of 1952, without waiting for the much more complete evidence provided by *Documents in Mycenaean Greek* in 1956. It was as well that Ventris was allowed to savor his triumph so soon. He was killed in a motor accident while the book was in the press, when he was only thirty-four years old.

The story of how the Greeks at length got back the credit for their own earliest history and art has now been briefly related. The contest between truth and error was long, and tortuous in its course. Yet I confess to being oddly moved by this strange story of astonishing discoveries and equally astonishing misinterpretations, which only reached its climax when Blegen with his spade at Pylos, and Ventris with his "grids" in a London suburb, at last revealed the real geography of the central province of our own remote past. The story's completion brings us back to our starting point, which was a journey to Pylos with Professor Blegen. Normally, this kind of personal experience has no proper place in an historical essay. But all rules may be broken if there is a good excuse for doing so; and in this case, there are two good excuses. In the first place, if I can make others even half-see Pylos, even half-hear the Pylos story, as I saw the place and heard the story on this journey, the gain will be far greater than any imaginable gain from a more conventional presentation of the facts.

In the second place, but quite as important, comes what I suppose must be called the human excuse. Among all my contemporaries and semi-contemporaries whom I have missed knowing, Michael Ventris is one of

38

the half dozen I should most like to have known; by all accounts he had great charm as well as great gifts. When chance took me to Athens some time ago, I was equally eager to know Professor Blegen; when I came to know him, I was the very opposite of disappointed; and it seems to me that it may not be amiss to try to suggest what manner of man is this great pathfinder into the unknown past of the West. So with no further apologies, I shall begin at the beginning, when I boldly telephoned the Professor to ask if I could call upon him. He immediately proved to be one of those rare scholars (nowadays almost a vanishing race) who are pleased when outsiders show serious interest in their subjects. The happy upshot was an agreement to go to Pylos together. "It's a beautiful place," said Blegen simply, as though to explain he was not conferring an unusual favor by this promise to make a journey with a stranger. "I haven't seen Pylos since this year's digging season ended, and I'd like to see it again."

On the day named, I picked up the Professor at his quiet house in Athens. He turned out to be a short, wiry man, looking much younger than his years, with a fine shock of thick gray hair and a pleasant, humorous face in which the main features are bright blue, always observant eyes. Field archaeologists, like the painters who copy pictures in museums, must get used to strangers blundering in upon them. At any rate, he seemed to take me as much for granted as though I had arrived with a full complement of letters of introduction from the trustees of the University of Cincinnati, where he held his professorial appointment until he retired from teaching. On the somewhat asthmatic airplane to Kalamata, which is the airport for Pylos, we talked about the development of archaeological techniques since Schliemann's day. Schliemann has been charged with being a mere treasure-seeker—which is unjust, since illuminating the past was his true motive. The method Schliemann used, however, was to dig for objects—preferably valuable objects—and he dug with such abandon, as Professor Blegen remarked, "that a lot of people think he may well have found the main

Linear B archive of the palace at Mycenae, and thrown it away again without noticing that the tablets were not quite ordinary lumps of dirt." The thought of the lost records of the palace of the Atreids made Blegen momentarily pensive; but he resumed the conversation before long. Nowadays, in brief, archaeologists dig for history, with infinite care, sometimes using brushes instead of spades; and they record each find, no matter how minute and trivial-seeming, in the most meticulous and precise manner, showing time of finding, precise location in the dig, physical position with respect to earlier finds, and so on and on. In rediscovering their site's story, archaeologists have three major aids. In the first place, unless the terrain has been disturbed, by erosion, for instance, or by later construction with deep foundations, archaeologists are aided by the logical rule that "lower is earlier." Any reader of archaeological literature knows that they also need another rule, for it is maddening that some archaeologists number the phases through which their sites have passed from the modern surface to the bottom, so that the most recent phase has the lowest number, whereas others more patiently wait till they get down to bedrock or virgin soil, and then number their phases from the beginning to the end of their site's history. But that is by the way.

As for the archaeologists' second major aid, it is the simple fact that broken pottery is both valueless and almost indestructible. Since the first jug or dish was potted, people have thrown away broken pots. In any normal dig, pieces of pottery always vastly outnumber any other class of finds. If properly recorded, they can be arranged in a continuous sequence. The local development of pottery styles and shapes can then be recognized; thus the pottery-sequence becomes a rather exact kind of chronological table, usable at other ancient sites where the same sorts of pottery may later be found. When Schliemann dug the Troy-mound, he had no notion of pottery's value as a time-indicator; therefore the enormous mass of pottery he found was not sequentially recorded. Even Evans still belonged, essentially, to the formative era of archaeology, and he too did not pay enough attention to pots. He based his Early, Middle and Late Minoan dates quite largely on the theoretical dates of imported objects, such as Egyptian scarabs, which he found at different levels in the Knossos ruins. If he had more carefully recorded the associations with pottery of his most exciting finds, and above all of the Linear B tablet deposits, there would be much less room for controversy, nowadays, about basic problems of Minoan chronology and even about Evans' own archaeological honor. Finally, the third major aid of the modern archaeologist, without which it would be far more difficult to construct dependable pottery-sequences, is the fact that human beings lay down their debris as oceans do, in distinguishable layers or strata.

This human habit was much more marked in the Stone and Bronze Ages than it is today, for people were less clean in their housekeeping and the houses were also differently built. In many cultures, including early Troy, people simply let all sorts of household debris—bones from their meals, broken dishes and the like—accumulate on their houses' floors until the mess became past bearing, when they brought in fresh clay, smeared it over the mess, smoothed all down, and began again. ("The people of Troy V were disgustingly clean, though," Professor Blegen interjected with a grin. "Any archaeologist prefers dirty housekeepers.") In addition, in places like Troy where mud brick was the most common building material, all houses in the end simply collapsed with age, whereupon the householders just flattened the ruins and built a new house at the resulting higher level. This is why undisturbed ancient sites like Erbil in Iraq— the Arbela where Alexander won a battle—have been built up by their inhabitants, millennium after millennium, until the modern town now stands on a wholly man-made hill. The layers of accumulation are generally rather clearly distinguishable. At Troy, for instance, where Schliemann had gone straight down to the level of the second city, like a bulldozer, Wilhelm

Dörpfeld showed that there had been nine successive cities on the site; and Professor Blegen then found clear evidence of no less than 46 successive strata of occupation—many strata in the longer-lasting cities, and only one in Priam's Troy—beginning in the time before men could work any metal but copper, and even copper was rare, and ending in the time of the Byzantine Empire.

"It's sometimes hard for people who aren't trained to see the differences," he told me with another quiet twinkle. "But *we* can see them. I remember, we took a zoologist to Troy one season, because we had collected so many animal bones, which we had kept carefully separated, stratum by stratum. When our zoologist had worked through the earliest boxes of bones from Troy I, he was much disturbed. 'No horses,' he said; 'how can there be no horses?' I told him to be patient, and to wait until he came to the boxes from Troy VI; but he was not *very* patient. So when he finally reached the boxes from Troy VI—that was the city destroyed by an earthquake and rebuilt as Troy VIIA, which the Greeks destroyed— we almost had another earthquake. He came running to Mrs. Blegen and me after one look at the new bones, shouting: 'Horses! Horses! I've found lots of horses!' He even accused me of snooping around the boxes before I gave them to him. 'How did you know it otherwise?' he asked me. But really it wasn't very hard to foresee when horse bones would turn up. There were close links between the culture of Troy in this period and the Mycenaean culture in Greece. The Trojan War was almost like a war between cousins, if not brothers. As you know, it is generally believed that horses were first introduced into Greece by the first Greek-speaking invaders—though I must say we only have actual horse bones from Troy and Lerna. If the general belief is correct, moreover, the Greeks must have been much helped in their invasion of Greece because they were horsemen. Think of Cortes' horses and how they affected the Mexicans. In the same way, and at about the same time, a new people also destroyed the fifth Troy and built Troy VI; so it was natural for horses to turn up in the Troy VI levels."

I could not resist asking the Professor why he was so sure that Troy VIIA was the unlucky city of King Priam; and he replied confidently that there were four excellent reasons for the identification. First, the date of this Troy was right. Second, this Troy had been put to the torch. Third, unburied human bones had been found in this Troy's streets. ("You'd never have that, except in a city that was sacked.") And fourth, most of this Troy's houses had been very small, hastily built, much crowded together and characteristically equipped with large numbers of huge storage jars sunk into their floors. ("The people, you see, must have crowded inside the city walls for protection, and laid in good stocks to withstand the Greek siege. Normally, the humbler people lived outside the walls, as in Troy VI.") There was more talk of the same sort, which gave one the feeling of listening to a great detective discoursing on clues. Very soon, however, the airplane reached Kalamata, and Troy was instantly forgotten in favor of Pylos. I all but expected the Professor to recite, "My foot is on my native heath," as he greeted the chauffeur of the waiting car, who was an old friend; and shook hands with the airport manager, another old friend; and eagerly ordered the chauffeur to "drive straight to the palace"—for he wanted to see his ruins much more than he wanted an early luncheon, which I had timidly suggested. Once in the car, I soon discovered two quite unforeseen traits in my companion. However deep in talk he might be, those blue eyes never ceased to survey the passing landscape, which was, for him, a short summary of the history of this part of Greece. "Venetian work; they ruled here too," he would say suddenly, as a small aqueduct showed up ahead, around one of the breath-taking hairpin curves which characterize the Messenian roads. Or, pointing to a seemingly undistinguished hill just coming into view, "Mycenaean remains up there—a small settlement. The whole countryside was dotted with them." Or, pointing to a village house

43

only remarkable in my eyes for the luxuriant, pink-flowered, tree-sized begonias growing in gasoline tins in its front yard, "Built in Turkish times, no doubt; not many of them left."

All this made me feel a bit like those spectators at tennis matches who are to be seen swiveling their heads backwards and forwards, from court to court, as they follow the play of the ball. But in my case the feat was more difficult, for I was continually glancing forwards and backwards, first at the immediate, real landscape when Professor Blegen found something worth pointing out, and then at the landscape of the past that he quietly but quite wonderfully conjured up in the intervals. His power to make the past real was the second Blegen trait that struck me. The conjuring trick began with that Mycenaean hilltop settlement. "The remains there are not very promising," the Professor remarked, "but they date from the

*Gold seal with crested griffin, from a Pylos tomb predating Nestor's palace.*

period before Nestor's palace." And with that he was off, at the archaeological equivalent of a hand gallop.

The first Greeks, he said, probably came into this rich Messenia
at the time of the general movement of the first Greek-speaking tribes into
Greece, toward the beginning of the second millennium B.C. Long before
Nestor's Pylos, there were other, pettier kingdoms, or perhaps one should
call them baronies, each with its hilltop fortress, and its tholos-tombs for
the ruling family, and its fighting men and artisans and peasants to till
the land—the last named, perhaps, from the old stock the Greeks had
overwhelmed. This was the state of Messenia until very late in the Age of
Bronze. In truth, the slow development of the western part of Greece is one
of the still unresolved mysteries. Mycenae, Tiryns, and all the other more
important early-founded kingdoms of the Greek Bronze Age were on the
eastern side of the country. In Crete, too, the earliest major centers were
at the eastern end of the island; and the same east-to-west movement took
place there that took place in Greece, although of course at an earlier date.
The reason may have been the greater accessibility of the eastern sites to
trans-Aegean trade; but no one quite knows. At any rate, Messenia only
came under centralized rule about 1300 B.C., and this was centuries after
the kingdoms of Mycenae and Tiryns were well established and beginning
to be strong and rich. According to the legend which Professor Blegen
accepts as probably representing the truth in a broad way, most of Messenia
was finally united in a single kingdom by Neleus, father of Nestor, and a
prince of Thessaly by birth. The legend does not indicate how Neleus came
down from northern Greece and won his Messenian kingdom. But some of
the smaller and earlier settlements, including one on the hilltop of Epano
Englianos, were burned to the ground and came to an end at the time when
the first part of the palace at Pylos was built by Neleus. Other settlements,
in contrast, survived intact until Nestor's palace also went up in flames.
So one may imagine some of the hill-barons making their peace and giving

45

their fealty to Neleus, while others resisted Neleus and his Thessalian warband, and suffered the consequences.

Finally, peace reigned again in Messenia, and Neleus chose the hilltop of Epano Englianos as the site of his seat of government. Perhaps he made this choice because the hilltop was already a fairly major center. Ironically enough, at any rate, those handsome royal tombs that helped to lead Professor Blegen to Nestor's palace turned out, when excavated, to belong to a time before Neleus and Nestor; and this suggests that the earlier rulers on Epano Englianos were also prosperous and strong. Certainly Neleus was exceptionally confident of the peace he had established. He never troubled to rebuild the walls of the old settlement on the little hilltop. Instead, unlike most of his kingly contemporaries of the Mycenaean age, he was content with a handsome but wholly unfortified palace. (This was why the memory of Pylos was lost for so long; the great defensive walls, giant-built the Greeks believed, were what preserved the memory of Mycenae and Tiryns.) Neleus' palace was constructed about 1300 B.C.; and here Nestor was presumably born, to rule, as Homer says, "through

46

*The hill of Epano Englianos.
The roof over Nestor's
palace is visible
to the center left.*

three generations of men"; and to enlarge the palace of his father; and to be succeeded by others of his line until the disaster struck of which I have already spoken.

Talking of these matters, we had crossed the range that separates Kalamata from Navarino Bay, and had cut across the rich coastal plain, with its banana trees and citrus plantations, and had wound upwards again, in the direction of Mount Aigaleon, whose great crag lords it over the local hills. Olive groves, fig orchards and vineyards in full fruit continuously alternated on the hillsides; and since this was the time of grape harvest, every hillside was strangely but beautifully ornamented with patterns, sometimes circular, sometimes of rectangles, of the deepest, most velvety brownish-purple—drying floors, where the newly plucked currant-grapes were being turned into raisins by long days in the golden sun. Quite abruptly, after a last fairly horrifying series of hairpin turns, we were confronted by a wire fence surrounding a steep-sided, table-shaped hilltop, like a much smaller, less stony version of the Acropolis at Athens. "Here we are; I'm glad to be back," said Professor Blegen, with obvious delight.

He positively leaped from the car and all but embraced the foreman of his excavating crew, Dionysios Androutsakis, who serves as palace guardian between digging seasons.

I have to confess that I was not well prepared for the first sight of the palace of Nestor. To protect the uncovered ruins from the weather,

*The palace of Nestor before the site was roofed over, photographed from the entrance portico. The foundation of the great gate tower is in the right foreground; opposite, left, is the archive room with a bench. The large area in the center of the photograph is the court of honor. Beyond it are the vestibule with sentry post and the megaron and hearth.*

the Greek government has put up an enormous steel structure. Members that appear to have been borrowed from a giant meccano set support what seems like a quarter of an acre of corrugated iron roof. Like most ruins, the ruins of Nestor's palace are low and dusty-seeming; and the immediate impact of these stumps of walls and bits of floors, lying under their protec-

tive corrugated iron, is the very opposite of romantic, haunting and beautiful. The visitor to the palace of Nestor who depends exclusively on the pleasures of the eye must be content with the view over the surrounding hills and down to the sea, which is incomparable. But I was lucky enough to have Professor Blegen, to give me another kind of view of the palace in its greatest days, with the helmeted sentries at the gates, and the subjects of King Nestor coming and going, to pay their taxes or present their petitions, and the King himself in his high hall.

Nestor's palace, it must be understood, was not at all like Versailles. Bronze Age Greek kingdoms were not grandiose nation-states. The whole area of Messenia ruled by King Nestor probably covered less than 100 miles along the coast and 50 miles inland. His entire armed forces probably did not number more than a few thousand men, together, of course, with those 90 ships that went to Troy. Bronze, it must be remembered, was a rare, almost semiprecious metal. As long as it was the only metal of military value, very small numbers of bronze-possessing fighting men could dominate rather considerable subject populations; but no Greek Bronze Age kingdom was on a really big scale. For Greece of the Bronze Age, Nestor's palace was very grand indeed, being the size of an exceptionally large modern country house, with main buildings irregularly covering an area approximately 180 feet wide and 150 feet deep. Thus it had more actual living-space than the palace at Mycenae, though it would have been dwarfed, of course, by the whole fortress-citadel complex from which Agamemnon ruled his lands. Nestor built his palace on the system still prevailing on the Greek islands, with most of the living rooms on the more airy second floor, and a ground floor given over to storerooms, offices and the like—except that the state rooms and some of the royal apartments were also on the ground floor, for easy public access. The ruins uncovered by Professor Blegen naturally show only the ground-floor plan; and as there were dozens of storerooms and offices, mostly very small, the ruins struck me as an unreadable maze on first inspection. Seeing me a bit cast down, Professor Blegen took over in his kindly way.

"We're standing," he said encouragingly, "where the road ended that led from the town below to the palace on the hill. The whole hilltop was cleared by Neleus and reserved for the palace alone. There (pointing to a large, circular depression in the pavement) is the foundation of the big column that held up the entrance portico. Look; you can see the column was fluted, from the impressions left by the flutings in that plaster molding

*Traces of a fluted wooden column in the palace of Nestor.*

which decorated the base of the column. There (pointing to a square, very massive foundation to the right of the portico pavement) was the great gate tower. The royal guards probably lived in it. And there (pointing to a stone platform on the left) was the place of the sentry at the gate.

All the other stands for sentries were placed to the right of the doors they guarded. But this sentry had another door to guard besides the main entrance of the palace; for there (pointing to another stone foundation to the left of the sentry's stand) were the offices of the collector of internal revenue, where we found the first tablets."

It was difficult to believe, for a moment, that the small, square chamber defined by the low foundation walls was the famous Pylos archive room, where the key to so much truth about our remote beginnings lay hidden, for so long, in the quiet earth. But there it was, with a low stucco bench running around the cramped walls, which may have partly served as a shelf on which the presiding palace official kept his baskets and boxes of clay tablet records, although there were probably wall shelves above as well. And there, in the slightly larger anteroom, was the base on which, in King Nestor's time, there stood a gigantic pottery jar into which Nestor's subjects poured their tax oil. The people of Bronze Age Messenia paid their taxes in kind, in olive oil and other things. To this very fact, we partly owe the preservation of most of the Pylos tablets, of which a total of 1,000 or more were finally unearthed in the archive room and its anteroom.

"If the tax oil hadn't been there when the palace was destroyed, ready to burst into the hottest flames and to cook the tablets thoroughly, most of the tablets would probably have disintegrated before we came along," Professor Blegen explained cheerfully.

The tablets, in truth, were not the permanent records of Nestor's scribes, or of the scribes of Knossos, or of Mycenae—where a few tablets were found by none other than Professor Wace when he finally resumed digging there. Permanent records, if any, were kept on parchment, on wood, or perhaps on paper traded out of Egypt; and they have long since disappeared. The tablets were temporary records—the accounts of each year, most probably—which were either pulped or thrown away or allowed to crumble into dust when they were no longer needed, as people used to

52

throw away used checkbooks before the Internal Revenue Service made the preservation of used checkbooks so important. Clay, being cheap, was used as the raw material for the tablets because the tablets were not required to last for more than a year or so. They range from notebook size to the size of the page of a large book. The scribes patted the finely purified clay into the desired shape (leaving fingerprints which are now being studied to determine whether individual scribes had their own accounting specialties). The damp tablets were then smoothed on one side to receive the Linear B hen-scratches; and after that the tablets were simply left to dry, which made them hard enough to last the required year or so, but no longer than a year or so in normal circumstances. Being made of clay, however, the tablets were baked into a sort of quasi terracotta when the buildings containing them were burned. This was how all tablets that have come down to us were in fact preserved. Palace burnings saved the palace records; in death, and only by death, the scribes of the tablets left their story behind them.

Many scribes were needed—Professor Bennett has tentatively identified the handwritings of more than forty among the Pylos tablets—because Bronze Age kingdoms like Nestor's were highly centralized and bureaucratically controlled. One reason for this bureaucratic centralization became apparent when Professor Blegen led the way onwards, from the archive room and tax collector's office, to the long series of storerooms for pottery and oil and wine. The truth is that Nestor's kingdom was also a major commercial enterprise engaged in a far-flung trade, mingled, very probably, with occasional bouts of piracy; and Nestor's palace was also, at least in part, a large commercial warehouse. The quantities of pottery stored in the palace were downright staggering. A single small pantry contained the fragments of 2,853 drinking cups, all shaped like champagne glasses with handles. A good many scholars therefore believe that Nestor dealt in pottery as well as other goods. Professor Blegen, who prefers to

*Heap of drinking cups from the pantry.*

think of Nestor as a great gentleman, much dislikes this part of the theory about Nestor-the-merchant.

"I just don't believe the King traded in anything as petty as pots," he told me, as we looked at the ruins of the wine cup pantry. "I suspect that they needed such a lot of wine cups because, on grand occasions, they used to break them after drinking from them, as was done with the wineglasses when toasts were drunk in some officers' messes in the nineteenth century. I know we found mountains of fragments on the slopes of the hill. But there's no doubt at all that oil was exported, both in crude form and after processing; and I think many other commodities were also traded."

The oil stores are the most extensive of the workaday rooms in the palace of Nestor, with row upon row of huge jars, into which, no doubt, the tax oil was transferred whenever the gigantic jar in the tax collector's office reached the brimming-over point. In these oil stores, too, was found a major clue to another archaeological puzzle. For decades, scholars had been arguing about the prevalence, among Bronze Age pottery remains in the Mediterranean, of a most impractical-looking, narrow-necked, narrow-mouthed type of pitcher which the experts, for their own strange reasons, like to call a stirrup jar. Stirrup jars were found in the Pylos palace, and in one of the oil stores were clay tablets recording the issuance of aromatics and other substances to "the unguent boilers." These

54

*Stirrup jars from Pylos (photograph by Carl W. Blegen).*

finds are thought to have greatly strengthened the previously made suggestion that the stirrup-jar pitchers, which had the virtue of being easy to
stopper, were the standard commercial oil containers; and it is further
agreed that a major luxury export of the Greek Bronze Age kingdoms was
probably the perfumed oil and ointment produced by those "unguent
boilers." All the Mediterranean peoples of the Bronze Age had an odd taste
for slathering themselves with perfumed oil. At Egyptian dinner parties,
as the tomb pictures show, the guests even put cones of scented ointment
on their heads and let the greasy stuff melt and run down over their bodies
as the evening's festivities progressed. Even the cemetery workmen of the
Theban City of the Dead once went on strike, in part at least, because they
had "no ointment," as their surviving list of complaints states.

Greece and Crete were, and are, the principal olive oil producing
regions of the Eastern Mediterranean, and every Greek hillside is odorous
with aromatic herbs. The evidence for a large oil trade at Nestor's Pylos is
reinforced by evidence from Agamemnon's Mycenae, where the stirrup-jar-
pitchers were also unearthed in an oil context. Professor Wace even called
the structure outside the citadel walls, in which he found most of his tablets
in his second round of digging at Mycenae, "the house of the oil merchant." (But this designation is also criticized, because many scholars believe that the oil trade, along with all other commerce, was a royal monopoly in the Bronze Age Greek kingdoms; and this rules out the existence

of a free enterprise oil merchant.) In oil exports, at any rate, and particularly in exports of costly perfumed oils, we now have at least part of the explanation of the vast quantities of gold found at Mycenae, and of the beads of amber from the faraway Baltic, and fragments of gold and silver and niello work, and the bits of amethyst and carnelian and ivory and other precious substances, which indicate that the palace of Nestor was very magnificent indeed before it was sacked and burned.

"The *Iliad* tells us," remarked Professor Blegen, "that Nestor's drinking cup was gold-studded and so heavy that only the King himself could lift it and drink from it. That must have been a bit hard on him as he got on in years. But it suggests that if we ever have the luck to find an intact royal tomb here in Pylos, which I don't think likely, the treasures will compare with the Mycenae treasures, almost all of which came from the tombs."

We had now made the circuit of the pottery pantries and oil stores. These were the outer rooms of the main palace building, in which the state rooms formed the central core. Our circuit had all but brought us back to our starting point, in the tax collector's office; and so we began again, passing the gateway sentry stand, crossing the threshold where the great gates once stood, and entering the court of honor with its traces of broad columned porches. "Suppose we were calling on the King, to pay our respects or for some other reason," said Professor Blegen, smiling as though in mild mockery of his own make-believe. "Then we should have been led in here to wait our turn." "Here" was a suite of two small waiting rooms to the left of the court of honor. One room was provided with a neatly stuccoed bench, and it also had a large stand in one corner. "The world's oldest surviving bar, as far as I can recall," said the Professor, with a grin. "Wine jars stood there, and one must suppose that guests were offered a drink while they waited on the bench for the King to receive them. The wine cups were kept in the next room; you can see them on the floor." And there they were indeed, in a broken mass calcined together by fire. Nestor's palace had been ready to receive guests until its last hour, but its last guests were bitterly unwelcome. Thinking of that final scene of ruin and pillage and arson, we returned to the court of honor, as the more welcome guests of Nestor must have done when called to the royal presence. Just as they had done, we passed another threshold with a sentry's stand to the right of it. This brought us to a long anteroom or hall. At either end of this hall there had been doors opening onto the two staircases that led to the upper story of the palace. In the hall's center had been the door of honor, which had been guarded by still another sentry. Going through, we stood at last in Nestor's throne room.

"Over there," said Professor Blegen, pointing to a place in the middle of the right-hand wall, "was where the throne stood. We have no part of it, for it was not stone like the great throne at Knossos. It would have been like the descriptions of very richly ornamented chairs in the tablets."

Marked out only by low foundations, the space of the throne room did not seem large; but in its heyday, as Professor Blegen vividly described it, this *megaron,* as the experts would call it, must have been a very fine room indeed. It was close to square—43 feet wide and 37 feet deep, to be exact. In the center of the pavement was the great ceremonial hearth, circular, with a raised border, and 13 feet in diameter. Around the hearth four huge fluted columns had once stood; and these in turn supported a large, square cupola or clerestory. Windows around the sides of this cupola were the throne room's source of light, and in the center of its roof there was an immense terracotta chimney, to carry off the smoke from the hearth—the pieces were discovered in the ruins, and it was the first such chimney ever found in any Bronze Age palace. The cupola's roof must have been about 30 feet above the smoking embers of the hearth, for the throne room was high ceilinged and the cupola, of course, was higher

still. This whole high, wide space, moreover, had been brilliantly colored
—the floors stuccoed, the walls frescoed, and (this one cannot prove but
cannot doubt) the wood of the columns and doors, wainscoting and ceiling beams, all brightly painted.

The whole palace had been decorated in this manner, except for

*The throne room,
photographed from a point
opposite the one on page 48.
In the foreground are
storage rooms for wine and oil;
the throne stood
against the wall, to the left
of the hearth as seen in
the photograph.*

the workrooms and storerooms; but the throne room, rather naturally, had received special attention. The stuccoed pavement was laid out in squares, with alternating geometric patterns of extreme intricacy in red, yellow, blue, black and white, with a fine naturalistic black octopus (no doubt honoring an already favorite Greek food) in a special square before the throne.

*The parapet of the hearth. Note the layers of stucco revealing repeated redecoration.*

The parapet of the great hearth was likewise decorated in black and bright colors, with dog-tooth flames below and complexly convoluted spirals above. All sorts of frescoed scenes covered the walls—a lyre player survives —with the space behind the throne reserved for two wide-winged royal griffins, heraldically confronted, with couchant lions behind them. All the colors, too, were fresh and clear; the numerous superimposed layers of stucco on the hearth parapet reveal that redecoration was ordered whenever shabbiness set in. Even the wall frescoes seem to have been removed and renewed from time to time, for great numbers of fragments, quite untouched by fire, have been found in a sort of dump on the hillside below the palace.

Altogether, the setting King Nestor contrived for himself evidently mingled splendor and gaiety in about equal proportions. One can be quite sure how it looked without seeing more than the dull and dusty

*Lyre-player fresco from the throne room at Pylos, restored by Piet de Jong.*

fragments that survive. As Professor Blegen showed me while we were studying the throne room, all the details I have given above were cautiously deduced from tiny but unchallengeable pieces of hard evidence, like the layered stucco of the hearth, which proves the frequency of redecoration. And as Professor Blegen also pointed out, one does not need to stop with the evidence provided by the throne room itself.

One is justified in picturing the vanished throne as being like the chair in one of the clay tablet inventories, which was "of crystal, inlaid with cyanus, tin (?) and gold," with back and sides inlaid in gold with human figures, stags' heads, bulls' heads and palm trees. On some such splendid seat, with its matching, golden-strutted footstool, one may reasonably imagine the King himself, for a ceremonial occasion quite probably wearing an immensely tall gold diadem like those that survive from Mycenae, perhaps with lilies and peacock feathers rising above the diadem's golden

61

points, as in the Knossos fresco bas relief, the portrait of the priest-king. In like fashion, the pieced-together frescoes found at Pylos, together with those from Knossos and from Tiryns, permit us to summon up the living appearance of King Nestor's court—the young men naked-torsoed, ringleted, wearing rich necklaces, with their middles fashionably cinched by the ornamented belts of their drawers; the ladies in long flounced dresses, bright colored and richly patterned; the guards in cone-shaped helmets encrusted with polished boars' tusks, carrying tall spears. Strange, it must have been, but beautiful as well, and no less beautiful because not too vast in scale or number.

From the hint of discipline in those door-guarding sentry stands, and from the clay tablets, we know too that, though small, this court was orderly and even hierarchical. The existence of a noble class may safely be inferred from the tablets, because the higher personages, like those characterized as the King's "Companions," are always named as "Alectryon son of Eteocles," for instance; whereas everyone else is in effect treated as "not born" in the detestable phrase of Proust's Faubourg St.-Germain. (But the parentage of sons and daughters of slaves was recorded, because this made them slaves too.) Also from the tablets, we learn that after the King, the

*The priest-king, painted stucco bas relief, from Knossos.*

*Procession fresco from Knossos.*

most powerful person in the state was the *Lawagetas,* which means "Leader of the War Host," whose office carried with it special lands of its own, on the same footing as the royal lands and those held by the gods. For the latest period, we can even identify the greatest individual landowner of Pylos, after the King and the *Lawagetas* and the gods. He was a certain Echelawon, while the last steward of the kingdom, or perhaps of the royal household, was a certain Alxoitas. Was it Alxoitas who sat daily in the tax collector's office, or was it one of his subordinates or colleagues? One would like to be sure, but the scribes' records of the inventories taken of the kingdom's cattle, and aromatics given to the unguent boilers, and other such transactions by this busy Alxoitas, do not tell us where we should have found him in his long-past office hours.

In contrast, it is pretty clear where we should have found the King himself in his less formal moments. On the left-hand side of the court of honor, in the last part of the main palace that Professor Blegen led me to, there were two modest but pleasant rooms which gave onto an enclosed court where water was piped in. Here, if Blegen is right, was the King's place of private work and relaxation. The enclosed court was built much later than the rest of the palace. It may be permissible to guess that the enclosure was ordered by the last King of Pylos, because Greece was already troubled; and the Pylian ruler was beginning to be fearful

*Fresco from the Queen's Hall at Pylos, restored by Piet de Jong.*

*Nestor's bath.*

of the future, and wished to be alone, sometimes, in a quiet place filled with green things in tubs and with a soothing sound of water.

In this corner of the palace, too, there is the Queen's hall, like a smaller, more delicately decorated version of the great throne room. The walls, here, bore an alternating pattern of feminine-seeming wingless griffins and lithe lions or leopards; there were floors painted with octopi and dolphins in the adjoining boudoir and toilet; and this suite of the Queen's also had its enclosed court, which still shows odd lines of holes in the stucco floor. These holes, Professor Blegen thinks, were most probably made for light movable fences used to keep the royal children within bounds, as we use playpens. And as though all this were not vivid and evocative enough, the Professor had saved the best to the last.

After the throne room his proudest exhibit was the bath of Nestor, which lies between the King's apartments and the Queen's hall. The bathtub, dumbbell shaped, generously large, of painted pottery, is still in place on its dais-like stand. The great jars that held water for the bath were also found in their accustomed corner, just as, in the Queen's toilet, water jugs were unearthed in a neat though broken row, having been ready to the last to be used for hand-washing or for flushing the pierced toilet stone. In Nestor's bathtub, moreover, there was a large wine cup, whether to be used for pouring water over the bather "or for pouring wine into him, we don't know," Professor Blegen remarked with a grin. Then, quite abruptly, he turned dead-serious and began quoting a passage from the third book of the *Odyssey*, which tells how Odysseus' son, Telemachus, visited King Nestor in Pylos in search of news about his father from Odysseus' old war comrade. The passage describes how "Polykaste, a fair girl, Nestor's youngest," led Telemachus to the palace bathroom; and after bathing him first, then rubbing him with oil,

> *She held fine clothes and a cloak to put around him,*
> *When he came godlike from the bathing place.*

"That happened here," said the Professor with confident finality, as we walked out into the late-afternoon sun, away from the stuffy shade of the corrugated iron roof. It had taken much time to examine all the many rooms of the main palace. When we finished, I felt sure Professor Blegen was right that Nestor had built this whole large structure at one time, to a well-drawn plan. Indeed the plan had been good enough to re-quire only the bare minimum of later changes by Nestor's two or three successors, who ruled the Pylian kingdom in the period between the old King's death and the day when the palace was overtaken by catastrophe. As we stood idle, enjoying the sunlight for a moment, Blegen explained the way the palace was constructed. The outer walls were faced with large, handsomely cut limestone blocks; but of these only a few survive, because the Venetians quarried the ruins for the cut stone in their time of rule in western Greece. ("We know they did it," said the Professor, "because we found a Venetian gold ducat just where the foreman of the quarrymen might have dropped it, deep in a foundation.") Behind the stone facing, there was rubble fill; but huge timbers were the structure's real supporting members. ("Look," said the Professor, pointing to a still blackened channel running through a foundation wall, "you can see where the timber burned, and the grain of the wood has even left its marks behind.") In its first phase, the interior of the palace may even have looked like English half-timbered work. Later, all the interior wall surfaces were smoothly plastered over, maybe to receive larger areas of fresco. But the timbers remained behind the plaster; and when the end came, the great quantities of wood, together with the huge stores of olive oil in the palace, ensured an inferno-like fire.

"It's too bad," said Professor Blegen, looking momentarily downcast. "To be sure, the sack of the palace was evidently pretty efficient, so we shouldn't have got any more fine things, even with a weak fire. So far as we can judge, the looters missed nothing of real value except a quantity of women's ivory toilet articles. In the fire, what was left of these ivory objects fell from the women's rooms on the second floor into one of the ground-floor storerooms, where we found large numbers of charred bits and pieces of ivory. We also found the remains of a silver cup, decorated with warriors' heads in gold and niello work; but that turned up near the main gateway, where it might easily have been dropped by a last looter running from the flames. All the same, if the fire had not been so very hot, we might at least have got one or two almost intact frescoes—something big like that; you never know. Still, we have to thank the flames for baking our tablets so well."

With that consoling thought, we resumed our inspection of the hilltop, on which the main palace built by Nestor was only the central and most important structure. To complete our picture of the whole palace, we went first to the older wing, which was presumably constructed by Neleus after Messenia had submitted to his rule. He had a free choice of

67

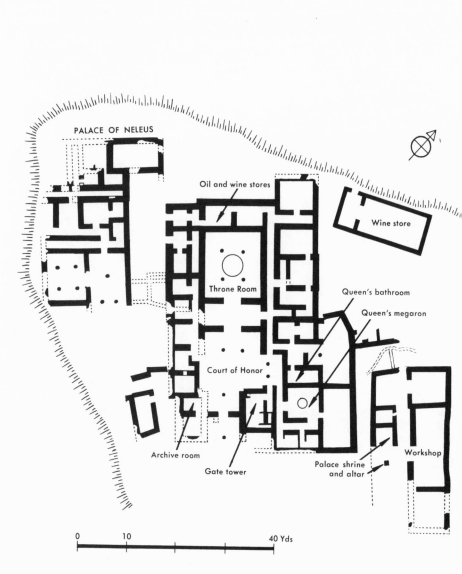

*Floor plan of Nestor's palace (after Blegen).*

site, like his unknown earliest predecessors (for there are ruins 600 to 700 years earlier than Neleus under Neleus' foundations). So he chose the site with the best view, on the very brink of the narrow hilltop, where nothing lay between him and the ocean far below except another ocean of bright air. Later, perhaps, after Nestor put up the main palace, the old palace of Neleus became the dwelling of the Crown Prince or the Queen Dowager of Pylos. It retained the necessary state rooms—a long, columned throne room, with a fine columned antechamber strangely frescoed with pink hunting hounds. Nearby there had been a kitchen, where many cooking pots were found. I had previously been puzzled by the apparent absence of any sort of cooking arrangements in the main palace. Hence I ventured to ask Professor Blegen whether Nestor, instead of turning his father's palace over to his mother or his son, might not have converted the old throne room of Neleus into his own banqueting hall.

It was the only time, in this whole journey with Professor Blegen, when I saw the smallest sign of the archaeologists' professional deformation—which is each archaeologist's utter absorption in his private picture of the past, to the almost complete exclusion of any other possible picture. The Professor, who believes in the Crown Prince-Queen Dowager theory, answered my question about a banqueting hall with a slight chill in his voice. "I doubt it very much," he said shortly. But a little later his gentle fairness got the better of him. As we were inspecting the place where the cooking pots were found, he volunteered a further statement: "I suppose there *is* a possibility that it was a banqueting hall. Indeed, one of the Greek archaeologists has made the same suggestion. But I still doubt it. The descriptions in Homer suggest that the Bronze Age Kings used their throne rooms for their feasts. After all, the great hearth in Nestor's throne room is quite big enough for roasting an ox."

Since the part of the palace attributed to Neleus stood on the steep brink of the hill, much of it has been altogether lost by erosion.

We had to clamber over the last, most tumbled part of the ruin, but here another problem that had been bothering me was resolved by my companion. "A main drain, there," he said, pointing to a stone channel running through the deepest foundations. "Must have got clogged once, for the whole thing had been dug up at one time. We can tell from the renewal of the stonework at the top of the drain. The fact is, the whole place is full of drains. They cared about plumbing, like the people at Knossos. They got their water from a spring on the next hill, which is a bit higher than this one. It was brought in by aqueduct—probably an aqueduct with wooden pipes. At any rate, there was an aqueduct of some sort, for we've found the traces."

From the old palace wing, we again crossed the little plaza in front of the great gateway. Beyond, there were traces of foundations which Professor Blegen thinks are the remains of a small private shrine attached to the palace. This seems likely because in this place stone fragments turned up of a "horn of consecration"—the same thing that is meant when the Bible mentions "the horns of the altar." These horn-shaped altar attachments were used in a good many Mediterranean cults. Before the Mycenaeans, the Minoans had them; and they have been found in Asia Minor and in Syria. The Pylos "horn of consecration" was comparatively small, which was natural, since the palace shrine was a tiny structure, hardly bigger than a good-sized closet. The chief sanctuary of Pylos, not on the palace hilltop but apparently not far away, belonged to *Potnia,* "The Lady," and this sanctuary held wide lands in the name of "The Lady." The principal male deity was Poseidon, and several of the other classical Greek gods were worshiped, probably including Demeter and Persephone, and certainly including Zeus and Hera, although the later King and Queen of Olympus were far less important, in Nestor's day, than the Lady-Earth Mother and Sea King-Poseidon. The "silent ones"—the dead—also received sacrifices, and there is more than a hint of a cult of a Clan Hero, or Divine Ancestor. If

70

*Gold ornament in the form of
an altar with horns of consecration and doves.
From the grave circle found by Schliemann
at Mycenae. Height c. 3½ inches;
sixteenth century* B.C.

*A model of a similar shrine from Knossos.*

this last interpretation of one of the Pylos tablets is correct, the little shrine of Nestor's palace was perhaps shared by the Earth Mother and the Clan Hero of the race of Neleus. The Neleids were of course god-begotten. All the more ancient royal lineages in Greece claimed divine origins, and even in classical times most people accepted the claim of the twin lines of Kings of Sparta to be descended from Heracles.

At the shrine, we were nearing the end of our ramble through the past, which had already taken many hours. Beyond the shrine's slight remnants, Professor Blegen pointed out the foundations of a large building that had been identified as the palace workshop by tablets recording chariot repairs, metalwork and leatherwork. Beyond this, again, was another large foundation where we paused for a while; for Professor Blegen, though abstemious, is something of a bon vivant, and this was Nestor's wine store, which the Professor likes to show off. The wine was not stored in the French manner, being kept aboveground in long rows of big jars, but it was handled with a degree of method that would do credit to a French *sommelier*. Many clay sealings giving vineyards of origin were found here, and the years of the different *crus* were also recorded. "We know they cared about the age of the wine," said the Professor proudly, "because Homer tells us so. When Telemachus landed in Pylos in search of Odysseus, they were celebrating the festival of Poseidon, down on the beach. As was only polite, Nestor offered the stranger meat and wine from the feast; and after he had eaten and drunk, when good manners finally permitted the question, Nestor asked him, 'Who are you? And from what lineage?' When Telemachus told Nestor he was the son of Odysseus, searching for his lost father, the old King made him come up to the palace— wouldn't take no for an answer, in fact, although Telemachus thought he ought to get on with his search. And the very first thing that Nestor did when they reached the palace was to call for the best wine. Homer specifies that the wine they broached was 'in its eleventh year.' "

So we came to the end at last. I had asked how he and Mrs. Blegen and the other members of his excavating team lived on the dig; and the Professor led me through the olive trees, on the untouched part of the hilltop, to show me their open-air dining table canopied by the largest, oldest olive of them all. "It's pleasant here," he said, "and we are like a family. I try never to have strangers. Professor Mabel Lang of Bryn Mawr, who has cleaned most of the frescoes, has done seven seasons with us; and Dr. Marion Rawson, who counted the 2,853 wine cups in that pantry, has been with us eleven seasons. On a dig, you have to live as a family lives— our house is over there in the village of Chora—and if you have to live as a family, it's better to be a happy family."

To leave the hilltop, we scrambled down a steep stone roadway, almost a staircase, that passed between the stumps of strong stone gate towers. This was probably the only part of his predecessors' fortifications that Neleus left standing when he built his palace. Not far away, the car was waiting, not without some show of impatience from the driver. He and Professor Blegen laughed about how hungry they both were as we drove down, through the gathering dusk, to the little port of modern Pylos. On the way, the Professor and I talked of the numerous confirmations of Homer that the archaeologists have now provided. They have come, so to say, in bits and pieces—at one moment, the discovery of the remains of a boar's tusk-encrusted helmet, which cleared up a passage long argued by the scholiasts, who could not imagine such a thing until they saw it; and at another moment, something big, like Blegen's own discovery of Pylos. Thinking about all this, I asked the Professor whether he really believed the story of Helen's love for Paris. But I never got an answer; for we had just reached the pleasant little hotel where we had reserved rooms. My question was lost in the exchange of surprised greetings between the Professor and two friends of his, who were taking a belated, very English afternoon tea on the hotel terrace. The friends turned out to be the Master of Downing College and Professor of Ancient Philosophy at Cambridge, W. K. C. Guthrie, and Mrs. Guthrie. The Guthries agreed to dine with us, and when darkness had fallen, and the lights of the fishing boats were showing in the bay over toward Sphacteria, we four sat down to an excellent meal of the good Greek hors d'oeuvres and shashlik and fruit, washed down with plenty of light resinated wine. Both professors were in good form—deep calling to deep, so to say—and it was an evening to remember.

The talk began with Pylos—it was then I learned how that first trench which laid bare the archive room had been solely planned to spare the olive trees—but in the end it covered rather more of the ancient Mediterranean than Odysseus saw in all his wanderings. The 46 levels of Troy; and the fate of the temple of Artemis at Ephesus; and the sound insight of Thucydides' opening summary of early Greek history; and the date for the fall of Troy proposed by the Alexandrian scholar Eratosthenes; and the competing theories about the origin of the Minoans; and L. R. Palmer's strictures on Sir Arthur Evans—all these and many other, comparable topics were touched upon in this wide-ranging conversation which struck me, not just by its display of learning, but also by its ease and lack of pretension. If you feel genuinely intimate with Eratosthenes, apparently, you talk about him as though he lived next door instead of nearly two millennia ago.

One passage of this long evening of talk deserves to be recorded at some length, moreover, because of its bearing on the accuracy of the evidence provided for us by the deciphered Linear B tablets. The scholar who has been boldest in using this evidence to reconstruct a picture of late Mycenaean society and history is the Oxford philologist already cited, professor Palmer, whose remarkable book *Mycenaeans and Minoans* has been a subject of sharp scholarly controversy ever since its recent appearance. There are several reasons for this controversy, beginning with the fact that Palmer outraged the numerous surviving Evansites by casting doubts on the accuracy, and on the general archaeological dependability, of

74

the Minoan chronology proposed by the great discoverer of Knossos. On this front, incidentally, Palmer has just renewed his attack, with quite impressive additional artillery from Evans' and Myres' own papers. To a lesser degree, Palmer has also been criticized for his boldness in using the Linear B tablets to make a coherent picture. It must be added that Palmer's picture closely agrees, except in matters of minor detail, with the picture that emerges from Ventris and Chadwick's *Documents in Mycenaean Greek*. He is largely supported by other scholars, like F. J. Tritsch. And his description of the Mycenaean economy does not go so far in its conclusions as the less colorful but more strongly outlined description by Professor Sterling Dow of Harvard. None the less, I wanted to know Blegen's judgment of the matter. So I asked the Professor, as our dinner was ending, what he thought of the way Palmer had interpreted his Pylos tablets.

It turned out that Blegen, who is a field archaeologist and not a philologist, had certain cautious reservations to make. It was a long job, he said, "a very long job," to arrive at sure and final readings of documents like the Linear B tablets, whose rather clumsy, sometimes debatable signs express—one might almost say embalm—a form of Greek at least four hundred years earlier than any Greek previously known to scholarship. Time would have to tell, he said; and he suggested that another ten years of work by the philologists would be needed before readings of the Pylos tablets could be accepted as dependable in detail. But to this he added that there was no question of Palmer's philological eminence, and he summed up:

"It all fits; it fits remarkably well, in fact. What he has found in the tablets is just what one would expect to find; and by that I don't at all mean he has read his own expectations into the texts. But I can't give any sort of final verdict. We must wait for time's verdict!"

So our evening ended, after we had all agreed to go on to Chora, the next day, to see Professor Blegen's archaeological workshop and the

75

*Frieze from propylon, Pylos.*

little museum the Greek government has built to contain the finds from Nestor's palace and the things unearthed in the surrounding region by Professor Blegen's Greek excavating partner, Professor Spyridon Marinatos. The following morning proved to be tranquilly golden, in the way of so many Greek mornings. The Guthries were excellent company. The conversation of the evening before was easily resumed as soon as the car started for Chora. The archaeological workshop was a fascinating establishment, where Greek specialists were busy fitting together broken pieces of pots in the manner of people fitting together the most taxing sort of picture puzzles. The little museum had promise of future charm; and the fragments of frescoes had great evocative power. Indeed, there was much to learn when Professor Blegen was pulling out drawer after drawer of bits of fresco, and showing the joins already made by Dr. Mabel Lang. Dr. Lang has undertaken to assemble all the Pylos frescoes in complete compositions; and when this has been done, the final result should be very much worth seeing. Yet I will not attempt to describe in detail the fine procession of white-robed maidens, and the wingless griffins and lion leopards from the Queen's throne hall; the small but extraordinarily vivid fresco of warriors storming a fortified place, and all the rest that we saw. In truth, this account of that journey to Pylos is already long enough for such a personal excursion. So I shall close it in the museum, with the Guthries exclaiming over the fresco fragments and Professor Blegen beaming with quiet pride, as well he might.

The surprise of Columbus, who never imagined that his sea route to India could be blocked by an unforeseen new continent, teaches that discoveries tend to play jokes on the discoverers. The rule applies in archaeology, as in other professions in which discovery is the grand aim and prize. Thus the Chinese scholars of the "Academia Sinica" who sponsored and joined in the celebrated excavation at Anyang, were naturally highly gratified by the justification of Chinese historical tradition provided by the Anyang oracle bones. The Sinologists who had condemned the Shang dynasty as imaginary were mainly Westerners, and the proof of the Shang kings' authenticity was something of a national triumph for the Chinese savants. At the same time, however, these Chinese savants were sorely wounded in their deepest sensibilities by what the Anyang dig revealed about ancient Chinese society. Here, alas, was a society altogether unlike the idealized Confucian picture of the past, in which wise rulers brought order and prosperity to "all under heaven" by the sedulous practice of benevolence and good ritual. Here, rather, was a society in which the rulers, if they were not asking their ancestors through the scapulomancers whether the time was ripe for war, were usually inquiring whether their next big-game hunting expedition would be lucky and kill many animals. Worse still, here was a society which practiced human sacrifice on a lavish scale, and sent many unfortunates to their death with each royal burial, so that every kingly ancestor might be well served in the afterlife. In the same fashion the remarkable discoveries that began at Mohenjo-Daro and Harappa not only proved that there was much historical truth in the Rig-Veda; they also showed that India's earliest civilization was quite repellently utilitarian, authoritarian and commercial, with very little to admire, in truth, except the drains.

These examples are relevant because Blegen's discovery of Pylos and Ventris' decipherment of Linear B had a comparable effect. They not only gave back to the Greeks the first superb creations of the Greek spirit; they not only placed Nestor and Agamemnon and Homer's other heroes in a solid historical context. They also showed that the real Greek kingdoms that leagued together against Troy were very different from the imagined kingdoms of the Homeric epics.

The social and political picture painted by the Homeric epics is nothing more, of course, than the incidental backdrop before which are played the marvelous dramas of the anger of Achilles and the return of Odysseus. Human character and action are the main themes. Yet the backdrop is richly detailed, and the details are also wonderfully vivid and convincing. There are a few difficulties, to be sure, like the odd fact that although chariots and chariot-teams are lovingly described, chariotry is never used in actual combat; instead, Homeric chariots are only employed, like the taxis of the Marne, to get to the scene of the fight. Over-all, however, the picture painted is logical and consistent. Even the political relationships implied in the account of the Greek coalition against Troy make perfectly good political sense. So does the larger picture of an heroic society, warrior-led, heroic in outlook and standards, in which the common folk count for very little and the scene is always dominated by the ruling elite of bronze-armed fighting men. Both the consistency of the over-all

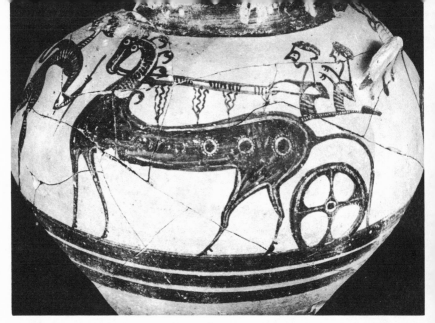

*Warriors in a chariot, on a thirteenth-century* B.C. *vase fragment from Mycenae.*

picture and the vividness of the details are best explained, I feel sure, by Milman Parry's theory of the composition of the Homeric epics, of which Sir Maurice Bowra is now the leading proponent. According to this theory, the epics were composed, or perhaps one should say, put into something like their surviving form, in the eighth century B.C., and therefore some centuries after Agamemnon's Mycenae and Nestor's Pylos had fallen into dust. But this great feat (or feats, if the *Odyssey* is later than the *Iliad*, as some suppose) was only the climax of a long tradition of oral poetry, deriving from Mycenaean times, and carried on through the centuries by bards who composed for recitation. From generation to generation, they passed on to their successors the main outlines of stories, the names of characters, devices of composition such as similes, and above all a whole mass of formulaic phrases varying from two words to several lines, which dealt not only with the ordinary mechanical matter of the epics, but also quite specifically with all sorts of details of daily

*Bronze dagger blade inlaid with gold, silver and niello depicting warriors on a lion hunt. From Schliemann's grave circle, Mycenae.*

life in the much earlier time when the oral tradition began. These details might sometimes be altered or understood very imperfectly, as in the case of the heroes' highly peculiar chariot tactics. But this too is a common phenomenon of epic traditions.

Despite the great gap in time between the destruction of Pylos in 1200 B.C. and the composition or assemblage of the Homeric epics in the eighth century, there is no reason to be surprised that Homer has now been justified by the archaeologists, and every bit as fully as old Schliemann could have wished. The heroic warrior class, still using bronze weapons which had long since given place to iron in Homer's time; the numerous kingdoms, located just where Homer placed them, with Mycenae first for wealth and power, just as Homer said; the richly decorated Mycenaean palaces like that of King Alcinous in Scheria, which must have seemed wholly mythical to the Greeks of Homer's time, who had no comparable palaces—all these main features of the *Iliad* and the *Odyssey*

81

were based, as we now know, on the solid facts of the Mycenaean age of Greece. Some Greek scholars—although they are now a minority—are still enraged by the belief of their colleagues like Bowra and Wace and Blegen that Homer is generally a reliable guide, at least as far as he goes. Bitter criticism from this minority greeted a recent pro-Homer publication, the *Companion to Homer* jointly edited by the late Professor Wace and F. H. Stubbings. But to an outsider this sharpness sounded like an echo of the sort of thing that Schliemann was subjected to after his discovery of Mycenae, which finally drove him to accept the Phoenician trading post theory. The point is that Homer has been proved reliable as far as he goes on so many occasions, and in such odd ways.

For example, one scholar, Martin Nilsson, long ago made the simple assumption that the place names most often mentioned by Homer were the chief Greek centers in the Mycenaean period. He then analyzed the special religious cults surviving in those places into Greek classical times. He found that the cult of Poseidon predominated rather heavily. He therefore concluded that in the Mycenaean age, Sea King-Poseidon was a more important deity than Zeus himself. The Pylos tablets have now confirmed this conclusion derived from Homer's geography; and by now the archaeologists have also buttressed Homer in yet another way, by finding Mycenaean remains at most of the places Homer mentioned. Again, a long-dead English scholar, Sir William Ridgeway, carefully deduced the system of Homeric land tenure from the stray references to this subject in the *Iliad* and the *Odyssey*. Decades later, Ridgeway's deductions have also been largely confirmed by the complex land registers in the Pylos tablets.

Yet in the Pylos case, as in so many others, the discovery's joke on the discoverers was still a pretty good one, and for a simple reason. The features of Mycenaean society so faithfully reflected in Homer, while largely proven to be true features, look altogether different when they are

82

viewed in the setting of their own time, which can now be crudely traced in the deciphered tablets. There is no hint in Homer that Nestor's kingdom and the others like it were tightly controlled, tightly administered states, highly bureaucratic in character and organization. There is little hint in Homer that these earliest Greek states, for all their warlike, semifeudal, Indo-European basic character, also partook of many of the characteristics of the sacred monarchies of the most ancient Orient. And there is no hint at all in Homer that Agamemnon, Nestor, Menelaus and the other kingly heroes were also merchant monopolists in a very large way of business, whose real quarrel with Troy quite possibly arose from King Priam's profitable control of the trans-Hellespontine trade route between Europe and Asia. Yet all these things not hinted at in Homer, which transform the whole picture of the Mycenaean age, are told us by the Pylos and Knossos tablets, and told with considerable clarity and insistency at that.

The picture painted by the tablets needs some introduction, however. To begin with, it is impossible to make any sense at all about the late Bronze Age without always bearing in mind the crucial problem of historic scale. The demographers calculate that in paleolithic times, when men lived by hunting, fishing and food-gathering alone, the entire human population of the globe cannot have greatly exceeded half a million persons. The more and more alarming increase of human numbers began with—and was only made possible by—the neolithic invention of Agriculture. The Bronze Age population of the Eastern Mediterranean was unquestionably much greater than the population of the late Stone Age.* Yet the population was still very small, and the whole scale of history in the Bronze Age was still minute, by our hideously inflated

---

* If the demographers are correct, the human population of the globe had reached 5,500,000—or less than half the population of greater New York—by the opening of the Bronze Age. This was an elevenfold increase, however, from the population of the old Stone Age.

standards. The Hittite Empire, for example, was one of the great powers of the second millennium B.C., strong enough in its heyday to trouble Babylon and strike fear into Egypt. The emergence of this major Indo-European state in Asia Minor was one of the factors that made the second millennium the world's first era of great power wars. The first battle in history whose course can be traced with reasonable confidence is the battle of Kadesh, late in our period, when the Hittite King Muwatallis repelled the northward advance of the young Pharaoh, Ramses II, on the banks of the Orontes in 1286 B.C. (For a long time everyone believed the boastful and lying account of this battle left by Ramses himself on the walls of the temple of Karnak. But the more recently discovered Hittite archives tell a different story, which is confirmed by the fact that Ramses had clearly meant to go farther yet was forced to turn back. The victory he claimed was in fact a defeat and very nearly a disaster, for the incautious young Pharaoh allowed himself to be caught between the river and the mountains by the entire Hittite army, when only the first of the four Egyptian chariot divisions had emerged from the mountain defiles.) Yet if you go to see the magically evocative remains of the Hittite capital at Boghazköy, you have to adjust your notions of the meaning of the phrase "great power" in the Bronze Age.

The walls of Hattusas, as the Hittites called their capital, are even more astonishing than the walls of Mycenae; and its site, on another saddle amid crags, is just as overwhelming. Yet the whole population of Hattusas and its suburbs must have been numbered, at most, in tens of thousands of human beings. This capital of an ancient empire that was no larger than a modest, one-industry small town today, gives food for thought. To be sure, the Hittites had certain advantages. At the outset, they had better chariots and horses than the older-established Babylonians and Egyptians; the latter, in fact, had no horses at all when the Hittite Empire first took form. The Hittites also pioneered the use of iron weapons instead of bronze. In the main, however, the Hittites were able to act as a great power simply because the other great powers of the Bronze Age were on much the same scale as the Hittite Empire. The truth is that throughout history both greatness and power have been—and are—strictly relative terms. A Bronze Age great power could have a capital the size of a modern small town and an army numbered only in thousands of men; and it was still a great power because the other great powers of that time were not much stronger.

Besides this crucial problem of historic scale, it is needful to bear in mind another problem of utmost significance. This is the problem of the profound influence of raw materials on historical patterns. If we look at the modern Middle East, which is the creation of the twentieth-century petroleum hunger, we can see at once that this problem is important, and may sometimes be decisive. To date, however, the problem has only been studied in bits and pieces, as in the remarkable studies of salt through the ages made by the Israeli government's scientific adviser on arid zone research, M. R. Bloch. Bloch's conclusions about salt only whet our appetite to know more. Salt is of course necessary to the life of any people that does not live on a salt-rich meat or fish diet; otherwise the internal saline solution of the human body cannot be kept in balance. Cereal eaters need a minimum of 2 to 5 grams a day. Bloch has reached the immensely exciting conclusion that the salt-pan method of evaporating salt from sea water was invented by the Minoan-Mycenaean civilization.* Since salt has always been a most important export commodity —probably the second commodity, indeed, to enter the human trade pattern, being preceded only by the primordial flint—Bloch's conclusion, if correct, helps to explain the prosperity of the Minoans and the Mycenaean

* Bloch's conclusion is challenged, however, by an odd gap in the Linear B tablets. They contain no mention of onions—or salt.

85

*Cretan one-talent weight
in porphyry stone, decorated
with an octopus.
From Knossos.*

Greeks. He further portrays the 6-foot rise in sea level that began before the time of Our Lord and reached its climax about A.D. 500 as a genuine world catastrophe, because it drowned most of the existing salt pans and other salt workings. It helped, he says, to bring on the European Dark Ages by causing salt starvation and destroying commerce in Northern Europe; and it also helped to spur the Roman Emperors Vespasian and Titus to their seemingly irrational conquest of the deserts around the Dead Sea. These were important as a salt source, just as the Middle East is now important as an oil source. This area was also desirable, of course, because of the great trade route that passed through Petra, which made the Nabataean rich. In addition, although it may seem hard to believe, parts of arid Jordan produced rich wheat crops at that period with the aid of reservoir irrigation. All the same, the rich cities that flourished then in impoverished little Jordan were presumably salt by-products, at least in part, as modern Kuwait and Jiddah are oil by-products.

The facts about salt, besides having their own bearing on the Minoan-Mycenaean story, help us to understand the fundamental importance of the central raw material problem of the Bronze Age—which was, rather naturally, the problem of bronze. This problem was central

86

because, as previously noted, bronze was at once scarce, hard to come by, and the only metal of serious military value. The main ingredient, copper, was of course common enough. But tin had to be alloyed with copper to give hardness and a good cutting edge—the needed amount was at least 5 per cent of tin for a mild bronze, and as much as 15 per cent for a hard bronze of the best quality. And tin was very uncommon indeed in the Eastern Mediterranean and the Near East. Local tin deposits began to be exhausted, in fact, as early as the third millennium B.C., and in the era of Sargon the Great unalloyed copper weapons actually came into use again in Mesopotamia, where first-class bronze weapons had been the rule before. According to R. J. Forbes, the tin shortage caused a trade to be organized with Western sources; and Bohemian, Saxon and Spanish tins thus found their way, mainly by chain-fashion exchanges, into the Eastern Mediterranean. Here and there, tin was also produced locally; as will be seen later, the happy accident of a tin mine may well have been a primary cause of Mycenae's wealth and power. Yet tin was scarce enough to make good bronze almost a semiprecious metal. Because bronze was costly, and because bronze was also the only metal that counted in war, very small numbers of bronze weapon owners could control very much larger subject populations. For this reason, a Bronze Age war could be tiny by our standards, involving only a few thousands of fighting men, or perhaps even less than that; and it could still change the course of history. For this reason, too, the order of society in the Bronze Age was naturally aristocratic—the aristocrats being those who owned bronze weapons—and when the king controlled his country's commerce and therefore its bronze supplies, the order of society was naturally monarchical. The discovery of methods of smelting iron, which is vastly commoner and easier to come by than bronze, was an event tending toward social revolution besides causing an immediate weapons revolution. The leading economic historian of the ancient world, Fritz M.

87

Heichelheim, speaks of the advent of iron as a "world revolution," undermining the old ways and creating "a new basis for civilized life." But in the second millennium B.C. iron was so rare that it was used for jewelry. Rings made from meteoric iron survive, from both Knossos and Mycenae.

If the problem of historic scale and the problem of bronze weaponry are both borne in mind, it is easier to understand the origins of Mycenaean Greek society. The scholars' arguments about the identity of the pre-Greek inhabitants of Greece would fill several volumes. The simplest and most convincing short outline has been supplied by Sterling Dow of Harvard. He points out that preclassical Greek sites show three successive levels of destruction, or "interruptions." After each destruction level, signs of profound cultural change appear. The last destruction level being assigned to the upheaval which destroyed Mycenaean civilization, that leaves two other destruction levels to be accounted for. This means that before the end of the Mycenaean age there must have been three successive occupations of Greece by peoples socially organized enough to leave remains of buildings. Neolithic peoples came first, and one of these built the fort at Dimini, with its curious, concentric lines of walls, like a military maze.

A metal-using people then entered Greece at some time between 3000 and 2500 B.C. They are thought to have come from Anatolia because of the resemblance of a good many non-Greek place names in Greece, such as Corinth, to numerous Anatolian place names. This people of Anatolian origin, with a rather primitive bronze culture, occupied most of Greece when the Greek-speaking tribes pushed in. Since the Greeks were almost certainly horsemen, it is reasonable to suppose that they ultimately originated somewhere in the great Eur-Asian plain, which is favorable to horse-rearing. But their immediate point of departure remains the subject of interminable and so far fruitless controversy. The last centuries of the third millennium and the beginning of the second millennium were the first great age of Indo-European folk wanderings. Why these great movements occurred—Pressure of increasing populations? Climatic changes in the Eur-Asian heart-land? Tales of wealth to be won beyond the horizon?—is another subject that can be and has been endlessly and thus far fruitlessly argued. In the centuries between about 2500 and 1900 B.C., at any rate, Indo-Europeans entered Iran, and the Aryans began their movement toward India; the Hittites, Mitannians and other Indo-European peoples turned up in Asia Minor and northern Syria; and Greek-speakers entered Greece.

Until just the other day, 1900 B.C. was almost universally cited as the approximate date for the first Greek occupation of Greek soil. Professor John Caskey of the University of Cincinnati has now offered a closely reasoned argument for putting back the date to 2100 B.C., but the consensus in favor of 1900 B.C. has not yet been shaken. The generally accepted date of 1900 B.C. therefore makes the Greek emergence the the last event in this mysterious, convulsive sequence of Indo-European emergencies onto the stage of history. Or it may be that we should say that the Greek entry into Greece and the destruction of Troy V by the people who founded Troy VI were the last *two* major events. Troy VI was founded around 1900 B.C; and there are other Greek links with Troy VI besides the fact that both invading peoples were horse breeders. In the Linear B tablets, for instance, the lists of workmen and the like show that the names Homer gives to his Trojan heroes—Eumedes, Antenor, Glaucus, even Tros and Hector—were common men's names in Mycenaean Greece, along with Greek Homeric heroes' names like Achilles. Close pre-war contacts between Troy and Mycenaean Greece are proven by the finds at Troy of Mycenaean pottery, and in other ways too. For these reasons, Blegen and some other scholars incline to think that the Trojans of Troy VI and of Priam's city were actually of Greek stock. This would explain why, in Homer, the two sides are always able to communicate without language difficulties.* But here again all is murk, shot through with dispute. Although a hunch of Professor Blegen's is usually worth more than the well-reasoned arguments of several other men, no one can be absolutely certain where the truth lies. When we envision the fall of Troy V and the Greek-speaking horsemen pushing down into Greece, however, we must not think of tribes in movement,

*(Whose) fighters drink the rivers up, (whose) shafts benight the air.*

    The power of a human group to multiply in favorable circumstances has never been exactly calculated; but it is very great. A few canoes, for instance, held all the ancestors of the large Hawaiian population found on the islands by Captain Cook; and the same holds true for the Maoris of New Zealand. This was what was in the mind of David Ben-Gurion—himself no mean historian—when he caused scandal in Israel some years ago by suggesting that the Children of Israel, when Moses led them out of Egypt, quite probably numbered less than a thousand. The Greek-speakers who invaded Greece not only enjoyed the superiority conferred by horses and better swords. They must also have benefited enormously from the terrifying effect on simple peoples of never-before-seen horses which we know from the accounts of Cortes' conquest of Mexico, as Blegen remarked to me. Hence, it is entirely possible that only ten or twenty thousand or even fewer Greek-speakers conquered the whole of Greece, which was then exceedingly sparsely settled in any case. (The sheer emptiness of the ancient world, or at least of large areas of it, is another crucial point that makes it hard to see the remote past in its true outline.) In the investigated sites, the arrival of the Greeks is usually,

* *But free communication is an epic convention, as Sir Maurice Bowra has kindly pointed out to me. At Roncesvalles, the Saracens are described as understanding Roland with no difficulty whatever.*

though not invariably, commemorated in the customary grim way, by a destruction level. The surviving earlier inhabitants of Greece are likely to have been reduced to a subject status, becoming hewers of wood and drawers of water and, above all, tillers of the fields for the new Greek overlords. Enough of them survived at any rate, as Sterling Dow states, "to communicate the names of natural features, town-sites and a few other words" to the Greek-speaking invaders.

If the invading Greek-speakers were few at the outset, which is probable but not of course certain, they multiplied rather rapidly after the various kindreds settled at Mycenae, Tiryns, Orchomenus, Gla, Iolkos and the other main Mycenaean centers. Having settled, they also began to prosper. As to the detailed outlines of Greek society at this stage in its development there is no hard evidence, and there probably never will be any. Judging by analogy, each invading tribe had its own royal kindred; or if they were all members of one tribe, the whole body of invaders looked up to one royal kindred. If the Greeks resembled the Hittites in the first phase of their empire, Greek kings were then chosen by election, generally among the available adult males of the royal family, the electors being the leaders or members of the other chief kindreds of the tribe. The kings, or other members of the royal kindred, may or may not have performed additionally as priests. If they were like the pre-Christian Scandinavians, the leading families were in part marked off from the common folk by their possession of hereditary priesthoods —which was also a common distinction of aristocratic families in Greece in the classical age. If we go further than this, and ask, *"What was it like in Greece, say about 1800 B.C.?"* the answer must depend very heavily on conjecture; yet simple political logic, plus bits and pieces of the surviving archaeological record, permit a crude picture to be painted with some hope of accuracy.

In each community, the petty king or local chief may be supposed

91

to have ruled from a *megaron*. This is a word of art for a building with a special plan, containing at a minimum a columned porch, leading to an anteroom, leading to a main hall centering around a great hearth. The *megaron* building plan was the germ from which evolved both the later Greek temples and the rich king's palaces of the late Bronze Age. But in 1800 B.C. even if this building plan was already in use, the king's or chief's house must have been far from grandiose, and the feasts in the hall must have been reasonably barbaric. After the king or chief, the bronze-armed warriors composed the rest of the upper class; but the life of Greek nobles at this early period must not be imagined as elegant or luxurious. When they were not fighting or seafaring (which they may have just started doing by 1800 B.C.), the warriors probably oversaw the flocks and herds, if they did not actually tend them. The women no doubt did the housework, aided by any slaves the warriors may have dragged home from their raids. That tradition survived until the end of the first era of Greece; even queens, as Penelope's example shows, regularly practiced fine weaving in the late Bronze Age. Below the noble class there were the commons, in whom Greek blood was very probably heavily diluted by the blood of the former people of the land. The more menial tasks must have fallen to them, and their life was even less luxurious; but in all but the worst years, everyone ought to have enjoyed a kind of rude and modest plenty. Populations were still small, the land was not yet overcrowded, and the fields should have produced enough for all despite the primitiveness of the farm tools.

Because the populations must still have been so small, the settlements themselves were also small. A king or chieftain's town was probably not much bigger than a large modern Greek village, but the plan must have been different, if we may judge by analogy. Even in the high period, whole towns or cities were never fortified; the great walls of the late Bronze Age citadels were erected to protect the king and his treasures, and to provide a place of refuge for the people in time of trouble. When trouble came, the people crowded in; otherwise the space within the walls was only inhabited by the king himself, his household and his guards, some of his officials and perhaps some members of the noble class. On this analogy, a Greek settlement of the early period probably had a fortified center, composed of a wall, earthwork or stockade surrounding the king's house, while the other houses of the settlement, large and small, straggled down the hillsides (for high sites were always chosen, for better defense); and shelters for the flocks and herds, and rough stables for the valuable horses alternated with the hut-like dwellings of the commonfolk. Such, at any rate, is the best picture that can be derived from educated guesswork.

Concerning this early period in Greece, in truth, we can only make educated guesses, partly guided by our more solid information about other peoples. But there is a sharp distinction between guessing what the first Greeks brought into Greece and listing what they did *not* bring into Greece. Of the things they brought, we can name only horses and improved bronze weapons, and a tribal, previously semi-nomadic way of life, with any certainty. But we may be quite certain that they did *not* bring in writing, or the kind of bureaucratic state administration that depends on written records, or the kind of highly centralized governmental and economic system that needs a bureaucracy to make it work. And precisely these things, which Homer does not so much as vaguely hint at, are the main features of Mycenaean Greek monarchy as revealed by the Linear B tablets.

Speaking as a political reporter, I consider the appearance of these unlooked-for features in the late Greek Bronze Age as the major problem posed by the decipherment of the Linear B tablets. How this strange social transformation may have occurred will be discussed later—appropriately enough in a final chapter reserved for the vast, obstinate, still enduring riddles of the Greek Bronze Age story. At this juncture it

93

is enough to say that the unlooked-for features of the late Greek Bronze Age states were quite certainly imported from outside Greece. The Greeks evidently began to have opportunities to observe the ways and imitate the techniques of other peoples rather soon after their descent into Greece. The forests that still clothed most of the Greek mountains in that era gave them ample timber for shipbuilding. The pre-Greek people whom they subjugated perhaps showed them the way to the sea. At any rate, they must have ventured out to sea fairly early, for by the middle of the second millennium B.C., the Mycenaean Greeks had undoubtedly become a wide-roving, far-trading people. By this time, for instance, Mycenaean commerce was overtaking Cretan commerce in Egypt.

Rather early on, therefore, the Greeks must at least have known about the centralized, planned form of society, even though they did not immediately imitate it; for this form of society prevailed in that era in Egypt, in many of the small states of Syria-Palestine, and above all in Crete. Their trade took them to all these places, and much farther afield as well. Mycenaean pottery, whose presence proves that there was trade, has been found right around the Eastern Mediterranean, northward up the Vardar valley; from Troy down the whole coast of Asia Minor; on Rhodes, Cyprus, Crete and almost all the other islands; down the whole Syria-Palestine coast from Tarsus to Gaza and beyond; along the Nile as far south as Aswan; and westward at coastal sites around the boot of Italy, in Sicily, and as far north as the island of Ischia. In addition, a design representing a dagger of Mycenaean form has now been discovered in Britain incised on one of the great megaliths of Stonehenge; and it is certain that the amber excavated at both Pylos and Mycenae must have come from the faraway Baltic. But the exchanges implied by the dagger and the amber were most probably made chain-fashion. The amber, for instance, will have been traded from tribe to tribe, down the long Baltic amber road of which the Vardar valley was one terminus.

94

The more direct trade of these enterprising Mycenaean Greeks has left so many traces that one leading authority on the subject, Sara Immerwahr, talks of the "existence of a Mycenaean commercial empire which flourished from about 1400 B.C. to shortly before 1200 B.C." And they did not stop with trade, either; they also established a Greece-overseas. They ruled Crete in the time when the Knossos records were kept in Linear B. They certainly had a trading colony, and they almost certainly founded a minor Mycenaean kingdom on Cyprus. They also had a trading settlement and probably a kingdom on Rhodes. Their merchants seem to have established more or less permanent Mycenaean quarters in more than one coastal town of Syria-Palestine; and they did not neglect Asia Minor. The Hittite cuneiform records from Boghazköy contain fascinating references to the *Ahhijawa*, who occupied a state with which the Hittite King Mursilis was the first to have dealings. The records also mention a king called *Tawagalawas*, whose interests met those of the Hittites at a place called *Milawanda*. In the thirteenth century B.C., once again, the Hittite King Tuthalias had to defend his southern border against *Attarissyas*, a "man of *Ahhijawa*." One of the most venomous scholarly disputes of this century surrounds these Greek-sounding names in the Hittite archives. The minority still asserts that the Greek-sounding character of the names is purest coincidence. The majority reply that the *Ahhijawa* were in fact Achaeans, that *Tawagalawas* was Eteocles, and that *Milawanda* was most probably Miletus in Caria.

Professor A. J. Beattie, the last disbeliever in Ventris' decipherment and therefore no mean practitioner of skepticism, has said that *Ahhijawa* "despite all objections raised, can only be" the Hittite way of spelling *Achaioi* (which was pronounced "Achaiwoi" in the second millennium). In addition, archaeology has now confirmed the existence of a Greek Bronze Age fortified Mycenaean settlement at Miletus, which increases the probability of the identification of *Milawanda;* and Professor

C. C. Vermeule has unearthed a Mycenaean cemetery at Halicarnassus. Indeed, the forecast now is that five or six sites of Mycenaean settlements will be eventually proved on the Asia Minor coast. Thus we may picture the Mycenaean Greeks of the high period not only establishing trading posts overseas, and conquering Crete, and attacking Troy, but also bidding for serious footholds on the Asian mainland and thus disturbing the mainland great powers. The Egyptian records of the end of the thirteenth century also mention the *Aqaiwasha*. They appear in what Professor Beattie describes as "the characteristically Achaean role of lending military aid to a rebel Libyan prince."

The curious fact is that until quite late in the Bronze Age, what the Greeks were doing abroad is rather clearer than what was happening to them at home. There are the myths, of course, some of which probably commemorate accurate traditions. The coalition of the "Seven Against Thebes" and the story of the destruction of the citadel of Cadmus in the next generation incorporate a tradition of particular interest. If a Greek coalition had to be formed to attack Thebes, it is possible that in the earlier period Thebes was the leading state of mainland Greece, occupying a position resembling that of Mycenae when the Trojan War began. By the time of the Trojan War, at any rate, Boeotia was no longer ruled from the *Cadmeia*. The Homeric ship list records many Boeotian ships, which means that the region was still rich and prosperous; but the Boeotians did not follow a single kingly leader, as the Mycenaeans followed Agamemnon and the ninety ships of Pylos followed Nestor. From the ship list, too, the experts have deduced the broad political pattern of all of Greece in the late Bronze Age; and the deductions have in turn been more and more largely confirmed by the archaeologists' spades.

The Peloponnese, to begin with, was roughly divided into either three or four major states, depending on whether Homer was right or wrong about the independence of Tiryns. If Homer was right in giving

*The fortification walls at Tiryns.*

Diomede an independent kingdom, Tiryns probably held most of the Argive plain, some other mainland territory and the island of Aegina. Mycenae, in the mountains just above Tiryns, certainly held a broad swath of territory, partly defined by the remains of Mycenae's road-net. The Mycenaean lands probably ran diagonally across the Peloponnese from the Corinthian gulf to the Aegean. Sparta was the kingdom of Menelaus, brother of Agamemnon, and may therefore have been a dependency of Mycenae in the days of Atreus. And to the west there was the Pylian kingdom, established by Neleus. In the interstices between these large states (but only large, remember, by Bronze Age standards) hill baronies of the type that existed in Messenia before Neleus no doubt survived to the very end of the Mycenaean story. In the Trojan War, according to Homer, Agamemnon not only manned 100 ships with his own men; he also lent 60 additional ships to "the Arcadians." The plural is significant, pointing to the conclusion that rather numerous hill baronies still existed at that time in poor and mountainous Arcadia. Above the Peloponnese, there were rather considerable Mycenaean states at Athens, Gla, Orchomenus, Iolkos and several other places, but Cadmus' Theban kingdom had been already overthrown by a coalition of other Greeks, as we have seen. Again hill baronies may have existed in the gaps; and there were certainly a number of smaller states as well, like Salamis. Homer says the great Ajax led 12 ships from Salamis against Troy. According to Homer, Crete also sent a large contingent to the war—no less than 80 ships under King Idomeneus—but the condition of Crete at this time is a deeply vexed question, which must be examined later.

If we ask about this later period the question that we asked about earlier Greece—*"What was it really like?"*—the answer can be given with more confidence. The archaeological record shows, to begin with, that both population and wealth had very greatly increased. We must guard ourselves of course, as always, against thinking in anything like modern terms. Sir Arthur Evans, who was never bearish about Knossos, estimated that Knossos at the height of its grandeur had a maximum population of 60,000 to 70,000 persons. By the standards of the Greeks when they first entered Greece, this was a gigantic metropolis. Very likely, it was also at least double the size of the largest Greek cities of the late Bronze Age. At Mycenae, for instance, buildings and tombs by then extended far beyond the high saddle among the crags; and there were suburb-like settlements on neighboring hillsides. Yet it is hard to believe that the whole space covered by buildings sheltered many more than 30,000 people, if that many. At Pylos, again, a town ran down the slopes around the cleared hilltop where the palace stood; but, although the town has not been excavated, one may be pretty sure its size was such that nowadays town would be the right word for it rather than city. This being the urban scale, it would be exceedingly surprising if the whole population of late Bronze Age Greece was much more than half the present population of Athens and the Piraeus alone, 1,850,000 people—and it may have been substantially less than this.

Of the total population, a very high percentage must still have been country dwellers, working on or getting their living from the land. In the poorer, more remote hill baronies, we may suspect that conditions were not enormously different from those that prevailed in the early settlements. To be sure, the baron or chief's hall may by now have been fashionably frescoed, perhaps by a second-class workman at cut rates because a surplus of artists had developed in Pylos or Tiryns. He, and his wife, and his eldest son may have had their gold necklaces-of-state; for gold necklaces seem to have been marks of caste. When he died, he was almost certainly laid away, with the earlier members of his line, in the family's tholos-tomb; for most families of importance clearly possessed such burial places by the late Bronze Age, if one may judge by the large numbers of these beehive-shaped stone vaults, both large and small, that

99

are continually being discovered in Greece. But although a hill baron and his handful of fighting men must have had better weapons than in the early period, and there may have been a scribe or two to keep the accounts, and far more of the land was cleared and all was better worked with better tools, life in the remoter country districts of Bronze Age Greece cannot have assumed an imposing or luxurious pattern.

In the major centers, it was very different. To see the difference, it is only necessary to consider the Treasury of Atreus, the greatest of the Mycenaean tombs. Its beehive-shaped cut-stone vault covers the largest space ever covered by a single vault in ancient times, until Hadrian put the vault on the Pantheon at Rome. The lintel stone of its great door weighs over 100 tons; and its main chamber is close to 50 feet in diameter and 45 feet high. It was richly decorated, too, the entrance with columns and plaques of carved green and red stone, and the domed interior with a pattern of metal ornaments—most probably gilt-bronze rosettes. To be sure, this was the grandest structure of this type put up in late Mycenaean Greece; but the so-called Treasury of Minyas at Orchomenus was nearly as grand and perhaps more richly decorated; and there were other great tombs at Mycenae as well. Besides tombs, immense fortifications were constructed by several of the major Greek rulers of the late Bronze Age. In this respect, Neleus and Nestor were exceptional. Furthermore, the designers of the fortifications seem to have become more ambitious as they went along; at Tiryns, for instance, the Cyclopean masonry using the largest blocks of stone is also the latest; in this part of the Tiryns fortifications stones seven feet in length were not seldom employed. Finally, the late Bronze Age was the pre-eminent era of palace-building. There must have been earlier palaces at all the major centers; but Professor Blegen is convinced that none of the great palaces of which traceable ruins survive was built before "Late Helladic III"—which means, at the earliest, only a century before Neleus built the first Pylos palace in 1300 B.C.

*Interior of the Treasury of Atreus at M*

The marvelous treasures found in the graves at Mycenae all date from before the late Bronze Age; and there is a perfectly good functional reason for this. In brief, the vastly more monumental and impressive tombs the Greek rulers took to building in the late period were not possible to conceal, were not designed to be concealed, and were highly unlikely to be forgotten by the people whose fathers or grandfathers or great-grandfathers had dragged the huge stones into place. The rulers who built them, and presumably filled them with treasure far surpassing the treasure Schliemann found, must have had the most superb confidence that their descendants would go on ruling, and incidentally protecting the tombs of their ancestors, for untold generations yet to come. But when this confidence proved to be sadly misplaced, the great tombs must have been instantly swept bare of all their valuables; their very conspicuousness ensured that result. There are indications that grave-robbing sometimes occurred before the Bronze Age dynasties fell; after their fall, there must have been a clean sweep of every still-remembered or observable tomb. It is not surprising, therefore, that the tangible proofs of the wealth of this last period of Mycenaean Greece are so much rarer than the proofs of the wealth of the period of Schliemann's never-robbed grave circle.

The absence of such tangible proofs of great wealth, plus one or two other indicators, have even caused some scholars to regard the end of the Mycenaean age as a period of impoverishment. One of the supposed indicators, for instance, is the fact that glass beads merely coated with gold leaf then came into use. But even in the early graves some of the things deposited were flimsily made, obviously as grave goods only. The substitution of gold-coated glass beads for real gold necklaces is only an extension of that practice. What kind of grave goods dead kings were provided with cannot really be judged in any case, since no late, unlooted royal tomb has yet been found. What kind of construction was undertaken can easily be judged, meanwhile—and more and more magnificent construction works do not fit

(TOP)
*Gold necklace from Mycenae.*

(RIGHT)
*Noblewomen in a chariot.
Detail of a fresco
from Tiryns.*

very well with a decline in wealth. To be sure, all trade with Asia Minor and the Syria-Palestine coast must have been disrupted, or even stopped altogether, only a few years after Professor Blegen's date for the fall of Troy. This is 1260 B.C. or thereabouts, and the "peoples of the sea" are thought to have made their first attack on Egypt around 1230 B.C. Before reaching Egypt, the sea peoples must have wholly upset the old trade patterns with the Near East. Just at the close, therefore, the commercially active Mycenaean Greek society may have been really impoverished by this disruption of the established trade patterns. But judging by what they built—and there are few better measuring sticks—the Mycenaean Greeks were very rich indeed, and were quite possibly getting richer, at least until they went off to the war against Troy.

As the main centers were no bigger than modern towns, the kings and their courts must have been highly noticeable. And as the kings were rich, and as the Bronze Age Greeks were clearly fond of display, not to say ostentation, we may picture Mycenae and Pylos and Tiryns as being extremely colorful in their heyday. Much of the architecture was richly colored, as the remains show. The members of the royal kindred and the noble class appear in the frescoes with many jewels and the women in fine dresses. Chariots and horse trappings were richly decorated, as the tablets record. From the frequency of processional scenes and the like in the frescoes, ceremonials appear to have been frequent. Altogether, even though they did not participate directly in the life of the conspicuous consumers, the artisans and commonfolk and slaves must have had much to catch their eyes. The people of one town must also have known a fair amount about the people—at least the more important people—of other towns over much of Greece. The passages in the *Iliad* describing the recruitment of the heroes and the gathering of the forces that went to Troy show all of Greece as a unity, not in a political sense, of course, but in a cultural and social sense. Homer also hints at more than a little visiting about, at any rate among the grandees. In the *Odyssey,* Telemachus goes by chariot from Pylos to Sparta, to see if Menelaus and his happily returned Queen Helen know anything about Odysseus' whereabouts. The remains of Mycenaean road systems, stone-built, with culverts for drainage, confirm these hints.

Although everyone seems to have known a good deal about everyone else, there must of course have been wide variations among the late Bronze Age Greek kingdoms. Complete uniformity is too unlikely. But if we now return to the evidence of the tablets, in order to see how this Greek society actually worked, the first strange fact that has to be faced is the almost complete administrative uniformity the tablets point to. The evidence merely consists, of course, of the two very large archives of Linear B tablets from Knossos and Pylos, plus about fifty tablets from Mycenae,

*Gold funerary diadem for a woman, made of thin gold plate.*
*From Schliemann's grave circle at Mycenae.*

plus scattered writing from other sites. The tablets tell us that when they were inscribed, the Knossian and Pylian kingdoms were all but identical, at least in their economic organization. The tablets from Mycenae in no way alter the picture, unless Wace was right about the existence of that free-enterprise oil merchant. Professor Bennett agrees with Wace but, as already noted, the majority holds that what Wace called "the house of the oil merchant" was really one of a series of external dependencies of the Mycenaean palace. In that case, by the way, what was said earlier about the larger size of the palace at Pylos may be somewhat misleading. If Agamemnon lodged the commercial departments of his palace in separate structures, whereas Nestor kept many of them under his palace roof, the palm for luxury has

*Head of a gold
and silver stickpin found
in the same woman's grave
in Mycenae.*

o be given to Agamemnon. All the same, Nestor's throne room was just a little bigger than the Lion-King's.

Nestor of Pylos, the ruler of Knossos and, one must presume, Agamemnon and all the other kings of the Greek Bronze Age had the special title of *Wanax*. This Mycenaean Greek word for king only barely survived into classical Greek; later, the common word for king became *basileus*. The *Wanax* was also different in kind from the rare Greek kings who still reigned in the classical period. A very major difference is a matter of dispute, however. Sir Arthur Evans long ago concluded that the ruler of Knossos was a sacred personage—a priest-king, probably thought of as the earthly husband of the Mother-Goddess, and therefore close to being a living god, just as the Pharaohs were living gods, and many of the Mesopotamian rulers were priest-kings and equated with gods. Professor Palmer, although a stern critic of Evans, fully accepts this Evans theory that the ruler of Knossos was a priest-king. He also holds that Nestor and the other mainland Greek rulers were priest-kings like the ruler of Knossos. But the leading American student of the tablets, Professor E. L. Bennett, Jr., has now attacked the whole idea of sacred kingship among the Bronze Age Greeks. Bennett thinks Palmer has read too much into the Pylos tablets, and he even doubts Evans' theory that sacred kingship existed at Knossos. Speaking as an outsider, it seems to me quite likely that the Minoan Minos was a true priest-king; since the Minoans, whoever they may have been, almost certainly came to Crete from the Asian mainland at a time when the institution of sacred kingship flourished in Asia. It also seems to me quite possible that when a Greek Minos supplanted the Minoan Minos, this Greek invader also took over all or most of his Minoan predecessor's sacred and priestly attributes. For one thing, it would have served his political convenience to do so, for the subject Minoan population would then have been more submissive. But it is much less easy to imagine the ruler being reverenced as a god or part-god in an almost purely Greek state like Pylos or Mycenae, with a warrior aristocracy inheriting some of the tra ditions of the Indo-European folk wanderings. As already noted, Nestor and Agamemnon and the other mainland rulers were unquestionably believed to be divinely descended; between the tholos-tombs of the Greek Bronze Age royalties and the Homeric epithets used for them, such as "god-born" and "like the gods," there is very little room for doubt about the belief in their divine ultimate origins. But a man descended from a god is not necessarily a sacred personage; he may merely trail ancestral clouds of glory, as it were, without possessing the personal aura implied by one of the Egyptian Pharoahs' common epithets, which was, quite simply, "the Good God." In the case of the Greek mainland states, in short, Bennett's skepticism about the existence of genuine priest-kingship seems justified to me. Maybe some of the Cretan-Asian forms were adopted on the mainland but was the true substance of reverence and holy fear behind the forms?

The answer to that question may not even be given when the last disputed reading of the Linear B tablets has been cleared up by the scholars—a time which is still far distant. Meanwhile it is already clear that even if a Greek king of the Mycenaean age was not the "one man, the unique man" because he was sacred, he was at least economically and administratively unique. In fact, the late Mycenaean monarchies certainly borrowed the administrative and economic methods of the sacred monarchies of the most ancient Orient, whether or not they also borrowed the religious excuse for those methods, which was the institution of sacred kingship. The simplest label for these ancient Oriental economies has been supplied by Max Weber, who described each state as being administered as a royal *oikos* (the word means "household" or "house"), with all its affairs regulated and administered from the center. Weber's concept may even have existed in the period when the sacred monarchies flourished, for the title of all the rulers of Egypt for over two millennia, Pharaoh, is simply an Egyptian word, *pr'o,* which means "the great house." As their surviving records

108

show, the Pharaohs went so far as to classify all the lands of Egypt and to prepare planting plans for every region. The Mycenaean Greek rulers did not apparently go to comparable lengths. Yet it is curious to read F. M. Heichelheim's account of the taxation systems, the ways of organizing labor and production, the roles played by the rulers in trade and agriculture, and other features of the economic systems of the ancient Oriental monarchies; for this account, compiled long before the Linear B decipherment, contains feature after feature which the students of the Linear B tablets have now discovered in the Greek royal economies of the late Mycenaean age. In general, the reader may assume that every detail of Bronze Age Greek palace administration and economic management which will be described hereafter had its parallel in Egypt, or in the Near East, or in both areas. Yet it must also be noted that these Oriental economic and administrative methods were apparently coupled with a social system that was specifically Greek rather than Oriental.

To begin with, the land registers and other evidence in the clay tablets prove that a Greek king of the late Bronze Age must have ruled by custom, following the old rules of the land, and not as a mere tyrant or even as an absolute monarch. When power is truly concentrated, especially in small states, stratification of society tends to disappear. There is little differentiation, so to say, except the crucial difference between the lonely ruler and the gray mass of the ruled. In the Greek society revealed by the Linear B tablets, on the other hand, we find signs of the kind of stratification that generally reflects a long tradition. After the king at the top, there is the *Lawagetas*, the "Leader of the War-Host," who may or may not have been the Crown Prince or another member of the royal kindred. Then came the class of men commonly referred to with noble patronymics, who have the title of "Companions" of the king. After them are the members of a seemingly much larger group, the *telestaῑ*, the "service-men" who presumably owed service to the king for the lands they held, on the familiar

109

feudal land-service pattern. After the service-men came the commons, who seem to have had a voice in their local, village affairs; and after the commons are the slaves. These last were evidently fairly numerous, and belonged to the sanctuaries of the gods as well as to the king and his lords. Artisans and craftsmen, of whom there were many with all sorts of specialties, could be either service-men, or members of the commons, or even slaves. But the great majority of the population unquestionably worked on the land, with many fishermen and sailors and sea traders in the coastal towns and villages.

There were three different kinds of landholdings, and the differences of landholding fit rather neatly with the still somewhat conjectural reconstruction of the class differences in the Greek Bronze Age. The king and the *Lawagetas* each had a *temenos*, meaning, in this instance, lands that went with the office. In later Greece, the word was used for the sacred land comprised in a temple enclosure. And besides this very special kind of land, there were two other more usual kinds of landholdings, *ki-ti-me-na* land and *ke-ke-me-na* land. The words have not been satisfactorily translated as yet, and they may never be. But Professor Palmer makes an impressive argument that since the service-men held the first of these two kinds of land, this was land carrying service obligations of a semifeudal character, whereas the other kind was common land which carried with it no semifeudal obligations. This picture of class differences and landownership differences, which has been deduced from the Linear B tablets, may of course be altered in detail or even revolutionized by subsequent work on the tablets or by further discoveries. Yet it must be said that it is just about the kind of picture one would expect to find, given the Greeks' Indo-European origins and the stage of their development in the late Bronze Age.

The first part of the picture that is unexpected, although equally well attested, is the tight administration to which this semifeudal early Greek society was subjected. Consider Nestor's Pylos, for example. As already noted, the whole area of the Pylian kingdom was less than 100 miles along the coast and 50 miles inland; and it may have been substantially smaller than this. Yet a primary division of Pylos into two separate administrative provinces is indicated by the Pylian palace scribes' unvarying practice of listing the kingdom's main towns in two separate groups, of nine and seven towns respectively. Pylos itself, we may suppose, was the administrative center of the larger nine-town province, but Professor Palmer believes that the seven-town province had a secondary capital of its own, at a place called Leuktron. Still following Palmer, each province had a governor and a vice-governor. The two provinces were further subdivided into districts, centering on their nine and seven towns; and each district had a *ko-re-te* and a *po-ro-ko-re-te*—in other words, a district officer and pro or deputy district officer.

This hierarchy of officials is deduced, very convincingly one must add, from the indications of the officials' relative standings, given by the texts having to do with gold and bronze deliveries. Obviously an official who was more highly rewarded, or was expected to contribute more heavily when the state was collecting bronze for the national defense effort, was likely to have had a higher standing than a man who got or gave less. The ratios were strikingly standardized. According to Palmer, the individuals whom he identifies as provincial governors "stand to" most of the supposed district officers "on the 'gold standard' in the ratio of 12:6 or 12:5," and the similar ratio for the district officers and the deputy district officers is, once again, "either 6:3 or 5:3." Still lower in the administrative and payments hierarchy came other officials whose title, *qa-si-re-u,* is plainly the same word, *basileus,* that meant "king" in classical Greek. How this word was so strangely upgraded—how the petty officials of the Mycenaean age became kings later on—has been interestingly explained by Sterling Dow of Harvard. Concerning the catastrophe that ended the Mycenaean age, he remarks that "the effect was not just the destruction of property . . . The

111

state was almost literally decapitated. The whole organization and the whole mentality at the top—that of the palace bureaucracy—went. Small local officials, numerous in each state, whose title had been *basileus* and was significantly kept, replaced the one *Wanax*. [In other words, each] state was broken up into smaller local units."

Before the great disaster Dow refers to, however, centralization was the rule. Little, primarily agricultural Pylos must have been exceptionally closely overseen, after all, if it had two provinces, two provincial governors, two deputy governors, sixteen district officers, sixteen deputy district officers, and numerous lesser officials stationed in the villages and attached to the guilds or corporations in which craftsmen often seem to have been organized. Yet this kind of elaborate administrative hierarchy was essential, if only because the king, or rather his palace bureaucracy, had an unappeasable appetite for the most detailed data on all sorts of subjects. They were particularly interested in subjects having to do with the taxable, military and labor resources of the kingdom. Judging by the tablets, the palace scribes were also remarkably fond of head counts, whether of people or of animals. A group of tablets having to do with issues of bronze to bronzesmiths, for instance, shows that the bronzesmiths of the Pylian kingdom were all known by name to the palace administrators, whose records also indicated which town each smith worked in, which smiths were in the service of the gods, and so on. There are other equally detailed lists of individuals, such as one concerning the clothworkers attached to a sanctuary in the town called Me-ta-pa; the women weavers were apparently slaves, and the list gives the parentage of each one, showing that at least one of the parents of each woman had also been a temple slave.

At both Knossos and Pylos, there are also immensely detailed censuses of the flocks and herds. One place in Crete, for instance, is shown as having exactly 60 rams, 270 ewes, 49 he-goats, 130 she-goats, 17 boars, 41 sows, 2 bulls and 4 cows. The similar Pylos censuses begin with entries

112

*Two views of a gold cup depicting a bull-catching.
From a tomb at Vaphio near Sparta, c. 1500 B.C.*

listing very large numbers of animals with no owner shown, whereas there is a note of the owner of each of the smaller groups of animals that complete each list. The animals with no owner shown are presumed to have belonged to the king himself. If this is correct, the King of Pylos possessed quite literally tens of thousands of sheep and goats. Incidentally, large cattle are extremely rare in these censuses, to the point that the bulls and cows in the Knossos tablets are individually named. They had names like "Dapple," "Dusky" and "Ginger," which make them sound charming. The chances are they were not charming, however, since the most likely reason for their rarity is the fact, suggested by the bull-frescoes, that the cattle of Mycenaean times had not evolved very far from the wild, extremely dangerous and very large *bos primigenius*. Assuming this inference is sound, cattle breeding must have been nearly as hazardous an occupation as bull-leaping itself—even if the cattle were generally allowed to run almost wild, as is suggested by the bull-catching scenes on the Vaphio cups.

The evidence that every creature in Pylos was subject to census, from the goats to the people, fits neatly with the evidence concerning labor-service and ration scales. The prevalence of labor-service is attested by the monuments. The mighty fortifications and great tombs at Mycenae, for instance, could not possibly have been constructed without the use of corvée-labor on an enormous scale. The tablets also show evidence of labor-service, in the form of records of rations issued to persons who do not seem to have been slaves. The rations were undoubtedly issued because these people had been called up for corvée-labor on roads or water channels or for some other purpose. Feeding those called up is standard practice wherever the corvée prevails and the government is reasonably honest. (But a close watch has to be kept on petty officials when the administration is corrupt, as in China in the last war, for instance, where the villagers called up for labor-service on the great Chengtu airfield complex for General Curtis LeMay's B-29 bombers, numbered over 600,000 men, women and children.) In

115

*. . on the south end of the citadel of Tiryns,*
*. . alled Great Casemate.*

the Linear B tablets, the groups of persons receiving rations while perform-ing labor-service are sometimes very large by Bronze Age standards, though not by Chinese standards. One Knossos tablet indicates that 493 "men of Lyktos," 522 "men of Tylissos" and 61 "men of Lato" got rations in this manner. Another concerns "women of Knossos," "women of Amnisos" and "women of Phaistos" and others. According to Professor Palmer, "the numbers [of women] catered for in all these places" can be calculated, even though the tablet is incomplete; and he estimates that in each place the number lay somewhere between 500 and 1,000. Incidentally, the watch kept by the Knossos palace scribes on the issuance of rations at Phaistos and the other places named proves that in the period of the Linear B tablets most of Crete was under the tight control of Knossos.

The settled and methodical habits of the Greek bureaucracies of the Bronze Age are once again indicated by the standardization of ration scales and their differentiation according to the status of the recipients. The basic ration unit seems to have been about one liter of wheat per day for a free man. If the rations were issued in figs, the quantities were the same as in the case of wheat; but if barley was issued, the daily ration was about two liters, since barley is less nourishing than wheat. Slaves received half the ration of free men. Women got a little less than half the men's ration. Children got half the women's ration. When rations were issued to persons of higher status, they got more than the basic free man's ration. Temple personnel, for instance, received about 1½ liters of wheat per day or the equivalent. All of this has many echoes. In Greek classical times, a free man's ration of grain was approximately the same as in the Mycenaean age; but the Mycenaean wine ration was twice the ration given in classical times, perhaps because the earlier wine was weaker. Again, the free man-slave ration-ratio reappears in Greek classical times; a Spartiate fighting man in the field got twice the ration of his accompanying helot servant, as we know from the rations allowed the Spartiates and their helots on Sphacteria.

after a truce had been arranged. But the main echoes of the Greek Bronze Age system come from the ancient Mesopotamian civilizations and Egypt, and particularly from the former. The figures given above are those calculated from the tablets by Professor Palmer, whose numerical detective work to ascertain the ration system is well worth studying at first hand, in his *Mycenaeans and Minoans*. In summing up, he says: "The [units of measurement, which he also analyzed] with their particular ratios, and the system of social rationing speak for themselves. That the system was ultimately derived from the Mesopotamian world is hardly open to doubt."

If the conjectures of the majority of scholars are correct, the commerce of the Greek Bronze Age states was also, in the main, a royal monopoly. Notice has already been given to the widespread rejection of Wace's view that the large building outside the walls of Mycenae which he called the "house of the oil merchant" was really the private house of a free-enterprise oil merchant. The building contained a room equipped with a special stove in which liquids could have been heated in double boilers. This was in fact the way that perfumed oils and ointments were made in the ancient world, as surviving recipes show. Hence Wace's house of the oil merchant is now thought of, instead, as Agamemnon's perfume factory, where oils and ointments scented with all kinds of aromatic herbs were prepared for home sale and for export.* This interpretation is reinforced by the Pylian evidence, which includes one tablet headed "How Alxoitas gave to Thyestes the unguent-boiler spices for boiling in the unguent." Thyestes received coriander, ginger grass and other things, including wine and honey, both of which were used in ancient perfume manufacture, the honey being added, no doubt, because of its moisture-retaining capacity. Alxoitas was undoubtedly a royal official, most probably the steward of

---

* *Many of the tablets Wace found have to do with spices and aromatics; but there is a difficulty, because a good many of them also have to do with wool.*

*Wine cups from Pylos.*

the Pylian kingdom as we have seen. The tablet was found in the palace at Pylos. Hence it is pretty clear that Thyestes was working for royal account.

From these and other indicators, in fact, it looks as if the Bronze Age Greek palaces were the administrative centers from which industrial output of various kinds was managed and directed. Within the range of Bronze Age possibilities—metalworking, cloth and embroidery production, perfumery, wine production, output of ornaments and luxury furniture, pottery production and so on—each palace may well have had its own manufacturing specialties. Although Professor Blegen dislikes the idea, the strong possibility has to be considered that pottery was a Pylian specialty. A good many of the experts think so at any rate; and it is a fact that such huge quantities of pots have not been recorded at any other Greek mainland site, although there were large pottery stores at Knossos. Moreover, Pylos was ideally placed to make good profits from exports of fine Mycenaean wares.

Since pottery is easily imitated, it is not often a profitable export; but when the differences in quality are very striking, pottery can be sold abroad at a good profit. Thus our greatest collections of Athenian wares

118

*Painted pottery from Pylos (photograph by Carl W. Blegen).*

of the high period come from Etruscan sites, because the Etruscans admired the inimitable triumphs of the Athenian potters. In the Eastern Mediterranean, in the Bronze Age, Mycenaean pottery was extremely popular; but in this highly civilized region, Mycenaean wares none the less had to meet the competition of skilled local potters. Thus pottery exported to the civilized centers is generally found in shapes that could have held something else when shipped—perfume or wine, for instance. More fragile pieces which could not be used as containers, like the champagne glass-shaped wine cups in the wine cup pantry at Pylos, are not often found; and if found, they are generally local imitations of Greek work. But in the Adriatic, northwest up the Greek coast from Pylos, there were ruder peoples, who would have found it very difficult to imitate the fine Mycenaean wares. Epirus, as will be seen later, was in fact one very probable center of the less civilized Dorian Greeks who were, in turn, the most probable destroyers of Pylos. Hence, the 2,853 wine cups in the wine cup pantry of Nestor's palace may well have been waiting to be packed and shipped up the coast for sale to the rough Dorian chiefs. As more recent experience shows, great profits are always to be made by selling things of fairly common use as luxury objects to less developed peoples, for whom these things

119

really are luxuries. Beads for the Indians are the obvious case in point. On this hypothesis, which is of course wholly based on circumstantial evidence, pottery became a manufacturing specialty of the Pylian palace because the proximity of Pylos to a profitable pottery market made this specialty a sound business proposition. To this, however, one must add the usual caveats. In the first place, the pots in the wine cup pantry were all undecorated; and export pottery was normally painted. But this is not decisive, in view of the fine potting of the Pylian ware. In the second place, Pylos was just as well placed to trade with southern Italy as with northwestern Greece; and Lord William Taylour's finds show there was an extensive Greek trade with southern Italy in Mycenaean times. On the other side of the balance sheet, however, there is the sheer size of the Pylian fleet in the *Iliad* ship list. Such a large fleet meant, above all, a busy peacetime trade. If there was such a trade, whether in pottery or other things, it is likely to have included northwestern Greece, since the best gains are always to be made on the "beads for the Indians" system. But on this question there can be no final answer until there is serious digging in Epirus to test the suggestion I have made.

In any case, the existence of a wide-ranging, lively commerce is revealed by surviving treasures of the Greek Bronze Age kings. These include objects incorporating imported raw materials as well as imported objects. Another proof of trade, already cited, is the number of pots and other things of Mycenaean Greek origin which have been found at many places around the Eastern Mediterranean and as far west as Sicily. Evidence of trade is also conspicuous in the clay tablet records. For example, the description of a throne-like chair in Chapter II comes from a Pylian inventory that lists no less than five tripod caldrons, each one differently decorated, but all stated to be "of Cretan workmanship." No other objects are mentioned as coming from Crete. The Pylian inventory contains no other mention of these big, three-legged bronze caldrons which continued in use as

120

*Ivory plaque found in Spata, Attica, c. 1300* B.C.

dinner party showpieces and objects for religious dedication well into Greek classical times, as the excavations at Olympia and elsewhere have revealed. It is tempting to guess, therefore, that tripod caldrons were one of the manufacturing specialties of the Knossos palace. If one may judge by the surviving Greek archaic examples, the caldrons were very large, complex in form, and rather elaborately decorated. Hence they called for specialized bronze-casting techniques, and this could have given the Knossos craftsmen an advantage in their manufacture. The same Pylian inventory lists objects of one sort or another which are either entirely composed of or are decorated with gold, rock crystal, ivory and ebony. All these substances must have come from abroad—the ebony and gold almost certainly from Egypt, which was the great gold source of the Bronze Age world; the ivory from Syria-Palestine, a great ivory-working center where elephants also

121

survived until the ninth century B.C., and perhaps from Egypt too; and the rock crystal perhaps from Crete, where bits of rock crystal are sometimes found to this day. Except for the tripod caldrons from Crete, however, the inventory makes no mention of the places of origin of any of the actual objects listed. Hence we may guess that the ebony, ivory, gold and rock crystal came into Pylos as raw material, to be worked up by the king's artisans. But the kinds of ivory decoration which are noted also leave open the possibility that ready-carved ivory plaques and decorative motifs were imported from Syria-Palestine, and were then used in Pylos as appliqués and inlays on furniture. If so, the trade went both ways, for Mycenaean Greek ivories have also been found at Megiddo in Palestine and elsewhere.

The inventory in question is also one of many proofs (like the much earlier tomb-finds at Mycenae) that the Greek Bronze Age palaces contained astonishing hoards of treasure. No one is quite sure what was being inventoried in this instance. Ventris and Chadwick concluded that the things listed were the contents of a palace reception room. Palmer has proposed instead that they were the grave goods buried with a Pylian grandee. E. L. Bennett, Jr., does not accept wholeheartedly either interpretation, and considers the question open. What is unquestionable, however, is that the objects listed were splendid to the point of being showy. Besides

*Women watching from a palace window. Fresco fragment from Mycenae.*

the chair "of crystal, inlaid with cyanus, tin (?) and gold" and its accompanying golden-strutted footstool, there was one table entirely made of ivory except for a marble central leg; there were eight additional tables, chairs and footstools made wholly or in part of ebony and ivory; there was a chair of ebony inlaid or otherwise decorated with golden birds; there were four tables and eight footstools of other materials inlaid with rosettes or other patterns in ivory; and there was still another particularly grand table of stone and rock crystal, nine-footed, and inlaid with "cyanus, tin (?) and gold." All this, remember, was in addition to numerous bronze utensils, which were also close to semiprecious at that time, plus bronze weapons, gold necklaces, libation jugs and so on. Of this accumulation of treasure in the palaces, Sterling Dow has the following to say:

"With their interest in astonishingly petty details, the tablets show a bookkeeping-shopkeeping mentality. The economy in some sense is planned. The object of the plan, or at least one object, is to fill the palace magazines with agricultural produce (Knossos) and the shelves with thousands of vases (Pylos), the sale of which would increase the royal treasures. . . . In other royal economies, i.e. in states where the king's income is very large (taxes, tribute, booty), and his expenses (army bodyguard, court, royal burials) are less, treasure can accumulate to enormous totals (cf. the Achaemenids and the Ptolemies)."

Dow, who was writing for specialists, did not of course mean to suggest that the Greek rulers of the Bronze Age piled up gold and other valuables on the scale of the Persian Great Kings, with their vast territories, millions of subjects and rich metallic resources, or the Ptolemaic Pharaohs, who planned the Egyptian economy almost as strictly as the economy of Communist China, with the sole purpose of producing surpluses for their own use. But if the difference in scale is remembered, the examples cited by Dow are still instructive. The simple size of the Bronze Age Greek palaces indicates that the upper-class consumers of the state surpluses were not

123

immensely numerous. The Pylian throne room, for instance, could not comfortably accommodate more than two- or threescore persons at a feast or ceremonial. And if the surplus consumers were not many, and the economy was carefully managed to produce a surplus, the resulting treasure accumulation must have been quite impressive enough to make the above-mentioned Pylian inventory nothing very much out of the ordinary. On this subject, Dow has more to say that gives food for thought:

"Within each . . . state . . . considering them from the point of view of the subjects, it seems clear that the authority of the monarch and his bureaucracy over a great many subjects was tremendous. People appear to have lived within an intricate framework of *system*, features of which were [economic] specialization under central control, with writing used to communicate and preserve orders and records. To some extent intricate and complex, the different functions—commerce and agriculture and manufacture—depended on each other. If treasure and the safeguarding of it were dominant concerns in the king's mind, subservience and care in fulfilling his duties in the system dominated the subject. The subject knew no other way of life."

In purely schematic terms, this is the best short summary of the nature of the joke that the great Linear B discovery played on the discoverers. What could be less like anything that was imaginable, as a probable description of the states ruled over by Homer's heroes? How could this have been forecast in the time before the Linear B tablets put Homer's heroes in a solid historical context? Yet Dow's schematic summary, effective as it is, none the less requires two footnotes. His reference to "writing used to communicate and preserve orders and records" represents one view of a most interesting matter. Many students think that knowledge of Linear B was not widespread in Mycenaean Greek society, and further hold that writing was only used for strictly practical purposes. They have good arguments on their side. The syllabic script is so clumsy, for one thing, that it would not have easily lent itself to poetry* or to any but dryly annalistic history. For another thing, the Greeks seem to have lost the art of writing at the end of the Mycenaean age, only becoming literate again when they made their Phoenician borrowing some centuries later. In addition, there is the curious fact that Linear A survives in religious inscriptions and in other ways, as well as in the clay tablet records, indicating a script at least familiar to a literate upper class; whereas Linear B has as yet been found only in the form of business and administrative documents, with no inscriptions to indicate use of Linear B by any but specialists. These facts certainly suggest that Linear B was known only to a narrow class of persons who either perished, or found no further market for their skills, when catastrophe finally overtook the Mycenaean Greek states. Yet neither of these arguments is conclusive.

Professor Bennett, who speaks as the leading American authority on Linear B texts, is firmly persuaded that a fair number of late Bronze Age Greeks—at least the noble and upper-artisan classes—were able to read and write. He too has strong evidence in the form of numerous small clay sealings with marks showing that threads passed through them—sealings which were clearly used, in fact, on thread-wrapped letters or documents of some foldable material like paper or parchment. Professor Bennett suspects that history and literature were written in Linear B, even though nothing of that sort survives because, of course, clay tablets would not have been used for such a purpose. As to this question, in sum, one has a free choice of the answer. For what that may be worth, I prefer Professor Bennett's answer, simply because literacy was often what is now so annoyingly described as a "status symbol" in the bureaucratically organized societies of the remote past. If literacy was an acquirement generally admired and

---

* But the rather similar Cypriot script was used for poetry. Four hexameters survive.

125

envied, all the more important persons in the late Bronze Age Greek states will have wanted to learn how to read and write. For doing so, they also had the additional motive of the prudent man who wishes to be able to check the balance sheets presented by his accountant.

So much for Footnote 1. Professor Dow's summary description of late Mycenaean monarchy also seems to me to demand another, even more important footnote because of what it leaves out—the art that comes down to us; the Homeric epics that preserve, in some sense, the remembered personalities of the great men of that time; the probable character and tastes of Echelawon and the *Lawagetas* and Alectryon son of Eteocles and the other noble personages in the Pylos tablets who would have gone to fight at Troy if born at the right moment. These Greeks of the late Bronze Age were artistic creators of a very high order, as we can tell from the exceptionally beautiful things they made and the charming frescoes they painted on their palace walls. Their art furthermore strikes me, as it has struck more expert persons like Professor Wace, as being specifically Greek in character; for it is humanistic, life-loving, full of sensuous enjoyment of every kind of beauty, and at its best endowed with wonderful inner tension and power. It is not the art, in other words, that one would expect to see produced by an anthill society of mere bureaucrats and serfs. And I think it is mistaken to suppose that late Greek Bronze Age society was at all anthill-like, solely because it was bureaucratically organized.

The Homeric epics drive home the same point, and so, I think, do Alectryon and Echelawon in a dimmer sort of way. There were in fact two different and contrasting elements in Mycenaean Greek society. One was the native element—the element descended from the Greek beginnings, as Indo-European horse breeders organized in tribes led by the fighting men. The other element was acquired—the higher civilization learned by the Greeks after they pushed into Greece, of which their social organization was only one aspect. From the interaction of these elements, Mycenaean society

126

*Detail of the Warrior Vase from Mycenae, dated c. 1180 B.C., shortly before the citadel fell.*

and Mycenaean art resulted. Unless we leave room for this interaction, and keep in mind its probable effects, both the art that comes down to us and the epics that commemorate the war against Troy necessarily become anomalous and even incomprehensible. To put the point more simply, it is needful to bear in mind that Mycenaean Greek society was not merely bureaucratic; it was also heroic. This is the special, peculiar admixture which produced Greek civilization of the late Bronze Age.

Why was Pylos destroyed? Who first looted and then burned the palace of Nestor? What brought the Mycenaean age of Greece to the sudden and terrible end, which is so starkly marked by the same ash-laden destruction levels at almost every known Mycenaean site? Professor Blegen long ago gave his own answer to these questions. In his 1939 report on his Pylos excavation, in which he told the scholarly world that Nestor's long-sought palace had at last been found, and revealed the existence of the first Linear B archive ever discovered on the mainland, he also said:

"The Dorian invasion, whatever its source and however it ran its course, has left a broad gash, like a fire-scar in a mountain forest, cutting through the archaeological panorama of ancient Greece. Many towns and settlements that flourished in the preceding Heroic age were henceforth abandoned or declined to a state of insignificance. Even some of the great and noted strongholds sank into virtual oblivion, and the places where they had stood were lost to the view of man."

In suggesting the invading Dorians as the destroyers of Pylos, Blegen was merely following the Greeks of the classical period. Their picture of their own past, which comes down to us in both Herodotus and Thucydides, made the Dorian invasion a cardinal turning point. According to this traditional picture, the Greeks came into Greece in two main waves. The first was the wave of the earlier Greek-speakers, whose entrance into Greece we have already traced. The classical Greeks called their ancestors of this first wave the "Achaeans," in this following Homer, and they credited the Achaeans with creating the civilization that is described in the Homeric epics. According to Thucydides, it was not until eighty years after the fall of Troy*—or long after all of Homer's heroes were dead and buried—that the second wave of Greek invaders broke over the peninsula. The people of this second wave were the Dorians, who were remembered as being much more crude and primitive than the Achaeans, but were believed to have possessed iron weapons instead of bronze. Still following the tradition, the Dorians destroyed all the Bronze Age kingdoms except Athens, where the Athenians boasted that the Acropolis had never been taken. They spread over all of the Peloponnese except mountainous, infertile Arcadia. And they also occupied Rhodes and most of Crete. One result of the invasion was the prevalence of the Doric dialect of Greek in the regions the Dorians conquered. In the Peloponnese, for instance, Arcadia was a dialect-island of the older speech, while Sparta, which had been Menelaus' kingdom, became the greatest of the Dorian states. Another of the invasion's results was a migration, or perhaps one should say a flight, of Greeks of the older stock to the coast of Asia Minor, where the people in the Greek cities founded at this time spoke either the Aeolic dialect, or else the Ionic branch of the Greek tongue which was also used at Athens.

Such, in brief, is the traditional account, except for one detail. The Greeks of the classical age also gave modern scholars the kind of

---

* *Professor Blegen, unquestionably the leading authority on this subject, confidently dates the fall of Troy about 1260 B.C. This supplants the formerly accepted date first proposed by Eratosthenes, which was 1184 B.C.*

present they like best—namely, a point to argue about for decade after decade—by customarily referring to the Dorian invasion as "the return of the Heraclids." The principal Heraclids of the classical age were the twin lines of kings of Doric Sparta. There would be no scholarly argument, therefore, if the customary phrase had only been "the coming of the Heraclids." Some scholars think this is, in effect, what the traditional phrase really did mean; for the word customarily translated as "return," which is *kathodos*, could also mean "descent" in older Greek. None the less, the translation of the word as "return" came to be general. But why was this terrible, fiercely destructive invasion called a "return"? Who was returning to what, and where had they been in the interval?

Partly because of these nagging questions, another theory about the end of Mycenaean Greece has been propounded since Professor Blegen wrote his famous 1939 excavation report. If this theory is correct, the Greeks whom Homer called Achaeans were merely the bronze-weapon-owning upper class of mixed Greek tribes, which also included large elements of more humble people of Dorian stock. The long siege of Troy kept most of the able-bodied members of the bronze-armed upper class out of Greece for ten long years. Almost unavoidably, therefore, it must have led to political troubles and a certain weakening of the Mycenaean nobles' authority at home. Something of this sort is in fact reflected, so it is suggested, by the lurid story of Agamemnon's return, and the murder of the War Leader of the Greeks by Clytemnestra and Aegisthus, and the subsequent bloody revenge taken by Orestes and Electra. The proponents of the new theory further suggest that the first Greek-speaking occupiers of Greece may have left behind, on the fringes of the Greek peninsula, so to say, some smaller, poorer tribes with leading families of purely Dorian lineage. These outliers, the theory continues, may have noted the weakness of the Achaean ruling class after the Trojan War. They may therefore have begun to move southwards, appealing the while to their fellow Dorians who formed the

131

oppressed social substratum of the Mycenaean kingdoms. And this intrusion of outlying Dorians under Doric-speaking chiefs may then have been remembered as a "return" in the Doric states of later Greece. For in these states, the expelled or massacred Achaean nobles would have been portrayed as illegitimate oppressors, while the assumption of leadership of the Dorian substratum by chiefs of their own stock would have been presented as a restoration of legitimate rule.

Yet the proponents of the new theory none the less think that the southward movement of outliers was essentially subsidiary. They hold in fact that the collapse of the Mycenaean kingdoms was mainly caused by a far-spreading surge of social revolution, most probably resulting from the social, political and economic disruption after the long siege of Troy. Before my trip to Pylos I had heard about the new social revolutionary theory from the brilliant director of the Greek government's archaeological department, the late Dr. John Papadimitriou. I found myself vaguely picturing the palace of Nestor being put to the torch by the oppressed commons of Messenia, out of patience at last with the endless exactions of the king and his lords. So I asked Blegen whether he had changed his mind since his 1939 report.

I quickly discovered that his view of the matter was not only unchanged; it was more firmly held than ever, if anything. His criticism of the social revolutionary theory was based, first of all, on its failure to account for the curious Greek dialect pattern of the classical age; but he also put strong emphasis on his belief that nearly all the Bronze Age palaces and fortresses came to an end at about the same time. Pylos, Mycenae, Tiryns, Gla, Orchomenus—all these and others were engulfed, so he thinks, in a single continuous wave of destruction. The *Cadmeia* at Thebes fell in the earlier local war already mentioned, and the Acropolis at Athens, which never fell as the old tradition asserted, were the sole exceptions to the general rule. But even at Athens great fear must have ɔeen felt at this moment of widespread ruin. The excavations of Professor Oscar Broneer have shown that the Acropolis was actually attacked; ιuts of the latest Mycenaean period were found to have been burned on the high slopes of the rock. They have shown too that a strenuous effort was made to render the Acropolis impregnable by ensuring its water supply. The haste of the well diggers is indicated by their use of temporary wooden steps to reach the trickle of water far below the earth. Because wood was used, the steps soon rotted. Hence the well dug deep into the rock, in the final crisis of the Greek Bronze Age civilization, was not seen again by living men until Broneer found its traces.

"Since this is what happened," Professor Blegen summed up, "I have no real doubts about the Greeks' tradition of the Dorian invasion. It fits all the facts as we know them, including the very important facts concerning the distribution of the Dorian and other Greek dialects in classical times. I could believe in one social revolution, at Mycenae for instance, or even in two social revolutions, at Mycenae and Tiryns, which are so close together. But it isn't sensible, in my opinion, to assume that all the Bronze Age kingdoms except Athens could have been destroyed by revolutions which broke out almost simultaneously, from one end of Greece to the other. Furthermore, the philologists who've been working on our Pylos tablets think they've found evidence of preparations for an invasion."

The archaeological record shows that Professor Blegen, who is nothing if not cautious, is well worth listening to when he simply voices a suspicion. Great weight must certainly be given to his judgment when he voices a positive opinion. To be sure, the chances are rather strong that his extremely positive opinion about the Dorian invasion will never be absolutely proven. If the rude villages and forts of the Dorian departure point should be excavated later on, for instance, no one could be quite sure that this really was the Dorian departure point. In the levels that

133

reveal the crisis of Mycenaean civilization, nothing has yet been found to which anyone can point with confidence and say, *"This is Dorian."*

Maybe, by a near-miracle, this will happen some day. For example, one can imagine a Dorian tribesman, inflamed by greed for loot, dropping his iron sword or dagger while sacking a Mycenaean palace, and not pausing to retrieve his weapon before the palace was put to the torch. The discovery of an iron weapon, in the ashes of a destruction level marking the end of a great center of Mycenaean Bronze Age culture, could most logically be explained on the ground that the intrusive weapon had belonged to one of the destroyers. If similar weapons were then discovered in a roughly contemporary non-Mycenaean site on the fringes of Greece, it would also be logical to assume that this was one of the departure points of the destroyers. Failing such an unlikely sequence of discoveries, however, the only course is to take the best opinion available. I therefore take Professor Blegen's opinion. To spare the reader the endless repetition of "If this is correct," "Assuming the invaders really were the Dorians," and so on and on, I shall regard the foregoing pages as a warning that there is a disputed point here. And I shall proceed, confidently following Blegen, on the assumption, hereafter unqualified, that the Dorians were the invaders who left the "fire-scar" which cuts so sharply "through the archaeological panorama of ancient Greece."

On this assumption, the geographical position of Pylos becomes particularly interesting. As noted already in passing, most of those who believe in the Dorian invasion also believe that the Dorian departure point was in far northern and northwestern Greece. Epirus, in particular, is thought of as a likely area of Dorian occupation before the invasion. Among the major Mycenaean centers of the late Bronze Age, Pylos, on the west coast of Greece, was the nearest to the ruder peoples in the northwest. As we have seen, the prosperity of Pylos may be in part explained by an export trade, in pottery or other goods, which followed the oastwise route to this northwestern region. If the Dorian invaders also ollowed the coast (as they must certainly have done if they came by sea, or mariners of that early period never lost sight of land if they could ьelp it), Pylos may have been the first really major Mycenaean center hat they attacked. This fits rather neatly with the comparatively early date—1200 B.C.—which Professor Blegen gives for the destruction of Nestor's palace. Very recently, important Mycenaean remains have begun o be discovered in Elis, to the north of Pylos; and the Dorians may of ourse have mopped up the Mycenaean Greeks of Elis on their way to ⁷ylos. The destruction levels reportedly support this view. However, if he kings of Pylos had also been making large profits by exports of My- ʼenaean luxury goods, such as fine pottery, to their ruder Dorian cousins, hen Pylos would have been the natural first objective of the Dorian in- vaders, simply because they would have heard so much about the wealth and grandeur of the Pylian kingdom. By the same token, the Mycenaean King of Pylos, with his lively commercial interest in the coastwise trade with the northwest, would have got some sort of warning of the warlike muster of the Dorians. This again fits with the harder available evidence, as will be seen. Among the circumstantial evidence, in truth, there is only one item that may seem to controvert this attempted reconstruction of the prelude to the destruction of Mycenaean Pylos. But this seemingly contradictory item is not really contradictory, if you happen to remember the Polish cavalry in the Second World War.

To begin with the seeming contradiction, it lies in the obvious fact that if the Dorians already had iron weapons, as the tradition asserts,*

* The tradition is strengthened by the fact that one of the very early iron in- dustries has been discovered in Illyria (modern southwestern Yugoslavia) with which peoples living in Epirus must have been in contact. Heichelheim dates this industry from "the late Mycenaean period."

the Pylians ought to have known about this great advance in weaponry. For if there really were Pylian-Dorian trade contacts, the fact that the Dorian fighting men were carrying a new sort of sword, of a different color and a different metal, must surely have been reported to the *Lawageta* and other leading fighting men of Pylos. Why, then, did the Pylians not make the obvious conversion from bronze to iron?

The answer to that question comes in two natural parts, I suggest (and here I speak boldly, for I am on political reporter's rather than archaeologist's territory). In the first place, the otherwise more civilized and advanced Pylians would have been reluctant to believe that a great advance in weaponry could possibly be achieved by their Dorian poor relations, with their different and therefore barbarous dialect and much rougher ways. In the second place, unless the Pylian fighting men were very different from any subsequent soldiers, they would have been inclined

*Fighting warriors, on a gold seal from the second grave circle at Mycenae, c. 1500 B.C.*

*Gold votive shield from Pylos —miniature object.*

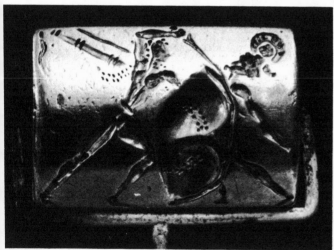

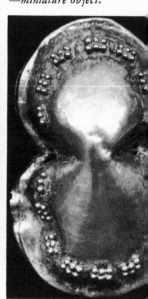

ͻ pooh-pooh the ugly, gray, innovating blades of the Dorians, even if the
Ɔorians had not been less advanced than the Pylians. Every soldier, one
ꞁust remember, always believes the weapon he has been trained with is
ꞁe best possible weapon, unless and until the harsh test of battle proves
ꞁe contrary. The Polish cavalry, charging Hitler's tanks with their lance-
ꞁennons bravely fluttering, were not lunatics as some people might sup-
ꞁose; they were simply the most extreme recent cases of soldiers believing
ꞁ the weapon they were trained with. The big-bomber generals of the
ⵑmerican air staff, who downgraded missile development because missiles
ꞁere costly and they were sure "nothing would replace the bomber," are
ꞁlso worth remembering in this connection. If we remember such recent
ꞁases, we shall no longer be surprised because the Pylian army did not
ꞁasten to exchange its glory-drenched, ever-victorious bronze swords for
ꞁwords made by a new method, and of a metal seldom before used in
ꞁreece except for an occasional piece of jewelry.

The failure to convert to iron is also understandable for another,
ꞁore technical reason. In brief, the earliest iron weapons may not have
ꞁeen immensely better, sword-for-sword, than the good bronze blades of
ꞁate Mycenaean times. Some students of the subject have even suggested
ꞁhat at this early stage in iron technology a swordsman must have had to
ꞁtop and bend his sword back into shape after a few hacks at his enemy.
Ɔne can all but hear the Pylian senior officers snorting with complacent
ꞁisdain because of the defects of iron. But in the manner of so many brass
ꞁats everywhere, the Pylian senior officers would then have failed to
ꞁotice the essential point—that iron, being common, could be used to arm
ꞁveryone, instead of being restricted, like bronze, to the armament of a
ꞁilitary elite. Whole hordes of iron-armed soldiers would soon overwhelm
ꞁ smaller, elite, bronze-armed force, even if the individual bronze swords
ꞁere better than the iron swords. One may picture the shock of the bronze-
ꞁielding Pylian elite soldiers when they discovered—too late alas—that

among the Dorians even the lowest of the low were permitted to serve in the battle line. Or they may have known this, too, in advance of the Dorian attack, but dismissed it as beneath their notice on the ground that "only gentlemen make good soldiers," in the way they used to hold that "rankers never make good officers" in the old British army.

So much for circumstantial evidence. Some day, when the Greek northwest has been better excavated, more will be known. Meanwhile, one can only say that the circumstantial evidence hangs together in a way that makes an intelligible and logical pattern, and that there is nothing in the archaeological record to dispute the logic of this pattern. Let us turn now to the harder archaeological evidence and, more particularly, to the evidence of the archive of Linear B tablets that has been found at Pylos. In his *Mycenaeans and Minoans*, Professor Palmer has remarked that ". a sense of emergency pervades the whole [Pylian Linear B] archive for all its sober and matter-of-fact appearance." But if this is correct, the first question is how long this "sense of emergency" detected by Palmer endured at Pylos.

The answer is that we cannot be quite sure. For all we know, people may have been running up and down the court of Nestor's palace barking like dogs, long before the first surviving clay tablet was inscribed. But this seems unlikely, in view of the clay tablet archive's "sober and matter-of-fact appearance." It is therefore interesting that the archive probably covers a very short period—a decidedly shorter period, I should say, once again speaking only as a political reporter, than the archaeological experts have as yet suggested. Because of the very nature of the Linear B tablets, the experts are unanimous that we have only the tag end of the records of Pylos and Knossos. This has to be true, because the tablets were not designed to last for more than a year or so. They have only lasted down to our own time because they were quite literally cooked in the fires that destroyed the Pylos and Knossos palaces. But as a political reporter am as much struck by the comparatively small number of the Pylos tablets as I am by their transformation into quasi-terracotta.

The number of surviving tablets is so striking because it is disproportionate to the number of scribes whose handwritings have been so carefully studied by E. L. Bennett, Jr. It may well be, for instance, that many tablets were stored in the upper story of the Pylos palace, and in the fire fell through to the lower floor in such a way that they were shattered beyond recognition before they could be preserved by thorough cooking. But if you simply suppose that the surviving evidence is not grossly misleading, the disproportion I have mentioned must be faced.

In brief, a few more than 1,200 Linear B tablets survive from Pylos, of which about 1,000 were found in the so-called archive room which Professor Blegen thinks was really the tax collector's office. (The numbers are approximate, because the experts are still making "joins" which turn two tablet fragments into one.) Yet Professor Bennett, even after reducing his earlier estimates, feels pretty confident that the tablets show the handwritings of more than forty scribes. All persons with bureaucratic experience can see that this many scribes ought to have produced more tablets.

To be sure, only eight scribes did a large part of the record-keeping that survives. To be sure, one must also assume that all the Greek administrators of the late Bronze Age, however busy they may have been with other things, were also scribes. The steward of the kingdom, Alxoitas, was a considerable personage, as his herds in the animal censuses show; but if he was not a scribe, able to check the accounts in person, he is dead-certain to have been a sadly inefficient steward. Furthermore, even the most secretarially specialized scribes must have had many other things to do besides preparing clay tablet records. Part of their time will have had to be given to compiling more permanent records, on sheets of leather or whatever else was used for this purpose. One of the most interesting documents from Pylos, for instance, is a long register of proposals for

landholdings. The register would surely have needed to be transcribed fo
permanence, when and if the holdings had been confirmed. Then, toc
consider the men who sat in the archive room-tax collector's office, wher
the largest single deposit of clay tablets was found. Besides listing ta
payments received, these scribes must have had to check the measure o
each new delivery of tax oil, before it lost its identity in the huge oliv
oil-receiving jar in the anteroom; and they must also have had to coun
or weigh deliveries of all the other sorts of commodities and/or edibl
creatures which were used to pay taxes in Pylos. But even after all thes
factors have been weighed in the balance, the yield of Linear B tablet
from Nestor's palace still seems surprisingly small, unless it is a drasticall
incomplete yield or unless the period represented is really very short in
deed. Anyone who knows bureaucrats, particularly bureaucrats with a pas
sion for detail and a fondness for list-making, also knows that about 1,20c
tablets—and far, far less than 1,200 complete documents—is a tiny outpu
for more than forty scribes. From the very smallness of the scribes' out
put, it therefore seems to me highly likely that the Pylos tablets actuall
cover a period of hardly more than a few weeks.

On the basis of the existing evidence, therefore, we canno
be sure that the last King of Pylos had very *early* warning of an im
pending attempt to invade his kingdom. But if Professor Palmer is half
way correct, we can be sure that the last King of Pylos had *some* warning

or the whole Linear B archive from Pylos is shot through with seeming-
vidence of preparations to repel invaders. To be sure, some scholars
ather haughtily say that there is no proof of emergency in the military
neasures described in the Pylian archive, but it seems to me they have a
lifficult though negative point to explain away. The palace at Knossos,
ike the palace at Pylos, was wholly unfortified and therefore equally
xposed to attack. The Knossos archive reveals an economic and adminis-
rative system all but identical with the Pylos archive. The Knossos tablets,
f which there are over 3,000, are also nearly three times as numerous
s the Pylos tablets. Yet there is nothing of a military nature in the whole
Knossos archive beyond written inventories of stores. One tablet mentions
,000-plus arrowheads, for instance—only enough for current equipment
f 200 men, it should be noted—and there are also chariot inventories
vith emphasis on the decoration of the chariots. But no hasty, active
nilitary preparations are recorded in the Knossos archive. Why should
his be so, unless the very active preparations described in the Pylos
.rchive had an emergency character? Is not this striking difference most
•asily explained on the basis that the King of Pylos had advance warning
•f his kingdom's doom, whereas the King of Knossos had no warning?
These are outsider's questions, but they are questions which insistently
lemand an answer from the experts who doubt Professor Palmer's and F. J.
Tritsch's interpretation of the Pylos tablets.

141

Among the Pylos tablets suggesting preparations to repel in vaders, pride of place must certainly be given to a set with the heading "How the watchers are guarding the coastal regions." The Pylian scribe kept a careful register, for the tablets appear to distinguish each coast watching unit by the name of its commander, as we would say "Tarleton Raiders." The commanders were apparently local magnates. After the presumed commander's name comes a place name, which is interpreted as being the place where the unit was stationed. Other personal names follow believed to be the list of officers, and then numbers of men are given showing the exact operational strength of the unit in question. At interva in the list, moreover, there is a further note, "And with them is the Com panion, so-and-so." Thus Klymenos' unit was at the place called Me-ta-p his company had 110 men in all; and the Companion attached to it wa Alectryon, son of Eteocles, who has already been mentioned. Being mem bers of the noble class, the Companions like Alectryon presumably owne war chariots; and it is logical to suppose that their function was to assu the swiftest possible liaison with GHQ. We also know that the greate of the nobles, Echelawon, was stationed with the leader of the War Hos the *Lawagetas*, apparently at a place called A-pe-e-ke on the Messenia Gulf; and A-pe-e-ke may therefore have been the GHQ.

Palmer makes a persuasive argument that the tablets cor cerning the "watchers guarding the coastal regions" mesh neatly with ar other set of tablets concerning "rowers going to Pleuron" and othe places. In this group of tablets, "rowers" are listed in sets of 40 sufficientl often to suggest that 40 men were the usual complement of a warship– or rather of the merchant ships converted to military purposes whic probably composed the Pylian fleet. As to the location of the fleet, almo none of Messenia's place names of the Mycenaean period survived int modern or even into classical times; but the palace scribes had the hab of listing the nine towns and seven towns of Nestor's Pylos in an ur varying standard order. This habit of the scribes has made it possible to reconstruct a conjectural geography of the Neleid kingdom. If the reconstruction is right, the units of coast-watching infantry covered the more remote flanks, so to say, being stationed along the two ends of the Pylian coastline. In the center of the coastline there is a long gap, where no coast-watching unit is recorded; but precisely here is where the places like Pleuron have been tentatively located; and here "rowers" were sent.

The concentration of the Pylian fleet, therefore, may also be tentatively located along this central sector of the coast; and the fleet's presence, in turn, may be supposed to have made it unnecessary to cover this particular sector with coast-watching units. If the *Lawagetas* knew his business, the thin screen of coast-watching units and the concentration of the fleet ought to have been backed up by a central reserve, perhaps mustered at A-pe-e-ke, if this was indeed the GHQ rather than a place that the *Lawagetas* and Echelawon happened to be visiting on an inspection trip when the tablet noting their presence there was written. Maybe the *Lawagetas* did not know his business, or grossly underestimated the power of a mass attack by tribes in which even the commonfolk had swords, or simply relied too heavily on the Pylian fleet. The tablets contain no mention of a central reserve, although it was folly not to organize one. But for the reasons already suggested, the time covered by the clay tablet record may be very brief indeed. Thus the main army may have been concentrated, and all the arrangements for provisioning it may have been made, even before our record begins. Certainly the main army of Pylos ought to have been put on a combat-training basis immediately after the first warning. Whereas the coast-watching units would have been sent to their lonely posts on the headlands as late as seemed reasonably safe, and collecting and arming the ships of the fleet would also have taken much longer than the call-up of the army in a state of Pylos' size.

143

The "rower" tablets not only describe rowers who are being sent to this or that place. They also list rowers who are "absent from" places where they presumably ought to have been. The Pylian armed forces, one must remember, numbered no more than a few thousand men at most, but they seem to have had decidely modern paperwork support, which ensured every man either being at his assigned post or being known to be missing from it. By the same token, somewhat more confused tablets concerning musters of bronzeworkers and other craftsmen indicate that the Pylian armed forces also enjoyed rather well-organized logistical support. On this point, Professor Palmer remarks that "the main concentration of 'rowers' (and would it be 'incautious' to imply the Pylian fleet?) was in Southern Messenia and units of craftsmen were being detailed to the same general area. . . . It would not be over-bold to entertain the notion that these bronze-smiths were to be employed as armorers. . . . [Other] texts list types of craftsmen, including 'bakers' and others whose sphere of activity is 'chariots.' The total impression is that these scattered texts reflect the assembly of artificers assigned to military duties."

Ventris and Chadwick, whose *Documents in Mycenaean Greek* was unavoidably based on a less complete examination of the material than Palmer's later-published work, are naturally less venturesome in their interpretations than the Oxford philologist, who was their friend and strong supporter. None the less, if an amateur may be allowed an opinion, I incline to think that one of the most impressive pieces of invasion-preparation evidence from Pylos is to be found in Ventris and Chadwick's *Documents*, in their series of translated tablets having to do with bronze. Here are records of collections of scrap or ingot bronze, from local officials such as those who had the title of *ko-re-te*—from all the Pylian administrative districts, in fact. And there is also a record of the issuance of bronze to bronzesmiths all over Pylos.

The bronze-issue tablets, of which Ventris and Chadwick repor no less than twenty-seven, are always introduced by a place name, and his is always followed by a phrase interpreted as meaning "smiths having received a bronze-allocation." After the smiths are listed and the quantities of bronze given to each are noted, there is another entry, "smiths having no allocation." These smiths too are listed, but without any notes of quantities of bronze since they got no bronze issues, presumably because there was none available for them. One object of listing the bronze-less smiths could have been to maximize war production, by having ready a handy register of unemployed bronzeworkers when and if more bronze had been collected. There is a similar hint of an attempt to maximize output in the fact that besides the regular bronzesmiths of the towns, the metalworkers in the service of the gods were evidently employed. One of the tablets records bronze issues to "the smiths of the Mistress." Moreover, when it is remembered how short a time was probably covered by the whole clay tablet archive, the quantities of bronze involved are also an impressive feature.

In the tablet concerning bronze collections from the district officials, the total collected was 1,046 kilograms, or just over a ton. In the bronze-issue tablets, the amount allocated to the 193 smiths who received bronze was 801 kilograms, or more than four fifths of a ton. For the Bronze Age, when bronze, as has been noted, was almost like a semiprecious metal, these weights of bronze were very considerable. The military purpose of the bronze issues is suggested by a curious fact concerning the two amounts of bronze most commonly allocated to individual bronzesmiths. The smaller amount, 1.5 kilograms, would have been enough to make 1,000 of the small Mycenaean arrowheads, while the larger amount, 5 kilograms, would have sufficed for fourteen Mycenaean swords or long spearheads. The total bronze issued to the smiths would have provided 534,000 arrowheads or 2,300 swords—a remarkable quantity of weapons, especially when it is considered that the numbers of men listed

145

in the coast-watching units totalled only about 1,000.

In addition, Ventris and Chadwick published another tablet listing "masons going to build" at Pylos and three other places. They thought that the masons must have been assigned to build fortifications, and Palmer of course, warmly endorses this idea. The tablet further shows that the masons were to be issued rations on a scale indicating that they were expected to be at work for twenty days. Altogether one has the impression of a rather desperate, sadly inadequate, last-minute attempt to fill the gap left by Neleus and Nestor's failure to build great walls at Pylos like the walls at Mycenae. In his day, Sheikh Mubarrak the Great was known as "the Wall of Kuwait," because, when the town elders pointed out to him that Kuwait's protecting wall was dangerously dilapidated, he replied proudly: "*I* am the wall of Kuwait." Neleus, and Nestor after him, presumably had the same self-confidence as Sheikh Mubarrak; but the time comes, in the history of all but the most fortunate states, when self-confidence is seen to be a poor substitute for an adequate national defense program.

Nor are directly military preparations the only activity of an invasion-suggesting nature which the Pylos tablets record. A whole series of tablets also appears to concern the movement of women and children to places of refuge, mainly to Pylos itself and to the place called Leuktron which may have been the Neleid kingdom's secondary administrative center. Professor Bennett's careful analyses show that these tablets were written by two different scribes. The part of the set for which one scribe was responsible also records the rations issued to these women and children. The other scribe's tablets merely give the numbers, without rations, from which it is deduced that the ration records for this second group of refugees were kept at Leuktron. Of this tablet series, Professor Palmer says that "the many discrepancies of detail about the composition of the groups [of women and children indicate] a fluid situation, and this im

146

ression is strengthened by the occasional notes entered in set C, for in-
tance, that 'X did not arrive.' " Another tablet notes the assignment of
inety of these same women and children as "Grainpourers," which is
nterpreted as meaning breadmakers, perhaps to replace the regular bakers
alled up for military duties.

Professor F. J. Tritsch of Birmingham University has made an
ndependent study of the same group of Pylos tablets, and has also reached
he conclusion that they "deal with fugitives from the danger areas . . .
who had taken refuge in and around the capital city, which was itself
preparing to meet the attack of the enemy." Tritsch has another most
triking detail to add. In brief, the religious sanctuaries of the Mycenaean
ge do not seem to have resembled the temples of later Greece; else they
vould have left impressive archaeological remains somewhere. But, how-
ver they were constructed, they were clearly repositories of much wealth,
owning slaves, holding lands in their own right, and receiving donations
f more slaves, of gold, of spices and of other things. All this is recorded
n the tablets. The chief sanctuary at Pylos, belonging to *Potnia,* the
Lady-Mistress, appears to have been at an as yet unlocated place called
Pa-ki-ja-na, probably not far from Pylos. As the kingdom's chief sanc-
uary, the temple of *Potnia* at Pa-ki-ja-na must have been especially
ich. One of the tablets records the presence in Pylos of fourteen women
laves of the priestess of the Pa-ki-ja-na sanctuary, together with the
'sacred gold" or "gold of the sanctuary"—the phrase can be translated
ither way. Tritsch adds, "the presence in the palace of the priestess'
ervants with the sacred gold has to be explained." And he concludes that
the expectation of sea-borne invasion was [most probably] responsible
or sending the gold treasure of the Pa-ki-ja-na sanctuary [which he thinks
vas also on the seacoast] to the nearby castle of Pylos."

Finally, still another series of tablets describes the collection
rom many villages in Pylos of stated numbers of units of a commodity

147

that was at first thought to be flax, and these tablets also note deliveries of this same commodity to the coast-watching detachments. The difficulty created by these apparent deliveries of flax to the coast-watchers was only increased when a Swiss scholar, Dr. H. Mühlestein, discovered that each coast-watching detachment received a number of units of this commodity exactly proportional to the detachment's strength in men. The hint was unmistakable that some sort of iron ration was being issued to the isolated coast-watchers, but how could the coast-watchers have needed an iron ration of flax? It was then remembered, however, that the word at first taken to mean flax could also mean linseed. Thucydides himself shows fat-rich linseed being used as an iron ration by the later Greeks when the Spartan hoplites were trapped on Sphacteria by the Athenian fleet. "Underwater swimmers," he says, "swam through the harbor to Sphacteria towing after them, by means of a cord, bags containing poppy seed mixed with honey and pounded linseed. At first they eluded discovery, but then watch was kept for them." Even the unexpected linseed fits into the invasion picture, in short.

As to the date of this invasion of Pylos, which was also the beginning of the end of the Mycenaean Greek civilization, Professor Blegen gives us 1200 B.C. Within fairly narrow limits, the date is unavoidably conjectural. What is not conjectural is the fact that the end of Pylos came with terrible swiftness. One may guess that, once their preparations were made, the more civilized Pylians were confident of their power to beat off the crude Dorians, even if the latter were much more numerous. At any rate, they did not panic. All the machinery of normal daily life instead continued to operate with ordered precision in the palace at Pylos. I have described how the wine jars stood ready in the guests' reception room, and how the water jars also were in readiness in the Queen's toilet, at the very moment when the palace went up in flames. Professor Palmer points out that the tablets mutely imply the same sudden en, brutal interruption of the busy daily round. In the archive room, he scribes seem to have been working, at the last, on the consolidated egister of proposals for landholdings which has already been mentioned. t was never finished; and the last tablet-page was found still uninscribed. )ne wonders whether the scribes were hastily armed and pressed into the anks of fighting men. Or did the last agony of Pylos find the scribes still t their work, to be driven from it only by the fearful sound of battle nounting higher, ever higher, toward the palace hilltop that Neleus, and Nestor after him, had thought would never need a wall?

"Alerted and organized," Professor Palmer concludes, "the 'ylians awaited the attack from the sea. The ruin of the palace and the ire that preserved the archives to our own times are eloquent testimony hat the attack was successful. . . . The scene must have been such as Homer painted: 'As when the smoke rising from a city reaches the bright ky far from an island that foemen beset, and the day long they contend n grievous strife from their city wall. At sundown the beacon fires blaze n rows and the glare reaches aloft for their neighbors to see, in the hope hat they will come in their ships and ward off their doom.' " But no ne came, and so "the bronze age of Greece [ended] with the storming nd firing of all the major strongholds of Mycenaean power."

Maybe it is silly (although I am not so sure about this in the ge of the H-bomb) but I am one of those who are much moved by his-ory. I am stirred by the triumphs, depressed by the defeats, and made nelancholy, above all, by the terrible transitoriness of human accomplish-nent which is, I fear, history's most obvious lesson. I first read Palmer's hapter, from which many of the foregoing facts and some quotations are aken, at the end of the same day when I had heard Professor Blegen ring the palace of Nestor back to busy life and all but people it again efore my eyes. Reading it just then had been almost too poignant; the hought of how the end probably came partly spoiled the second day of

149

my journey to Pylos. When we at last boarded the plane to go back to Athens, Professor Blegen for the first time struck me as a bit tired; and I myself was gorged with new facts and impressions. Yet there was one final question I could not resist asking, and I asked it just before we reached Professor Blegen's house in Plutarch Street. When Nestor's palace was burned, I inquired, was that the end of the story; or was there any further chapter? The Professor replied with his characteristic gentle smile:

"Not at all; the story didn't end there. If we can trust the ancient Greeks, who were a lot nearer their own past than we are, refugees from Pylos escaped to play leading roles in several other Greek cities. At the beginning of classical times, the chief family in Miletus were Neleids. Pylians also founded Colophon, according to the poet Mimnermus—'When from the lofty city of Neleian Pylos we came on shipboard to the pleasant land of Asia'—and Mimnermus wrote his poem about his home town, you must remember, in the seventh century B.C. Finally a prince of the house of Neleus apparently escaped to Athens. The last King of Athens, Codrus, who was said to have fallen 'a sacrifice for the people' in the great battle that saved Athens from the Dorians, was remembered as having Neleid blood. Furthermore, both the Peisistratids—the family of the Tyrant—and the Alcmaeonids—the family of Alcmaeon who rebuilt the temple of Delphi, and of Pericles himself—had traditions of Neleid descent. No one seems to have doubted that these great families really were Neleid in origin; and if it wasn't doubted at the time when plenty of backbiting people would have been only too anxious to make fun of this kind of faked genealogy, I see no reason to doubt it now. Experience teaches, I believe, that it's always wisest to give the benefit of the doubt to tradition. Anyway, I *like* to think Pericles descended from Neleus and Nestor."

I like to think that, too. I told the Professor so; and the thought brightened our parting.

The destruction of the Greek states of the late Bronze Age brought to an end a whole way of life, with a finality far exceeding any of the comparatively petty upheavals of our own time, such as the Russian revolution. Mycenaean Greek society—this society centering around the kings in their rich palaces—this society led by warriors but planned and head-counted and directed and taxed by palace bureaucracies—had been civilized, artificial, fruitful and in many respects beautiful. Yet "one may conjecture that [it had also] been fragile." The quotation is from *The Greeks of the Bronze Age*, by Sterling Dow, who continues:

"Destroy the palace and the whole community was wrecked. This happened. Pylos, the last palace to be built, was perhaps the first to go, circa 1200 B.C., the rest very soon, in the next decades. The Dorian destroyers were savage enough to have ended less fragile organizations than the palace bureaucracies. As it was, the disruption of commerce brought down the whole of society. This fragility explains why, even without Dorians on the Acropolis, Attica also went under. The economy was geared to certain exports and imports; they ended, and the invaders were soon ravaging the Attic countryside. The Acropolis they could not take, but destruction was complete without that."

151

Although he wrote without detailed knowledge of the data provided by the Linear B tablets, F. M. Heichelheim made precisely the same point. "The crucial flaw" of the Bronze Age royal economies, he remarked, lay in their almost absolute dependence on "continuous planning by the central state authorities"; when this was interrupted, it meant "the end of all civilized life . . . so that later generations [had] to begin from very primitive village . . . conditions again." This was an impressive insight.

As can be seen, Dow thinks that at most a generation may have elapsed between the burning of the Pylos palace and the moment when the tide of destruction at last began to recede—perhaps the moment when the Dorian invaders broke off the siege of the high rock of Athens, though not before they had effectively destroyed the bases of Athenian Bronze Age society. Professor George Mylonas, who assisted Dr. John Papadimitriou in the excavation of the most recently found grave circle of Mycenae, gives 1100 B.C. as the date when the citadel of the Lion-Kings was finally put to the torch; and if Mylonas is right, Mycenae may have outlasted Pylos by a full century. Certainly every Bronze Age ruler must have hastened to strengthen his defenses after he got the fearful news from Pylos; and most of the other major centers were certainly much easier to defend than the unfortified palace of Neleus and Nestor. Professor Blegen none the less thinks that all the major centers fell within a very short time. He even suspects that the ships of Pylos were being mustered not solely to defend the coast but above all to be ready for a quick getaway. I cannot judge the archaeological facts which cause these divergences, but I must say that the pattern which emerged after the great invasion makes better political sense on the assumption that the first onslaught of the Dorians was followed by a fairly long period of seesaw fighting, with some Bronze Age fortresses holding their own for a time and others quickly going up in flames as Pylos did.

152

It will have been far easier, for instance, for a Neleid prince from Pylos to make a place for himself in an Athens already fearful and indignant but not yet under attack. Above all, considerable groups of refugees must have had to cross the Aegean, in order to plant even village-sized roots of the later Greek cities of Asia Minor. According to tradition, Athens was the way station of many of the refugees. But even if this is correct, large numbers of persons can hardly have left the other Mycenaean centers for Athens when the besiegers were already storming their city's walls, or after their homes were in ashes and under the noses of their conquerors. Moreover, unless the Athenians were improbably generous in their own moment of danger, emigrations must surely have been organized in the cities of origin, in order to provide the emigrants with the barest necessities of success such as seed for a crop, tools to clear the fields, and weapons for the men. It is hard to see how this can have happened, except before the cities fell. A date of 1100 B.C. has now been given by the archaeologists for the earliest new foundations on the Asia Minor coast, which does not fit badly with Mylonas' date for the fall of Mycenae. In any case, whether or not the Dorian conquest took less or more than a generation, the defense of the old ways failed in the end. That is the key point. All the Bronze Age palaces went up in flames, except for the long-vanished palace which then crowned the Athenian Acropolis; and the former system of society was utterly destroyed.

The best proof of the thoroughness of the destruction is to be found in the Linear B tablets themselves. For one thing, the tablets show the Greek kings of the Bronze Age with the proud title *Wanax,* which was all but forgotten in the later period. For another thing, the script of the tablets also vanished from men's memories. Professor Dow sensibly argues that this onset of "illiteracy was due to the failure of interest on the part of the older people in teaching the young to read and write; [and to] an equally complete failure of interest on the part of the younger [in learning]. . . . The failure of interest . . . was caused by the utter collapse of a system which engrossed the lives of those who wrote and those who read. When the system collapsed overnight, the incentive to literacy was not all that went with it, but people's very lives. There were no more careers for the palace bureaucrats, the craftsmen, the officers, even for the more highly trained slaves. Probably most of them had to go dig in the fields. There was a reversion to primitive economy."

A primitive economy is precisely what the archaeological record reveals. There was no great stylistic break at the end of the Bronze Age, although the first iron weapons turn up in graves dated soon after the Dorian invasion. But although pots continued to be made in the same shapes and with comparable decoration, for example, everything was infinitely poorer and meaner and sparser and rarer. There was in fact a dark age; and this Greek dark age that endured until the first beginnings of the magical Greek upsurge in classical times was no short period either. The evidence indicates it lasted for a very long time, until the beginning of the new period in Greece marked by the geometric pottery style, about 900 B.C.

If one takes inventory, all the survivals from the Greek Bronze Age do not weigh very heavy in the balance against all that was lost—except for the Homeric epics. We cannot tell whether intact poetry of the high period survived, as Wace maintained and T. B. L. Webster comes close to maintaining,* but we can now be certain that a great many memories and stories and descriptions of life in the higher period must have been pre-

---

* *Sir Maurice Bowra is somewhat more cautious than the late Professor Wace, but he has made a strong case for the view that the Homeric hexameter is actually a Mycenaean verse convention. One main difference between Mycenaean Greek and later Greek was that the earlier form of the language was less contracted. The later Achaioi, for instance, was pronounced "Achaiwoi," or something like that, in Mycenaean times. The hexameter, Sir Maurice points out, can be written far more easily with the uncontracted language; the dull clay tablet records even contain phrases, here and there, that can be scanned as parts of hexameters.*

served—otherwise the Homeric epics would not be such accurate though strangely incomplete guides to Bronze Age Greece. In this last connection, I am much struck, as an outsider, by the implications of the general scholarly opinion that the *Iliad* and the *Odyssey* were composed in one or more of the cities of Ionian Greece in the eighth century B.C. The locale helps, I think, to explain what I have called discovery's joke on the discoverers. For many centuries after the end of the Bronze Age, the Greeks of these cities on the coast of Asia Minor must have had extremely vivid recollections of their refugee origins; as is shown by Mimnermus' line, already quoted, these origins were not soon forgotten. In refugee or dramatically ruined families and social groups, memories of past glories, of heroes of old time, of mansions long since in decay, and of picturesque social customs now abandoned, all tend to be remarkably tenacious, whereas memories of the less glamorous features of the social system that produced these former glories (and what is less glamorous than bureaucracy?) tend to fade fast from men's minds. In short, selective recollection, like that in Homer, is a natural process in such circumstances. In the American South, a way of life was also destroyed with great swiftness; and one can actually study this process of selective recollection at work after the Southern way of life had vanished. Consider, for example, the difference between the authorized and the complete editions of one of the great Civil War documents, the incomparable Mary Boykin Chesnut's *Diary from Dixie*. This diary of the wife of a great Southern plantation owner who served in Jefferson Davis' sub-cabinet was first published forty years or so after the Civil War by Mrs. Chesnut's Charlestonian heirs, who edited it heavily before publication. The complete edition was published nearly half a century later—and by Northerners. The complete edition contains passage after passage vividly describing every dark feature of the slave economy—the Negroes on the auction block, their plight on the harsher plantations, the fear of their slaves that lurked in so many plantation owners' minds, the embittering

155

suspicion that their husbands had slave-mistresses which lurked in the minds of many plantation owners' wives, and so on and on. But if you read the authorized edition you find nothing inappropriate to the trying title which Mrs. Chesnut's heirs supplied—all the bravery, and luxury, and final tragedy of the slave-owning South are there, but the ugly underpinnings of the slave system are hardly noticed in the heirs' edition of *Diary from Dixie*. In fact the heirs' edition, which good Charlestonians still prefer, resembles Homer in the special sense that it is quite accurate except for the omissions; but the omissions are important enough to change the whole picture as soon as they are restored.

So we may imagine an aged grandfather in ninth-century Colophon or Chios or Smyrna—all three places later claimed to have given birth to Homer. We may picture him telling his grandchild of the wonders of his own several-times-great-grandfather's time—of all the splendors of Nestor's palace, and the wise king's gold-studded drinking cup, and the bronze-armed warriors, and the great feasts in the king's hall, and the heroes who went to Troy. And we may suppose that he said nothing, because he remembered nothing, about such other topics as the royal steward Alxoitas and his bureaucrats, and the taxes, and the labor-service, and the whole state organization the Linear B tablets have at length revealed. As history, that is how our story perhaps ended.

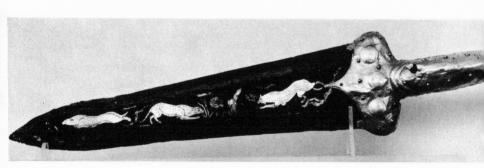

*Inlaid dagger from a tomb near Pylos.*

There has been another, much more recent sequel, however, of a more curious and ironical sort. In brief, Blegen's discovery of Linear B tablets at Pylos, and Ventris' decipherment of the script, effectively settled one controversy but started eight or ten others. The truth is that the very answer to the riddle that was successfully read has confronted the scholarly world with an almost excessive supply of quite new riddles. The reader who prefers riddles with their answers attached had best stop here. But in my opinion the new riddles are intensely interesting, so I shall try to summarize them as fairly as I can. With only one exception, all these plaguing but absorbing riddles have to do, in one way or another, with the nature of the relationship between Crete and mainland Greece. Thus the essential first step has to be a short return to where we started, in order to give thumbnail sketches of the Minoan and Mycenaean stories. As the story with deeper roots in the past, the Minoan story has pride of place.

Sir Arthur Evans long ago provided his Minoans with a history reaching back into the dawn time of human civilization. His earlier dates have now been discarded, as too remote in time; but most of the learned world still accepts his division of the Minoan story into three main epochs: Early, Middle and Late Minoan. It may be that the majority of specialists will always adhere to this division, but after the upheavals of recent years, most notably that caused by Ventris' decipherment, a majority of those who still use the Evans system do so in the manner of Humpty-Dumpty using words. He told Alice, as will be recalled, that you must just use them to mean what you want them to mean. Among the experts, in truth, there is the widest diversity, ranging from the surviving Evansites, who cling to his system with a minimum of change, all the way to the veteran of Minoan archaeology, Dr. Doro Levi, the famous continuator of the Italian excavation of the Phaistos palace, who thinks that the grander eras of the Minoan story opened as late as 1800 B.C. It seems to me that the simplest summary of those parts of the story which no one doubts has been offered

157

*Faience votive plaque—a cow with calf—from Knossos, the earliest period of the second palaces.*

by the distinguished French archaeologist now continuing the excavation of the lovely palace at Mallia, Professor Henri van Effenterre. Because of the uncertainty increasingly surrounding the Evans system, van Effenterre has written (in *Preuves*):

"The history of Minoan Crete has been effectively contracted into two basic periods: that of the 'first palaces' and that of the 'second palaces,' roughly corresponding . . . to the nineteenth through the seventeenth centuries B.C. for the first period, and to the sixteenth through the fifteenth centuries B.C. for the second period. The era before the palaces is still very little known. One can neither give its duration, nor describe its beginnings. . . . It was the time when neolithic peoples colonized Crete, found there favorable conditions of life, grew in numbers, and formed the network of village communities which was thereafter the basis of the economic life of the island. In the present state of our knowledge, this earlier era belongs to prehistory. History begins with the construction of the palaces."

Such, then, is the basic framework—an early period of unknown duration, followed by the period of the first palaces, extending from about 1900 B.C. to about 1600 B.C., followed by the period of the second palaces, extending from about 1600 B.C. to about 1400 B.C. Fleshing out this simple framework is not easy, for the experts' disagreements begin at the beginning, with the time when the first neolithic people arrived in Crete. Evans put the date very far back, and with some reason, since the accumulation of debris by these stone users forms a considerable part of the hill of Knossos; the neolithic deposit under the palace is the deepest known at any European site. Others have brought the date down to a much more recent time. At any rate, the epoch that really matters, when the neolithic culture started to prosper and develop, appears to have opened about 3000 B.C. Again, there is disagreement about when metal using began in Crete and about whether the appearance of metal also implies the appearance of a new people. In his *Crete and Mycenae,* Professor Spyridon Marinatos places the first small beginnings of the Cretan Bronze Age as early as 2800 B.C. The average opinion would give a later date, around the middle of the third millennium. As to a new people's arrival, Evans thought the first Minoans

*Objects from the Cretan pre-palace period:* (LEFT) *a gold pendant from Mallia;* (RIGHT) *a stone pitcher and bowl from Mochlos. Third millennium* B.C.

were the intruding metal users; van Effenterre thinks the first palaces were built by recent new arrivals; and Doro Levi suspects that the Cretan stone users and the builders of the first palaces belonged to the same race. You can take your choice, in short. In any case, the more important point to note is that Crete had become a prosperous island before the first palaces were built. There are no grandiose remains, as from the subsequent periods, but fine gold jewelry appears in graves of the pre-palace era, as do admirably worked vessels of hard stone like those from the earliest eras of Egypt.

What then caused great palaces to be suddenly and almost simultaneously built at Knossos, Phaistos and Mallia is another much-disputed subject. The most common view is that of J. W. Graham, who suggests in his excellent *Palaces of Crete* that there was a "cultural explosion," rather like spontaneous combustion in a hay barn, which resulted from the long though gradual increase of wealth and population in the preceding period. Or you may prefer Professor van Effenterre's view that a new people arrived, to give the needed impulse. At any rate, beginning in about 1900 B.C. or a little earlier or later, great palace structures rose at the three main sites in Crete. Evans believed that even at this stage Crete was already ruled by Knossian Minos. But the legends tell of Minos ruling Knossos, his brother Rhadamanthys ruling Phaistos, and Sarpedon ruling Mallia; and this is now thought to symbolize the political reality of a Crete divided in the period of the first palaces into three main kingdoms. Each of the three palaces had its adjacent region of special fertility, and Phaistos, with the beautiful Messara plain lying spread out below the prow-like hilltop where the palace stood, was decidedly the richest of the three. Hence it is not surprising that Professor Levi's recent probings into the level of the first palace at Phaistos rather strongly suggest that in this early era Phaistos was an even more important center than Knossos.

Since the remains of the first palaces are everywhere overlaid by the ruins of the second palaces, this first era of Minoan grandeur also

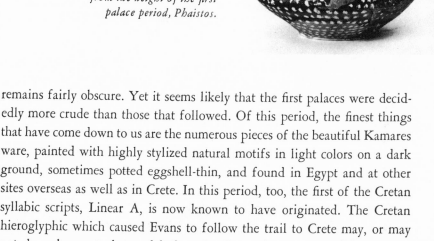

*Kamares-ware cups,
from the height of the first
palace period, Phaistos.*

remains fairly obscure. Yet it seems likely that the first palaces were decidedly more crude than those that followed. Of this period, the finest things that have come down to us are the numerous pieces of the beautiful Kamares ware, painted with highly stylized natural motifs in light colors on a dark ground, sometimes potted eggshell-thin, and found in Egypt and at other sites overseas as well as in Crete. In this period, too, the first of the Cretan syllabic scripts, Linear A, is now known to have originated. The Cretan hieroglyphic which caused Evans to follow the trail to Crete may, or may not, have begun to be used before the first palaces were built. Formerly it was universally supposed that the period of the first palaces was also the period of the developed hieroglyphic script. But at Phaistos, Doro Levi has now found Linear A fragments in the levels of the older palace there. This leaves little room for doubt that Linear A at least originated in the period of the first palaces. The builders of the second palace at Phaistos did not stop at leveling the site before they began again. Probably as an anti-earthquake precaution, they covered almost all the leveled ruins of the first palace with an immensely thick layer of stone-hard cement. This makes excavating the lower levels hideously difficult, but also makes it all but certain that anything found in a lower level really belonged to that level. What comes from a first palace level at Phaistos comes in effect from an anciently sealed vault.

The prosperity of the period of the first palaces came to an end about 1700 B.C. or a little later, when all of them were destroyed. Most believe that an earthquake caused this catastrophe; but J. W. Graham has suggested either a raid from mainland Greece or the combination of an earthquake and a Greek raid in the wake of the earthquake's destruction. There followed a kind of trough in the Cretan story. In his *Crete and Mycenae*, Professor Marinatos states that "not a single building can be attributed with certainty" to the century between 1700 and 1600 B.C. which he describes as "empty" and "transitional" but not "a time of decline or disaster." This unfruitful stretch of time, which van Effenterre includes, as we have seen, in his period of the first palaces, was then followed by an

*Bull-leaping fresco from the last period at Knossos.*

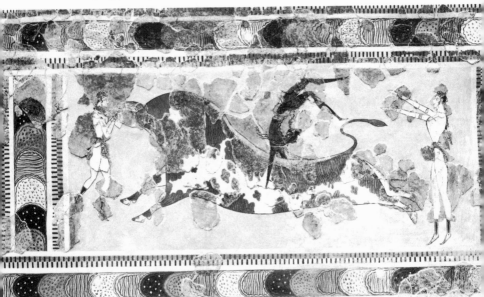

*Detail of a procession painted on the side of a sarcophagus, c. 1400* B.C. *From a tomb near Haghia Triada.*

extraordinary time of progress and fruitfulness. This began when the period of the second palaces opened about 1600 B.C.

Examining the ruins of the second palaces, one can see why Knossos added the word "labyrinth" to the Greek language and thus to our own. (The root, of course, is "labrys," the sacred double ax, which played so large a part in the mysterious Minoan cult.) Yet these huge, seemingly maze-like buildings have their own logic, as has been shown by Graham, who is the chief student of their architecture. At Knossos, at Phaistos and at Mallia a great central court provided the necessary space for the bull games the Minoans loved; and this was enclosed by the palace's main structures. The façades were decorated with colonnades and porticoes; broad ceremonial staircases led to the upper floors; there were enfilades of grand

163

rooms for public or ceremonial purposes; there were luxurious domestic quarters for the members of the reigning families; huge magazines received the produce of the land and provided storage for the palace treasures; lightness and airiness were increased where necessary, with no danger of exposure to the harsh winter winds, by the provision of many light wells; and there were warrens of little rooms for servants and palace administrators, special areas reserved for the palace cults, and entrance courts and other courts to supplement the great central courtyards. In addition, every device from plumbing to fresco decoration was used to make the second palaces pleasant, indeed luxurious, habitations for rich rulers and pleasure-loving courtiers. Some of those devices could well be imitated today, at least in lands of Mediterranean climate; the grander rooms of the second palace period, for instance, could be entirely opened to the full light of day, or half-lighted, or darkened, or they could be protected against the wind on one side or the other at will, simply by opening or closing the rows of french doors with transoms above which formed their outer walls.

Besides putting up these astonishing structures, as the architecture suggests, the people of the second palaces had a high civilization technically comparable with any of the contemporary civilizations of the Bronze Age, and more attractive than the others too, because less hieratic, more open, more human and life-loving. In this period, too, besides the main palaces, great numbers of rich villas and mansions were built all over Crete; and near Phaistos, the royal villa of Haghia Triada became a miniature palace lacking only the characteristic central courtyard. Evidence for the most widespread use of the Linear A script has been found in the remains of the structures from the second palace period, although at this time the hiero-glyphic script was still retained for occasional ritual use. Most of Crete was linked together by a stone-built road net, seemingly centering on Knossos; and this is one of the items of evidence in the dispute that still rages about the political organization of the island at this time. In brief, the view of

164

*Knossos, West Corridor, with stora*

Sir Arthur Evans, that Knossos ruled all Crete almost from the outset, no longer finds many defenders; but a considerable number of the experts hold that the territories of Phaistos, Mallia and almost all the rest of Crete were subordinated to Knossos from the beginning of the period of the second palaces. Others, like Professor van Effenterre, do not believe in the unification. As an outsider, I am much impressed by the opinion of Doro Levi; for the marvelous Phaistos palace is now *his,* so to say: he has found indications that Phaistos actually outshone Knossos in the period of the first palaces; yet he thinks that Knossos exercised some sort of central authority in the period of the second palaces.

The period of the second palaces did not endure in full glory for very long, however. In the late sixteenth or early fifteenth century B.C., a catastrophe overtook Crete. Professor Marinatos has proposed the extremely ingenious explanation of a volcanic eruption on the island of Thera, exceeding the power of the terrible eruption of Krakatoa as the geological evidence shows, which all but overwhelmed nearby Crete by causing a devastating series of fearful tidal waves and post-volcanic earthquakes. This happened, in Marinatos' opinion, about 1520 B.C. Whatever the date, and whatever the cause, the evidence for a catastrophe is pretty clear. After this, the Phaistos and Mallia palaces do not seem to have been rebuilt, and Knossos was the sole palace that survived, to experience yet another destruction in the mid-fifteenth century, and to be rebuilt yet again. How long Knossos survived, who occupied it, and when this occupation ended have been subjects of increasingly sharp controversy ever since Ventris' decipherment of the Knossos Linear B archive proved decisively that Greeks ruled there at the close of the history of the palace of Minos. Evans dated the final destruction of the great pile to 1400 B.C. After this, so he said, the place was abandoned except for wretched squatters who carried on a debased cult among the ruins. The majority of the experts still accept the Evans date for the end of Knossos. Yet the members of an increasing minority believe that the date must be incorrect. The alternative views thus far put forward will be summarized later, as we proceed with our collection of riddles. It is clear, at least, that the Minoan story ended with Knossos and most of Crete under Greek control, and with Linear B as the new administrative language, replacing Linear A.

As can be seen at once, the Minoan story has its own inherent riddle, quite independent of the Greek story. *Who were the Minoans?* As has been noted already, the hieroglyphic and Linear A scripts are still undeciphered; but it is sure that they are not Greek. Hence the people or peoples who devised these scripts were not Greeks either.* To make matters worse,

* *The hieroglyphic script appears in an early and a late form; and the famous Phaistos disk, with its mysterious spiral inscription, shows still another script, quite different from either of the Minoan hieroglyphic scripts and from Linear A. Someday someone may find out the truth about this strange disk, with its characters that seem to breathe magical power (and may of course merely conceal statistics of the oil trade). Meanwhile it must be said that all the theories concerning it have to be marked unproven, and some of the proposed interpretations must be given a worse mark than that. There is a good chance, moreover, that the place of origin of the Phaistos disk was outside Crete.*

*Phaistos disk.*

the mass of material normally needed for decipherment is lacking in both cases. However, there are enough Linear A tablets and inscriptions to tempt venturesome scholars, and work on Linear A has also been greatly stimulated by the decipherment of Linear B. Going on the assumption that similar signs in the two scripts had similar syllabic sounds, Professor Cyrus Gordon of Brandeis University has reached the conclusion that Linear A conceals a Semitic language. Making precisely the same assumption, L. R. Palmer has reached the very different conclusion that Linear A conceals the Luvian language. The Luvians were an Indo-European people who entered Anatolia somewhat before the Hittites. The excavators of Beycesultan, a site in what was probably former Luvian territory, have found a shrine with great altar "horns" in which they see Minoan links. They have also found the ruins of a palace whose design, they believe, is akin to the design of the Minoan palaces in their grandest period—the period of the second palaces.* The Beycesultan palace was destroyed, most probably by the Hittite King Labarnas, a century or more before the beginning of the period of the second palaces in Crete. Professor Palmer has therefore concluded that there were two successive groups of Minoans— the originators of the Minoan civilization, who lasted until the end of the first palace period and used the hieroglyphic scripts; and Luvian invaders, driven to Crete by the Hittite advance in Anatolia, who built the second palaces and devised the Linear A script. He further believes that he has deciphered an actual Luvian inscription, *Ja-sa-sa-ra-me,* meaning "My Lady," on a stone altar found in the Dictaean cave, which was an important shrine in Minoan times and later. In addition, Palmer boldly allots to the Luvians the earlier centuries of Greek history; the Luvians, he says, were

* But this claim of the Beycesultan excavators, Seton Lloyd and James Mellaart, is stoutly rejected by J. W. Graham in his The Palaces of Crete. Graham also rejects Sir Leonard Woolley's even more emphatic claim of prototype status for the palace he excavated at Alalakh in Syria.

the first Indo-European intruders in the Greek peninsula, arriving toward the beginning of the second millennium and only being displaced by the Greeks about 1600 B.C. Finally, Palmer suggests that the Luvians were also the people who founded Troy VI and still inhabited Priam's Troy—in which case the Trojan War was a last Greek-Luvian test of strength.

Palmer's Luvian theory has provoked considerably more scholarly asperity than his strictures on Sir Arthur Evans. George Mylonas, for instance, has made archaeological mincemeat of the Luvians-in-Greece part of the theory. In addition, Doro Levi's discovery of Linear A fragments in the first palace levels at Phaistos creates what looks like an insuperable difficulty for the Palmer theory as outlined to date. Yet Levi himself has lately written that "in recent years archaeological research aimed at throwing light on the . . . origins of the Minoan civilization has moved toward the shores of Asia Minor." He has been excavating at Iasos, with the result thus far of showing that the island culture of the Cyclades had significant mainland links; and he holds that "several sites" in Anatolia, including the Beycesultan palace, "have disclosed architectural forms, aspects of religious beliefs, and artistic elements close to the Minoan ones." In addition, the great Swedish expert on Mycenaean pottery, Arne Furumark, has made an analytic study of the Linear A texts, following the methods of Michael Ventris with Linear B; and he has reportedly reached the conclusion that Linear A conceals an Anatolian, Indo-European language—which *might* be Luvian. As a further sample of the present state of the problem, I may perhaps quote the "conclusions" offered by a leading Soviet scholar, V. V. Sevoroskin, in a recent number of *Nestor*. "(1) Two genetically related 'Hittite' languages—Minoan and Proto-Lycian—underwent an influence of a non-Indo-European 'Pre-Luvian' CVCV-language. . . . (2) The non-Indo-European Minoan language influenced the Indo-European Proto-Lycian language; this process took place in Southwest Anatolia. . . . I think that this question is interesting enough to deserve further investigation and dis-

169

cussion." Among the would-be decipherers of Linear A, meanwhile, Professor Palmer freely concedes that his Luvian thesis requires more substantial proofs. Professor Gordon, in contrast, regards his Semitic decipherment as fully proven, even claiming to have read quite long inscriptions; but the Gordon view as yet commands almost no support from other scholars. Further theories about this tempting mystery are to be expected; but proof is another matter. Hence the origin of the Minoans must still be left where Sir Arthur Evans left it, in doubt.

So much for the first riddle. We have at least nine more riddles to go. But since all these remaining riddles involve the Cretan-Greek relationship, let us first have a look at what happened at Mycenae, which has the longest archaeologically demonstrable history of any of the major sites on the Greek mainland. Building on the foundations laid by Schliemann, Chrestos Tsountas and A. J. B. Wace, Professor Mylonas has constructed the version of Mycenaean history which we shall follow. According to Mylonas, the first Greeks came to the high, strong site among the crags at about the time of the Greek entry into Greece, around 1900 B.C. They massacred or subjugated the former inhabitants. They multiplied and began to grow rich. Or, rather, we should perhaps say that they began to grow rich unless they were remarkably idle and feckless; for they had fertile, almost empty land to till, timber on the hillsides to make ships, and quite possibly the most profitable mineral resources within reach, as will be seen. It cannot be said positively that they began to grow rich, simply because the remains they have left are poor. Graves from this very early period are mean, and grave goods are far from impressive—as might well be expected in the case of people who had only recently been at least seminomadic.

No great structures reveal wealth in this early period, either— but this again is just what one would expect. In the first phases of such a community, the increase of prosperity and population is a slow, imperceptible process, seldom marked by dramatic changes in habits of life. It is only

*Electrum death mask from the first grave circle outside the citadel of Mycenae.*

when a kind of critical mass is reached that the dramatic changes begin; and this seems to have happened during the seventeenth century B.C.*

The beginning of change is indicated by the first of the two Mycenaean grave circles (but the latest discovered, which Dr. Papadimitriou and George Mylonas jointly excavated). Mylonas dates the first grave circle to 1650 B.C. The earlier burials were by no means showy, but the mere fact that a grave circle was constructed must be regarded as telling in itself. Moreover, before the end of this first grave circle, which perhaps overlaps with the first-discovered but later circle excavated by Schliemann, the members of the Mycenaean ruling house were already wealthy enough to honor the dead with such costly grave goods as bronze swords, gold, silver and

* *F. H. Stubbings attributes the changes to the arrival of new leadership from Egypt, in the person of the legendary Danaus. But this suggestion has not as yet received wide support.*

171

*The Nile scene
on the bronze dagger found
by Schliemann.*

rock crystal vessels, gold and rock crystal jewelry and the like. Some of the
finds from the first grave circle are truly remarkable, such as the early royal
death-mask made of electrum and the perfectly designed rock crystal vessel
in the form of a duck. Yet it should be noted that these things make no
great show, compared to what came later. A great and very rapid further
increase of wealth is clearly indicated by the treasures in the royal grave circle that Schliemann found within the citadel, which is now dated between
1600 and 1500 B.C. Mylonas believes, with Professors Marinatos and A.
Persson, that the new funeral customs and the wealth the graves reveal
both reflect Egyptian influence and contacts. The ostrich eggs found in the
graves almost certainly came from Egypt. The golden death-masks look like
a borrowing. So does the new habit of depositing rich grave goods. Above
all, the dagger found by Schliemann, inlaid in silver and gold and niello-
work with a marvelous scene of a cat hunting birds among reed beds of
papyrus, portrays an actual episode of life on the Nile, although the dagger
itself, beyond much doubt, was made in Greece. The Egyptians expelled

172

heir hated dynasty of foreign occupiers, the Hyksos kings, not long after 1600 B.C., and the rising against the Hyksos is believed to have begun considerably earlier. Ahmose, the Pharaoh who finally took the Hyksos capital at Avaris, is believed to have employed mercenaries to aid his resistance movement; and it is possible that the King of Mycenae of those days made large profits by sending soldiers to Egypt, the Bronze Age land of gold, just as the Grand Duke of Hesse rented his Hessians to George III for service against the American colonists. We have seen that somewhat later *Aqaiwasha* aided a rebellious Libyan prince against the Pharaoh; and the employment of foreign mercenary or slave soldiers was not uncommon in the Bronze Age—one of the frescoes in the Knossos palace actually shows a captain of the palace guard with members of his company of Negro troops, who were probably slaves.

Departing for a moment from Mylonas' version of the Mycenaean story, another possible indication of the source of Mycenae's wealth is to be found in an almost forgotten paper by O. Davies, published in the June, 1929, number of the *Journal of Hellenic Studies*. Davies carefully examined the remains of Bronze Age mining at Cirrha, which is the seaport of Delphi on the Corinthian gulf. He found that a principal industry of the place had been "the mining of tin," which had been done by the open-cast method, thus leaving great cuts in the hillsides. The mines themselves had been completely worked out, leaving no trace of the ore; but the ore was smelted at high temperatures in "crucibles of coarse very hard clay"; and deposits on the inner surfaces of surviving crucibles were shown by analysis to be stannic oxide, thus providing "positive evidence for tin." Mycenaean pottery was found associated with the main tin workings. Being on the northern shore of the Corinthian gulf, Cirrha was not in the Peloponnese. But as has been said, the territory just across the narrow Corinthian gulf is generally believed to have formed part of the domains of Mycenae. Davies concluded his account by noting that "Delphi itself indulged in mining in a small way," and suggesting that Mycenae was the chief exploiter of the Cirrha mines. "Mycenae," said Davies, "has always been supposed to have indulged in trade with the Corinthian gulf, though it has been doubtful in what that trade consisted; here, however, is found at least one useful commodity near at hand, which could then be exported as far as the islands and Crete and possibly even to Asia Minor and Egypt." As the Cirrha tin workings began very early indeed, and as Bohemia, Saxony and Spain are the other nearest known tin sources of the Aegean world in the second millennium B.C., the tin of the Cirrhan mines, if Davies was right about them, must have been extremely profitable from an early date. Hence it may easily have provided the impetus for Mycenae's initial forward surge. And if Mycenae exported Cirrhan tin to Egypt, as Davies suggested, the trade contact could have led to the export of mercenaries first suggested by Marinatos and Persson. In sum, tin and mercenaries may well have combined to earn the first riches revealed in the Mycenaean grave circles.*

After Schliemann's grave circle, there came later tombs; but the next really major item in Mycenae's archaeological record is the improvement of the citadel's previously modest fortifications† by the construction of the first Cyclopean walls. They were dated about 1350 B.C. Were the first Cyclopean walls built because prosperity had brought to Greece a sharp population increase, leading to territorial disputes, and thus creating an

---

* It must be added that excavators from the French School at Athens conducted an elaborate dig at Cirrha about a decade after Davies, without confirming his findings. But they were not mining specialists as he was; they did not seek out Davies, to review his evidence with him; and their failure to find what he found is an argument from absence —always dubious in itself. Davies' crucibles need to be located, however. Professor Mylonas, it should also be added, is not skeptical about Davies' findings on the spot at Cirrha; but he regards the connection with Mycenae as unproved as yet.

† These have left no trace and must be assumed, however.

urgent need to protect the royal citadel against raids from neighbor kingdoms, like Tiryns down in the plain? No one knows, but it is sure that the first walls betoken power, and power which then increased; for beginning in about 1250 B.C. further great works were undertaken at Mycenae. The Lion Gate was built. The fortifications were extended and strengthened. The Treasury of Atreus was constructed, quite possibly to receive the actual last remains of the great king who was Agamemnon's father. Yet the conquest of Troy under Agamemnon's all-too-human leadership was the climax of the Mycenaean story. There are indications that not long after that fear seized upon the fortress-citadel, as it seized upon the Acropolis of Athens. The secret cistern with a fortified approach was then provided, so that besiegers could not cut off the people in the citadel of Mycenae from their water source, the spring of Perseus. But all this was unavailing. Even before construction of the protected cistern, Mylonas thinks Mycenae successfully weathered a first crisis, in which the so-called "House of the

*Staircase to the secret cistern in the citadel of Mycenae (taken from below).*

Oil Merchant" outside the walls was burned.* But there was a second siege when the great walls were stormed; for a layer of ashes that Mylonas dates to about 1100 B.C. shows how the Mycenaean period of glory came to a bitter end.

Such, then, was Mycenae's story, which can now be laid down alongside the Minoan story, like an approximately dated measuring stick. In 1900 B.C., to begin with, when Mycenae had become Greek but was still no more than a village, Knossos was becoming the site of a great palace. And the next riddle is: *What role the Minoans played in the Aegean in the first period of the Greek beginnings, and how this role affected the Greeks.*

As usual, the scholars disagree. Lately it has become fashionable to cry down the old theory of Minoan prosperity based upon thalassocracy. The existence of this thalassocracy is quite unproved, it is said, and therefore (an illogical "therefore," please note) no such thing ever existed. For the very little that may be worth, I am more impressed by the contrary argument, most recently made by Sterling Dow. Certainly it is grotesque to imagine the Minoans ruling over a kind of Aegean Bronze Age version of the British Empire, of the sort Pendlebury seemed to have in mind in the quotation given in the first chapter. But in this context, we should think of the word "thalassocracy" as meaning something vastly less ambitious—for example, a system of overseas trading posts, some of which may have been administered or garrisoned from the center, all knitted together by a wide ranging sea commerce and guaranteed by rudimentary sea power. As an island people, owing a considerable part of their prosperity to oversea trade, the Minoans may quite easily have ended by organizing a thalassocracy of this primitive type; and there are many facts to suggest that they did so.

* British excavators have just uncovered a house within the citadel that burned at this time. Interestingly, Professor Mylonas dates these first burnings to 1200 B.C., the Pylos destruction date.

176

The evidence is strong, to begin with, for the existence of a wide et of Minoan trading posts, or outpost/colonies. Long after the Minoans hemselves had vanished from the stage of history, the memory of their presence was conserved by no less than eleven places, all called Minoa, mostly on the Aegean islands, but including one as far west as Sicily (with which the legends connect Minos of Knossos) and two on the Greek mainand. One mainland Minoa was on the shore near Megara; the other was t Monemvasia, where the Franks who briefly gained a foothold in Greece luring the Crusades built a great medieval castle. The Minoans no doubt hose this latter site for the same reason the Franks did, because it was n the sea, yet had easy access to the rich lands of Sparta. None of the ormer Minoas has been successfully excavated as yet; but their mere names ell a story. In addition, excavation has clearly attested the existence of Minoan posts or settlements at other places outside Crete, such as Trianda n Rhodes.

As for the existence of Minoan sea power, to protect the commerce of these posts or settlements with the mother-island, it cannot now be proved and probably never will be. Yet there is circumstantial evidence hat Thucydides was right in giving Minos of Knossos the credit for being he first ruler to organize a navy. To begin with, there is the pattern of building in Crete itself. The Minoan palaces and their dependent towns were entirely unfortified, for all practical purposes; yet piracy has been a Mediterranean specialty from the beginning of history until very recent imes. Being unfortified, the palaces and towns of Crete were obvious targets for pirate raids. Furthermore, they were remarkably tempting targets; or the more important palaces were much larger, on the average, than the ater Greek palaces, which must mean that the palaces were rich, and the owns also had many large and luxurious upper-class houses. If the Minoans saw no need for fortifications in these circumstances, one is almost compelled to assume that they relied on a navy which was at least strong enough to prevent piracy along the coasts of Crete. The requirements of such a navy it must be remembered, cannot have been grandiose or costly in the first half of the second millennium. All that was needed was the development of slightly specialized ships with well-armed crews, which would then be stronger than any casual sea marauder. A small number would have sufficed If such ships were developed to protect the coasts of Crete, moreover, it would have been downright shortsighted not to use them for the additional purpose of protecting the major sea lanes. In a vacuum of other sea power, very little sea power can be made to go a long way.

On this head, a fascinating line of speculation is opened by the remarkable remains, including fine Mycenaean as well as Minoan pottery and quite unprecedented, life-sized cult statues, which Professor John Caskey has lately found on the island of Kea (ancient Ceos), off the coast of Attica. The fifth-century poet Bacchylides preserved an obviously more ancient legend of a raid on Ceos by Cretan Minos, who married the local princess, begot a son, and then went home, leaving half his troops behind On the evidence to date, Professor Caskey considers that the primary connections of his site on Ceos were with Crete. The place is fortified, but only on the side where there was danger of a raid from the mainland which seems to reinforce Caskey's tentative view. On the other hand, the latest Minoan or imitation-Minoan pottery found on Ceos plainly dates from close to 1400 B.C.—which is considerably later than the time when some of the other Minoan outpost/colonies are thought to have been destroyed or abandoned. One may conjecture, therefore, that this network of overseas settlements, or trading posts, or places with special Cretan links—whichever they may have been—decayed in patches, with some succumbing earlier than others to the growing Mycenaean competition Finally, if we abandon conjecture altogether, we are still left with the almost unavoidable conclusion that the Minoan influence on the Greek beginnings must have been very great indeed. Whether or not Thucydides was right about the navy of Minos, the Minoans certainly engaged in overseas trade from a fairly early date. Their traders are most unlikely to have neglected the Greek mainland; the two Minoas on the mainland also confirm this. And for these reasons, at this stage in the Bronze Age, Minoan influence was about the only significant foreign influence to which the Greeks can have been exposed.

*What happened thereafter, when the Greek mainland settlements began to grow stronger and wealthier?* is the next riddle. Or, rather, it is the next series of riddles, for what happened must have been a complex series of interacting developments. In trying to see what these developments may have been, we have some guidance (although by no means enough) from a number of well-established facts. These few certainties in the tangled and incomplete record may be summarized as follows:

I. Some at least of the Greek mainland settlements were already strong and beginning to be wealthy by the late seventeenth century B.C., as is shown by the rich later burials in the first Mycenaean grave circle, whose first graves date from around 1650. Even if part of this wealth came from mercenary service overseas, as seems possible, part of it must also have come from sea commerce such as the tin exports already mentioned. The very fact that Greek soldiers served in Egypt—if they did serve—implies prior trade contacts with Egypt, and ships to get the soldiers to Egypt after they were hired. Moreover, the mainland Greeks had also begun to plant outpost-colonies overseas by the middle of the second millennium. One such was Enkomi in Cyprus.

II. In this period, Greek commerce with Egypt also competed with and in the end far surpassed Cretan commerce. Blegen and Wace counted the foreign pottery found at various Egyptian sites dating from the middle of the second millennium; they discovered that the pots of mainland Greek origin outnumbered those from Crete by over five to one.

III. It appears that the Minoan outpost/colonies also declined or were deserted at about this same time. On Rhodes, Trianda was deserted for instance, while Mycenaean Enkomi, on Cyprus, continued and prospered. (In fact Cyprus survived as a kind of Mycenaean enclave into the new era after the Dorian invasion; here alone, in later Greek times, a king was still a *Wanax,* for instance.)

IV. At some moment as yet undetermined, mainland Greeks from Mycenae or elsewhere invaded and subjugated most of Crete, and a Greek *Wanax* ruled upon the immemorial throne of Minos at Knossos. And at some equally indeterminate moment after the Greek conquest, the Knossos records began to be kept in the Linear B script.

As can be seen, Greek power increased; Minoan power meanwhile declined, either relatively or absolutely; and in the end, Greeks seized control of Crete. These were the three main developments. From the fact already in the record, they cannot be doubted. As can also be seen, however the central historical riddle is *What happened at Knossos, and when?*

In other words, how did the Greeks gain control of Knossos and under what circumstances, and at what date; and once there, how long did they maintain their control of Crete, and who then caused the conflagration that cooked the Linear B archive of the palace of Minos? The second part of the question is really just as important as the first. A good many of the Minoan specialists, particularly those belonging to the older tradition, have thus far dealt with the Greeks in Crete in a way that strongly recalls the Mad Hatter trying to stuff the Dormouse into the Teapot. One or two are not even convinced by the Ventris decipherment (although they have honorably refrained from charging fraud in the shrill manner of Professor Beattie). The majority admit the decipherment; they briefly admit that, since Linear B was Greek, the Greeks must have got to Knossos somehow; and then they leave it at that. Yet it cannot be left at that. Any logical scheme must not only bring the Greeks to Crete; it must lso account for the end of this first Greek kingdom in Crete, when the great Knossos palace was destroyed on a day, as the archaeological record shows, when the wind was blowing hard from the south. I think it best o begin with the scheme which conserves the largest possible part of the orthodox version of the Minoan story. Yet I find myself somewhat embarassed, for the most convincing scheme of this character, having both a beginning and an end, was proposed some time ago by Sterling Dow of Harvard. When Dow delivered his paper to the Stockholm Congress, few doubts about the main outlines of the orthodox version of the Minoan story had been voiced in any quarter. Since then, doubts have been more and more oudly and cogently voiced, and Dow himself, so he informs me, now has an open mind about where the truth may lie. Hence I am driven to outline an answer to the riddle *What happened at Knossos, and when?* which is no longer regarded as the certainly accurate answer by the man who originally gave it. Yet it is a possible answer, as follows:

BETWEEN 1480 AND 1460 B.C., Greek raiders from Mycenae seize Knossos and subjugate Crete. Crete then becomes a colony, ruled by a vassal king under the High King at Mycenae.

ABOUT 1450 B.C., the "palace style" is born at Knossos. This is the decorative style in which Wace saw mainland affiliations, which led him to propose a Greek conquest. At about the same time, the Greek rulers of Crete use the Minoan Linear A script as a basis for their invention of Greek Linear B.

IN 1400 B.C., as Evans said, the Knossos palace and all the other palaces in Crete are destroyed. This ruin is wrought by order of the High King of Mycenae, in exasperation with his Cretan colony.

AFTER 1400 B.C., once again as Evans said, Crete becomes a backwater. "The evidence of archaeology," remarked Dow, shows that "Crete was reduced to being isolated and quiet" after 1400 B.C.

181

To this scheme, only one footnote is required. In order to explain the apparent anomaly of a Mycenaean conquest and occupation of Crete followed by a destruction ordered from Mycenae, Dow suggested that there was a Cretan resistance movement which eventually proved too strong for the Mycenaeans to master. The Cretans, he pointed out, "are dagger people," who have repeatedly shown themselves masters of the tactics of resistance. "There may," he said, "have been a long series of incidents culminating in some such act as the assassination of a *Wanax* . . . Mycenae presently had had enough. To hold the island in chains was out of the question. They lacked the man power. They could find—and did find—more tranquil fields to dominate [than Crete]. And so, in utter exasperation, Mycenae pillaged, massacred, burned, and withdrew."

The second possible answer to the riddle *What happened at Knossos, and when?* was first suggested by C. W. Blegen, in his customary quiet but firm way. This answer then won over L. R. Palmer, who has since made a crusading fight to persuade all and sundry that this is the correct answer. The result has been a vast deal of acrimony between Palmer and the adherents of Sir Arthur Evans; for the Blegen-Palmer answer is squarely based upon the assumption that Evans grossly misread the archaeological evidence produced by his own great excavation at Knossos. It has to be based on this assumption of a misreading by Evans, since the heart of the matter is a radical change in Evans' crucial date for the final destruction of the great palace at Knossos. Palmer believes that he has found solid proof of this misreading, in the Knossos daybooks kept by Evans' Scottish assistant, Duncan Mackenzie, which are preserved at Oxford. It must be added that it is not needful to suppose that Evans' error, if any, was willful and intentional. Evans, it has to be remembered, was not a modern archaeologist; he had no training whatever, in fact, in the microscopic nuances of modern stratigraphic excavation. He was a man of daemonic energies, doing ten men's work at the head of a regular excavating industry—year after year

182

he employed 250 workmen. At Knossos he was also dealing with one of the most stratigraphically complex sites ever excavated; for the palace had been endlessly improved, repaired, damaged by earthquake or fire, rebuilt, extended, reconstructed, altered, and so on and on until the last great fire consumed the huge building for good and all on that day when the wind was blowing hard from the south. For all these reasons, Evans can too easily have got his strata wrong, and therefore his whole story wrong. Among the Italian and French archaeologists, there are many who think that Evans did just that. The scheme, built on the assumption that Evans was wrong about the terminal date of the Knossos palace, may be outlined as follows:

UP TO 1450 B.C. OR THEREABOUTS, the Minoans [really Luvians, says Palmer but not Blegen] continue in control of Crete, while Greek power grows on the mainland.

ABOUT 1450 B.C. AND PERHAPS AS LATE AS 1400 B.C., Knossos is conquered by a Greek raid and most of the rest of Crete comes under Greek rule. The Palace of Minos thus becomes the center of a new Greek kingdom.

AFTER THE GREEK CONQUEST OF KNOSSOS, the new Greek kingdom in Crete flourishes for a couple of centuries. The Knossos archives are now kept in Linear B. The famous throne room at Knossos, admitted by Evans to be a reconstruction of this part of the palace, is also built rather late in the history of this Greek kingdom in Crete, since the "model for the reconstruction [says Blegen] is the hall of state in a mainland palace built [after 1400 B.C.] and more specifically [even as late as 1300 B.C.]."

SHORTLY AFTER 1200 B.C., and soon after the ruin of Pylos, the Dorians invade Crete, which they are supposed to have reached rather early in their destructive course. The Mycenaean Greek kingdom in Crete is extinguished by the invasion. The great palace at Knossos is sacked, burned and left in ruins by the Dorians, on that same day when an ill-omened wind blew hard from the south.

This radical revision of the orthodox view of what happened at Knossos has recommended itself to Blegen and Palmer, and more recently to others as well, because it has two major advantages. In the first place, the revision justifies Homer. Whereas Evans held that the Knossos palace was occupied by wretched squatters after 1400 B.C., Homer tells a quite contrary story. In the *Odyssey*, Idomeneus, king of Crete, is described as ruling over many races—Achaeans, Dorians,* Pelasgians, Kydonians and Eteo-Cretans—the last three being non-Greek races, rather obviously. The realm of Idomeneus is stated to include "a hundred cities," among them Phaistos, Gortyn and Knossos, the "dancing floor of fair-haired Ariadne." And Idomeneus is credited with leading eighty ships to Troy, which puts him just after Nestor of Pylos in the table of political-economic precedence established by the *Iliad* ship list. If the Knossos story continued to 1200 B.C. and beyond, instead of ending in a holocaust in 1400, the story leaves ample room for Idomeneus; otherwise Idomeneus has to be elaborately equivocated out of sight, except by the diminishing minority of scholars who think there is no truth in Homer anyway. This seems to me an advantage of the first order. So does the other advantage of the Blegen-Palmer revision. On this topic, Professor Blegen says:

"One cannot fail to be struck by the scantiness of salient differ-

---

*This is the only mention of Dorians anywhere in the Homeric epics. If Idomeneus had the kind of kingdom that Homer described, his subjects cannot have included Dorians, although Crete became a pre-eminent Dorian center after the great invasion. The matter has occasioned interminable, impassioned scholarly debate.*

ences between [the clay tablet archives from Pylos and Knossos]. . . . By and large, the tablets from Crete are so astonishingly similar to those from the mainland in most epigraphical and other respects as well as in the nature of their contents, that one can hardly avoid reaching the conclusion that the documents are more or less nearly contemporary products of a homogeneous society. Certainly they do not exhibit obvious criteria pointing to a chronological range of 200 to 250 years." Having thus shown the grave difficulties involved in supposing that the Knossos tablets were baked in a palace burning in 1400 whereas the baking of the Pylos tablets occurred in 1200 B.C. Blegen goes on to an impressive disquisition on the Greek love of novelty, and the resulting almost continuous evolution of Greek letters and script styles—the kind of evolution of which there is no sign at all in the Knossos and Pylos tablets. Finally, however, with customary fairness, Blegen appends a note:

"I would not stress too much [the script's failure to evolve] were it not for the fact, now clear, that we are dealing with Greeks and their works. In some systems of writing, conservative traditions long kept changes to a minimum. Dr. Julius Lewy tells me . . . that in some periods [there are] few if any criteria for distinguishing chronological differences of two or three hundred years [between cuneiform tablets]. The content of the [cuneiform] texts is often the only guide within several centuries."

Such are the impressive arguments for the second answer to the riddle *What happened at Knossos, and when?* The counterarguments put forward by John Boardman in his defense of Evans are also most impressive. Purely politically, however, the Blegen–Palmer version of Minoan history is more persuasive. Furthermore, the centuries between 1400 and 1200 B.C. are shown to have been a prosperous time in Crete by numerous items in the archaeological record. Phaistos and Mallia may have been abandoned, but there are Mycenaean houses in the Mallian palace's subordinate town, which Professor van Effenterre is now uncovering with remarkable

185

results.* On the same lovely hilltop as Phaistos, too, at Haghia Triada, a large Mycenaean *megaron* was built over the remains of the luxurious palace-villa of the period of the second palaces; and an impressive agora, or market, also was constructed. Homer's picture of Idomeneus, as close to Agamemnon in the importance of his kingdom, is in fact sustained by the archaeological evidence, whatever may have happened at Knossos. I cannot even hope to begin to judge the stratigraphic questions which are involved in the dispute about the date of the Knossos palace's destruction; so I must leave the reader to choose as he pleases among the alternative answers provided by the experts. To this, however, I would add two further points of some importance. Once again speaking solely as a political analyst, I must say that the two answers to the Knossos riddle thus far offered by the experts do not seem to me to be the only possible answers. And I must also say that when the dialogue among the experts produces final answers concerning the Minoan-Greek relationship, these must certainly incorporate a really satisfactory answer to still another riddle of a different sort, as follows:

*What is the explanation of the close similarity, almost amounting to stylistic identity, of the finest Bronze Age objects found in Crete and on the Greek mainland?* For various partisan reasons, many scholars have treated this last riddle in my series as though it did not exist; yet its existence and its central importance seem to me undeniable. To indicate the outlines of the problem, let us see how a few of the marvelous finds in Crete and Greece compare with one another.

---

* *Among the remains of the earlier, Minoan period he has found a great public place or square, separate from the palace and its courts, together with an astonishing underground crypt with no traces of cult, which he takes to have been the assembly place of the town elders or leading men. Even if van Effenterre's interpretation of the crypt is not accepted—and it is certainly bold though persuasive—the mere discovery of the handsome, quite separate public place alters the old, wholly palace-centered picture of Minoan society.*

*The Mycenaean lion's-head rh*

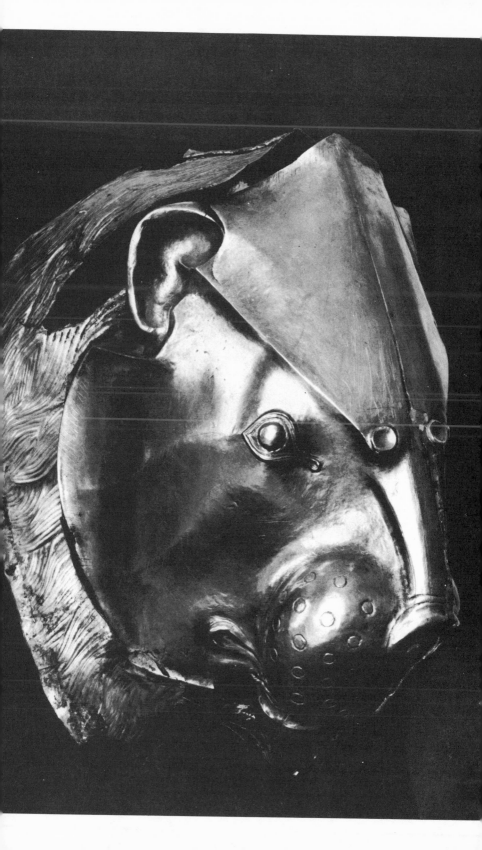

At Mycenae, in grave IV of the grave circle dating between 1600 and 1500 B.C., Schliemann found a great gold rhyton or ritual vase, which has the form of a lion's head. The head has several highly individual style marks. The ears are almost human in shape. Two curious dot-like bosses mark the ends of the eyebrows. The junction of the eyelids is prolonged, forward of the eyeball, in a way that conveys a ferocious expression. Above all, except for the mane, the whole lion's head is divided into highly plastic yet severely simplified sculptural planes. Every one of these four highly individual style marks appears in another superb rhyton in the form of a lioness's head, found in the palace at Knossos, and dated between 1550 and 1500 B.C. In addition, the hair along the lioness's jowl is indicated with almost the same formal pattern used for the lion's mane. The vase from Knossos is of a different material—marble-like limestone rather than gold—and since the lioness-head is shown stretched forward, the shape is longer and sculpturally stronger. Yet the resemblances are far more striking than the differences.

*The Minoan lioness head from Knossos.*

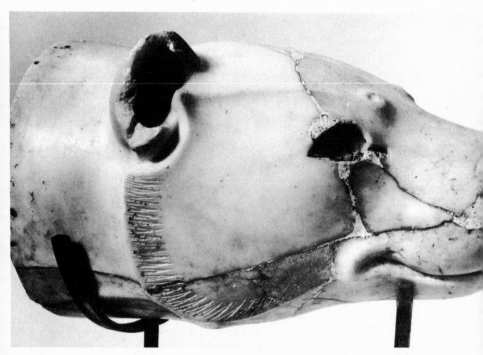

*e silver bull's-head rhyton from Mycenae.*    *The steatite bull's-head rhyton from Knossos.*

Also in grave IV at Mycenae, Schliemann found another rhyton in the form of a bull's head of silver, with gold-inlaid muzzle, a gold rosette on the forehead, and golden horns. From the Little Palace at Knossos comes a comparable bull's-head vase, of black stone (steatite), with shell-inlaid muzzle, crystal-inlaid eyes, and gilt wood horns. The Knossos bull's head, like the lioness head, is dated between 1550 and 1500 B.C. Once again, the materials used in the two objects are different, but the resemblances are more striking than this difference.

Then there are the two famous golden cups found in a tholos-

189

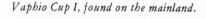

*Vaphio Cup I, found on the mainland.*

*Detail from the Cretan sports rhyton from Haghia Triada.*

tomb at Vaphio in Laconia, which must be compared with three equally famous black stone (again steatite) vessels from the Cretan palace at Haghia Triada. The gold cups are decorated with scenes of bull-catching in repoussé work. The two most important of the stone vessels are the harvesters' vase, showing a marvelously lively procession celebrating a harvest, and a great rhyton carved with bands of sporting scenes, of bull-jumping, boxing and wrestling. The supposed dates are again close—between 1550 and 1500 B.C. for the vessels from Crete and about 1500 B.C. for the mainland cups. The great bulls that dominate the décor of the Vaphio cups strongly recall the bulls in the bull-jumping band of the Haghia Triada rhyton, but the way the cups' few but masterly human figures are handled is even more striking. The posture of the bull-catcher being gored on cup I is all but identical with the posture of the bull-leaper being even

190

*ail from Vaphio Cup II.*

*Boxer detail, Cretan sports rhyton.*

more horribly gored on the Haghia Triada rhyton, even though their bulls are throwing the two unfortunates in quite different ways. Again, on cup II, a young bull-catcher is desperately tightening a noose around an unknowing bull's leg. The noose-tightening catcher is shown, like the boxers on the Haghia Triada rhyton, at a moment of intense muscular effort. The stylization of the straining muscles, so economical yet so effective, is identical. And the problem of depicting these figures in violent action in shallow relief is also solved in identical fashion, by turning the upper torso and broad shoulders, Egyptian-wise, to face the beholder, while the head and the body from the waist down are shown in profile. The treatment of the male bodies on the harvesters' vase shows the same idiosyncrasies, but here the most striking feature is the way that each of the many harvesters' small faces has been given its own individuality. Exactly comparable is the way

191

Three Cretan vases:
(UPPER LEFT) *the harvesters' va*
(RIGHT) *the sports rhyton;*
(LOWER LEFT) *the chieftain's va*
*All from Haghia Triada.*

the youthful, handsome, noose-tightening bull-catcher on Vaphio cup II has been differentiated from the older, plainer, less lucky man who has fallen under the enraged bull on cup I. Several of the same idiosyncrasies reappear in the third vessel from Haghia Triada, the so-called chieftain's vase.

The resulting problem was simply solved by Sir Arthur Evans. He said that all these objects came, if not from the same workshops, at least from neighbor workshops. He explained all the best objects found in Greece as the civilized Minoans' exports to the savage Greeks. But it really is not as simple as all that, although more modern scholars, like Friedrich Matz, continue to solve the problem precisely as Evans did. To begin with, there is the curious question of the materials used for these objects. All the Greek-found ones were made of precious metal, whereas all those found in Crete were mainly made of much less costly though no less beautiful stone. Yet the glow of gold was evidently admired in Crete\* —and therefore the choice of stone was not the result of a super-refined Japanese sobriety—since it is generally agreed among the experts that the three incomparable vases from Haghia Triada were originally coated with thin gold leaf. Suppose the Cretans were actually rich enough to be just as lavish with precious metals as the Mycenaean Greeks. All other things being equal, the actual mathematical odds are then close to 1000 to 1 against all of the four objects found in Greece being of gold and silver and all of the five most closely comparable objects found in Crete being mainly of stone. Of course, all other things were not equal. The Greek-found objects came from unlooted tombs, and no unlooted royal tomb of the Minoan age has yet been found in Crete. That weights the averages enormously heavily.

\* *Just as stone was also used in the mainland. Fragments survive of objects similar to the Cretan stone vessels. But here we are comparing the* finest *objects surviving in Greece and Crete.*

Yet there is still an anomaly here, the existence of which is confirmed by the really startling disproportion between the total Cretan and Greek yields of Bronze Age ornaments and objects in silver and gold. Somewhere or other, one cannot help feeling, the archaeologists who have combed over Crete so carefully ought to have found at least one very grand and glittering piece, to compare with the richest from Greece. But instead there are a few small silver vessels and only one small, lightly made gold vessel; and there is also the odd comparison between the finely designed bronze pitcher found by Evans at Knossos and the pitcher, all but identical in design but made of silver, which was found at Mycenae.

The implications of the anomaly above outlined are of course almost entirely political and economic. Speaking subjectively, I cannot help but feel that another kind of anomaly also needs examination. In brief, the Cretan-found objects are less precious in substance, but the more

*Silver pitcher from second grave circle, Mycenae, fifteenth century* B.C.

*Bronze pitcher from Knossos, fifteenth century* B.C.

*Limestone frieze from the second palace at Knossos.*

hours I have spent looking at them the more they have seemed to me superior in quality. Nor is this judgment wholly subjective. If we glance once again at the Vaphio cups and the stone vessels from Haghia Triada —especially the sports rhyton—we find something that is fairly staggering to discover in the middle of the Bronze Age. We find, in fact, that in addition to using the Egyptian twisted torso, the artists have made several attempts to depict human figures seen from the side and in action, with no distortion whatever. The problem, which was not tackled again so far as I can recall for another thousand years, was of course to show the arm-shoulder part of the body in a convincing manner, without trying to escape from the limits of bas-relief. In the Haghia Triada sports rhyton, the problem is solved with considerable success in the figures of the gored bull-leaper and a helmeted boxer who has sunk to his knees. The Vaphio cups are generally considered to be later in date than the great stone vessel from Crete; in the figures of the gored bull-catcher and the man who has fallen beneath the angry bull, the cups also show attempts to avoid the Egyptian twisted torso; but despite the close similarities to the Cretan-found designs, these most difficult parts of the designs on the Vaphio

195

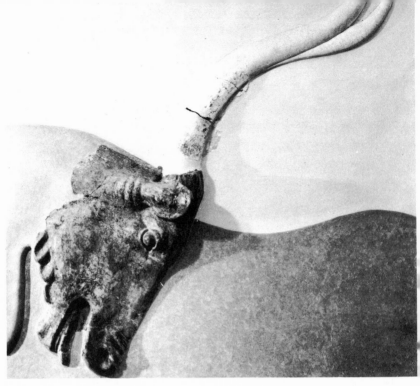

*Bull's-head stucco relief, Knossos.*

cups are conspicuously less assured and less successful. But if the cups were exported from Crete, or made on the mainland by Minoan craftsmen-émigrés, and if they are later in date, why this seeming deterioration? And just how do all these marvelous objects, so alike and so different, really relate to one another? These are complex questions. Yet an even worse complication appears when we move on to certain things of widely separated dates, which were intimately linked together by Sir Arthur Evans himself.

In brief, these things are the magnificent stucco relief of the head of a charging bull and an elegant decorative motif—a band of half-rosettes separated by framed spirals—both of which come from Knossos; and an exactly similar decorative motif and a fragmentary relief of a charging bull (one of Lord Elgin's bits of loot from Greece), both of which were origi-

*Detail of procession fresco, Tiryns.*

nally parts of the grandiose portal design of the Treasury of Atreus at Mycenae.* Evans was the first to point out that his finds at Knossos were all but identical with the Mycenaean fragments. He further dated his Knossos finds rather early. *Ergo*, he said, Wace's Mycenaean dating was all wrong, and the Treasury of Atreus must also be put early in the Mycenaean sequence. Anyway this wonderful structure was basically Minoan work, he also added. Today, however, no scholar any longer challenges Wace's late date for this great tomb or suggests that the Minoans had any

---

* *This was Evans' opinion. Others are not so sure, and some also think the relief may have been incorporated in the portal design, but only when it was already an admired antique.*

part in it. F. Matz, who is one of the strong defenders of the Evans tradition, is thus reduced to speaking of the "Minoan decoration" of the Treasury of Atreus, without mentioning the fairly important fact that the Knossos bull's head and decorative motif are still given a sixteenth-century date, whereas the exactly similar "Minoan decoration" of the Treasury of Atreus is universally given a thirteenth-century date. Surely there is something quite wrong here. But what is it?

I have already labored this point at excessive length, but there is a little more that really must be said. The frescoes must certainly be considered. After the glorious cupbearer, the most celebrated of the Knossos fragments is probably the so-called "Parisienne." She came from a fresco which Evans thought showed a religious scene, and Professor Marinatos

*"La Parisienne," detail of Knossos fresco.*

believes is a picture of a fashionable picnic. The Parisienne is dated by Marinatos to somewhere between 1500 and 1450 B.C. Yet the pretty girl from Knossos is clearly the first cousin, if not the sister, of the girls in a procession fresco from Tiryns; and the Tiryns girls must certainly be dated after 1400 B.C. and probably after 1300 B.C. The Knossos fresco is more talented and vivid; in particular the line is much bolder, freer and more emphatic than in the Tiryns fresco. But the differences are not very much greater than you would find in a drawing by Constantin Guys (which the Parisienne suggests) and a contemporary drawing by a less gifted imitator. Friedrich Matz sees "Minoan tradition" but "150 years later" in the Tiryns fresco. The gap is at least as long between the usually accepted dates of the similarly linked frescoes of royal griffins in the Knossos and Pylos throne rooms, and a very different view about these frescoes has been stated by Professor Blegen. Blegen concluded his attack on the orthodox date of the Knossos throne room with the remark that its griffin-painted walls "offer further evidence [that the Knossos throne room has been dated much too early] since [the Knossos frescoes] are executed in a style very close to the frescoes from the palace of Nestor." Again, there is something wrong here, but just what is it? In the same fashion, the startling links between many of the seals found in Crete and on the mainland also deserve exploration. So does the problem of the superbly executed inlaid daggers from various sites in Greece—luxury objects if there ever were any—which have no parallels from Crete.

Yet enough, and more than enough, has already been said about individual objects. As the reader will have noted, the dating difficulties are serious. Yet I venture to think that there is an even greater difficulty, which has as yet received much less attention. This I would call the difficulty of *localization*. To be sure, certain classes of things found in Crete and on mainland Greece are inherently localized. The wonderful inlaid daggers and the death-masks of precious metal are localized in Greece, to begin

199

with, because none has ever been found in Crete; just as Linear A tablets are localized in Crete. The experts can also distinguish Cretan pottery from Mycenaean pottery, in the same way (and I would heretically add, for the same reasons) that experts on European porcelains can quickly distinguish Sèvres from Vieux Paris, Vieux Paris from Chelsea, Chelsea from Bow, and Bow from Meissen. But the majority of the very finest things found in Crete and Greece with dates from the seventeenth century B.C. onwards, are not localized in any inherent way. They are only localized, in fact, because the find-spots have been recorded. Take away the record of the find-spots. Then ask an imaginary expert (he has to be imaginary, because all experts know every find-spot) to name the most likely find-spots of the majority of the objects and decorations I have listed. About the objects the expert would then have to say, in all honesty, "Well, on general grounds of style and design, these things could have been found in Crete or on the mainland; but these are of carved stone and their execution is incomparable, so I should guess they were found in Crete; whereas those are of precious metal but slightly inferior in quality, so I plump for mainland Greece."

As can be seen, this seems to create an enormous problem. Naturally, the problem does not exist for men like Friedrich Matz, who remain convinced that Sir Arthur Evans was dead-right about his Minoans, even though he was dead-wrong about Linear B and the Greek occupation of Knossos. For Matz, as for Evans, all the finest things found in Greece are either Minoan exports or reflections of Minoan influence. Matz may be correct at that. L. R. Palmer may also be correct in contending, as he does contend, that Evans got his Knossos levels so wrong that he antedated some of the best things found there, thus stealing from the Greeks, as it were, marvels that were in fact produced in the Greek period at Knossos, when the palace records were kept in Linear B. For the time being, however, it would seem to me simpler and safer to speak of the emergence of a

200

Greco-Minoan style during the seventeenth century B.C. We may then conceive this Greco-Minoan style as the product of a unitary art tradition having two related, interacting centers, in Crete and on the mainland. And we may leave to further research the crucial decision whether the style was always dominantly Minoan, or was part-Greek from the outset, or was first dominantly Minoan and then dominantly Greek. The style was plainly unitary, and was very wonderful, too; but no one can say whose style it was at any given moment, until we have the ultimate answer to the historical riddle: *What happened at Knossos, and when?*

In short, a dependable interpretation of the art demands a dependable version of the history. When examining the conflicting versions of this history that have been offered thus far, and when trying to synthesize the current findings and opinions of the many experts on Greek and Cretan art, I can only add that I have been much struck by a curious phenomenon. In brief, there have been two quite sharply contrasting kinds of response to the Ventris decipherment of Linear B. Among those experts with a vested interest in the orthodox version of the Minoan story, a great many have responded to the considerable shock of the Ventris decipherment in almost the way the nineteenth-century Greek scholars responded to Schliemann's great discovery at Mycenae. They have tried, in other words, to conserve every bit of the orthodox version that could conceivably be salvaged; and they have sought to push the Greeks into the smallest possible corner of Cretan history. But there has also been a different kind of response. Palmer, the philologist, and Blegen, the great specialist on Trojan and mainland Greek archaeology, have already proposed a radical revision of the old orthodoxies. Open-mindedness verging on sympathy for Palmer is also observable among the Italian and French archaeologists, as well as some of the Greeks, who understandably fretted a little under the former dominion of Sir Arthur Evans. The Canadian, Graham, also has indicated marked doubts about Evans' early date for the destruction of the Knossos palace. Faced with this conflict of authorities, I cannot judge who is likely to prove right in the end (although I shall be much surprised if the Luvian part of Professor Palmer's theory is ever shown to be correct, at any rate in anything like its present form). But even as an outsider, there are two judgments which I think I am competent to make. In the first place, the whole history of scholarship shows that when a basic element of an established theory has been shown to be dead-wrong, it is extremely dangerous to react by trying to defend and preserve every other element of the challenged theory. The safer and wiser reaction is to recognize that a theory which was wrong in one part may be wrong in other parts, and therefore to begin a fundamental reappraisal of all the facts—"a new analysis, without passion," such as Professor van Effenterre has suggested. At least that much is called for by the upheaval in the old theories about the Aegean Bronze Age that began with Blegen's discovery of the Pylos tablets and ended with Ventris' revelation that Linear B was Greek after all. In the second place, this fundamental reappraisal is unlikely to be made with real assurance of success unless those who make it bear in mind that basic political processes in the Bronze Age are really highly unlikely to have differed greatly from basic political processes in other eras. But here we are touching on the topic of this essay's last chapter.

Archaeologists, and even historians specialized in periods for which archaeology provides the main evidence, quite often share a common human failing. The political processes in the remote eras they are studying are mainly revealed by objects, by strata, and by ruins. Hence they tend not to allow for the diversity, the complexity and the peculiarity of all political processes. One of my first learned friends was a famous student of the early Chinese bronzes. As he was a man of the nineteenth century at heart, he believed in progress. As he believed in progress, he could not conceive that the bronzes showing the most refined casting techniques could possibly belong to the beginning of the series. As these were the pieces which the Chinese experts attributed to the Shang dynasty, he joined the other Western students of the subject who held that the Shang and Hsia dynasties were both mythical. And as he was an unhappy man, he used to console his own melancholia, when it occurred, by down-dating the Shang bronzes in the great collection over which he presided—thus encouraging himself by vindicating progress. The bronzes' date tickets were getting perilously close to the time of Our Lord when Anyang was dug up, and all the dates of my friend's Shang pieces had

to be moved back many centuries. Being an honest scholar, he correcte
his own error; but he died soon after.

While writing this essay, I have been honored by the kindness o
many of the leading students of the Greek Bronze Age, and on more tha
one of them I have perhaps unfairly tried a little test suggested by th
unhappy experience of my Chinese bronze-expert friend. In the Vienn
treasure rooms, in brief, there is a remarkable garment. This cape of wove
silk is decorated with two motifs—the tree of life, straight out o
Sumerian Ur—and two carnivore-herbivore combats—straight out of th
ancient Asian animal art, except that the weavers have used camels as th
victims of the attacking lions. In addition, the cape has a woven border i
the form of a prayer to God in Arabic, with a date early in the twelft
century A.D. which is given in the Muslim reckoning in years after th
Hegira. "Where," I have asked, "do you think the cape must have bee
woven?" Syria has been the most common answer. The correct answer wa
never given, yet it has a certain bearing on the mystery of Greek develop
ment in the Bronze Age—since who used what script when is such an im
portant factor in this mystery.

In brief, the coronation cape of the Holy Roman Empire wa
woven at Palermo in 1134 A.D. for Roger II d'Hauteville, some sevent
years after the first Norman landing in Sicily, and a good forty-six year
after the Normans quashed the last opposition of Sicily's previous Sarace
rulers. Yet a royal garment woven with a prayer to God in Arabic and date
by the Muslim reckoning would have been the last thing to worry th
Sicilian Normans. When this small band of warriors made their landing o
the island, Sicily was Christian at the base (which aided their conquest) bu
Saracen-administered and half-Arabic in culture. Having gained control o
this society considerably more complex than any they had known, the Nor
mans were not merely rapidly Sicilianized; they were even partly Arabized
The heir of the Norman kings, Frederick II Hohenstaufen, was brought u

t Palermo speaking Arabic from childhood; indeed his Arabic tastes were
ıne of the Vatican's arguments for calling *Stupor Mundi* a sort of junior
.nti-Christ. Arabic was still one of the languages of Frederick's court and
:hancery a full century and a half after the Norman conquest of Sicily
ıegan. And it was Frederick, of course, who wore the wonderful cape at
ıis own coronation as Holy Roman emperor, and thus added it to the regalia
ıf the empire.

The two cases I have cited are very much in point, because they
eveal the pitfalls that may lie in wait for those who draw superficially
ogical deductions from objects alone—which is a common, natural and
ıften unavoidable archaeological habit. Sometimes objects present anomalies
which may never be fully understood, as in the case (at least to date) of the
:oarsening of Chinese bronze techniques after the Chou conquest of the
šhang.* Sometimes, too, objects present seeming anomalies which are
:asily understandable when the underlying political processes are also
ınderstood, as in the case of the coronation cape. For these reasons, it
:eems to me only sensible to seek guidance whenever and wherever guidance
an be found outside the objects themselves. For many archaeologists—
ıome of them, I should add, among the very greatest—this kind of search
or additional, external guidance is sheer heresy. I suspect this is the main
eason why the dominant political processes of the Greek Bronze Age have
ıever been analyzed, so far as I am aware, simply as processes.

History has no laws, which is why historical analogies can never
:ell us what must have happened or what is surely going to happen. But
ıistory is at least separable into many different sorts of political processes.
Jach of these processes also has its own characteristic probabilities. Hence,
f we can identify the nature of an otherwise mysterious process in the re-

---

* *A process Dr. Li Chi of the "Academia Sinica" has now shown to have begun
ıt the end of the Shang—only adding to the puzzle.*

mote past, we have already gained much. The probable course and probabl results of the process can then be estimated; and thus we know what is likel to have happened, or at least what may have happened and what cann be ruled out as having happened. In the study of the past, as in the study of the present, there are two kinds of errors that must be carefully avoided One is certainly the unthinking use of historical analogies—which leads t nonsensical assertions in the style of "the Russian" or "the Chinaman" or "the Frenchman" never, or always, does this, that or the other. But th other error, which is every bit as dangerous, is historical parochialism— which leads to the kind of twaddle talked about modern Asian politic processes by virtuous persons who have never been there. Moreover, histor cal parochialism can be quite as misleading to students of the remote pa as to cloistered editorial writers of great newspapers. For example, all kind of false conclusions are likely to be reached if the Greek conquest of Cret is equated, let us say, with the British conquest of India; for it is just abou dead-certain that these two historical episodes were as far apart in kind a they were in time.

Self-excuse is the motive of the foregoing long digression. Th truth is that I am about to plunge onward into uncharted territory. I mea to try to analyze the key episodes of the Greek Bronze Age, not in terms o pottery periods but solely as political processes. I cannot justify this furth venture by offering the reader a *smörgåsbord* of expert opinions. Among th students of the Bronze Age, to be sure, sharp political insights have not bee uncommon. For example, when the theory of Minoan rule of mainlan Greece was first being called into question, a great expert astutely remarke that if the then-current arguments from the objects alone were rigidly ap plied, they would lead to the conclusion that Etruria was under the rule o Athens in the period when the Etruscans were such avid buyers of fin Athenian pottery. But such an isolated insight is quite different from th procedural study of an entire episode. This has not been attempted, so fa

206

*owl from Knossos, c. 1550–1520* **B.C.**

s I know; and I believe that valuable additional light will be shed by the
ttempt. Yet I must add one further warning. One of my learned friends,
ɔ whom I showed an earlier draft of this book, remarked that I was offer-
ng a "new version, most interesting but highly disputable" of the history
f the Greek Bronze Age. I am doing nothing of the sort, because I know
ery well that I am incompetent to do so. I believe, however, that the num-
er of quite possible versions of Greek Bronze Age history has been unduly
estricted, precisely because the key episodes have not been studied as
processes. Look at the key episodes procedurally, and you find an unex-
ectedly enlarged range of choice—even though certain choices already
nade by certain experts also begin to seem unexpectedly dubious. As to the
inal choice of the correct version of the Greek Bronze Age story, that can
nly be made by further professional exploration of the problems involved
n this story.

207

What, then, are these key episodes which I have been so abstractly discussing? The central one, too long perhaps to be called a mere episode, is the transformation of Greek Bronze Age society, from the primitive form of the Greek beginnings in Greece into the extremely specialized and elaborate form that is revealed by the clay tablets. But I suspect that the best clues to this puzzling transformation are to be found in the other key episode, which is the Greek conquest of Knossos; and this is where I propose to start. It may seem odd to talk about a procedural analysis of this invasion of Crete, which cannot be precisely dated, about which, indeed, almost nothing is positively known except that it placed a Greek upon the ancient throne of Minos. But let us see where the attempt leads.

It must be noted, to begin with, that the experts have always thought about this conquest as a process—but their thought has been subconscious, as it were. Thus Sir Arthur Evans simply took it for granted that any conquest must always produce a "break." Hence he was firmly convinced that Minoans must always have ruled at Knossos until the final destruction of the palace of Minos, because he found "no break." Thus most students of the problem now take it for granted that any conquest must at least be followed by a partial language change. Hence they assume that non-Greeks must have ruled at Knossos while the Knossian scribes used Linear A, and they further assume that the arrival of the Greeks must have been promptly followed by the invention of Linear B. What makes these assumptions questionable is the strong likelihood that Evans was thinking and most of the modern experts on the Bronze Age are still thinking about the wrong kind of conquest. Their models are the conquests in the long series that began when Cortes and Pizarro subjugated the ancient pre-Columbian civilizations, and ended only the other day when the tide of Western imperialism at last began to recede. All these conquests did indeed produce very radical cultural and political "breaks" with the pasts of the conquered civilizations. All of them also produced, as a minimum

hanges in the local administrative languages; and in the former Spanish
nd Portuguese territories in Latin America they also produced permanent
hanges in the everyday languages of the conquered peoples.

But if you consider the problem politically, you can see at once
now misleading it is to think of the Greek Bronze Age warriors who beat
lown the last resistance on the hill of Knossos as in any way resembling
he members of the Honorable East India Company, or even the brave but
greedy men-at-arms who followed Cortes and Pizarro. None of the Western
mperial conquerors ever gave an instant's thought to adopting the customs,
he culture and the administrative methods of the subjugated peoples, precisely because they were intensely conscious of belonging to more advanced
and highly developed societies. In other words, the sequels that Evans supposed, and so many still suppose, must flow from all conquests are in fact
he sequels of a particular kind of conquest—*the conquest of a less advanced
by a more advanced society*. Concerning the Greek conquest of Knossos and
most of Crete, there is a special point that had better be got out of the way
at once. In brief, when the conquered society and its conquerors are in
roughly equal stages of development, history shows that you must expect
a rather mixed and unpredictable pattern of results, as in the case of
Rome's conquest of Greece. It is imaginable (though I think only barely
imaginable) that Greek mainland society had pulled abreast of Minoan
society when the invasion of Crete occurred. But if this was the way of
it, the Greeks almost certainly came into Crete so late that the last part of
Sir Arthur Evans' version of the Knossos story is even more erroneous than
L. R. Palmer has suggested. From the beginning, moreover, it has been
almost universally assumed that this was not the way of it. It has been
assumed, in fact, that the Greeks came into Crete as rough, unlettered
warriors, who beat down the resistance of the more civilized Minoans
solely because of their superior warlike qualities.

In this far more probable event, the Greek conquerors certainly did not think of themselves as coming from a society more enlightened and advanced than the great, already ancient Minoan civilization which they subjugated. Confident in their own courage, they no doubt were; but in all other respects they must have held the Minoans in considerable awe, as the possessors of technical, cultural, artistic and political secrets that were unknown to the ruder Greeks. Furthermore, when they arrived in Crete, the Greeks can hardly have numbered more than a few thousand fighting men, and since Bronze Age shipping did not lend itself to large-scale population transfers, the infusion of Greek blood into Crete can hardly have been massive at the outset. In short, the odds are extremely strong that the Greek conquest of Crete belonged to another special class of historical episode, namely, *conquests of more advanced societies by warrior minorities.* And this quite different kind of conquest also has its own powerful inherent tendencies, which are almost exactly opposite to the tendencies of

*Faience town mosaic from Knossos, first palace period.*

onquests of less advanced by more advanced societies.

You do not have to indulge in mystical Toynbee-nonsense in order to find reasons why this other kind of conquest has inbuilt special tendencies. As a practical matter, a warrior minority that seizes control of a more advanced society is like a child who suddenly gains possession of a costly, complicated piece of machinery, needing operating skills quite outside the child's experience. A child in this situation can do only one of two things. Either it can smash the newly acquired machine to bits, from sheer ignorance or fear or lust for destruction, or it can grasp the value of its new prize, learn from the skilled persons who know how to operate the machine, and finally grow up to be very like its teachers. When the Dorians invaded Mycenaean Greece, they chose the first alternative. They smashed Mycenaean Greek society to bits. In the same fashion, the prosperous and flourishing society that existed in Iraq under the Abbassid

Caliphate was smashed almost to bits by the conquest of the Mongols unde
Hulagu Khan.*

* In the time of Harun-al-Rashid, the population of Iraq is estimated to hav
been 25,000,000. The best opinion is that the sequel of Hulagu Khan's conquest was
reduction of the population by no less than 20,000,000 souls, resulting from the reversio
of most of the cultivated land to desert. But the chances are rather strong that the historian
who have rarely administered great irrigation systems, have been unjust in supposing tha
Hulagu Khan and his Mongols desired this gigantic catastrophe. The point is that th
complex irrigation system which produced the prosperity of this area under the Abbassids
depended on annual cleaning of the channels by large levies of corvée laborers. The cleanin
had to be regular, because silting was heavy. If there was no corvée, the remoter channel
in which waterflow was most sluggish, at once silted up; that much of the harvest was lo
the next year; and that many fewer people were available for the next year's corvée, becaus
a good many people had nothing to eat. And if there was no corvée the next year, the whol
process once again repeated itself, narrowing still further the society's human and produc
tive base. In this manner, the Abbassid irrigation system rapidly failed for good an
all under the Mongols. As this was the way the catastrophe happened, it is downrigh
unlikely that Hulagu Khan actually wanted to extirpate four fifths of the population he ha
just conquered. But he did not comprehend the water management and corvée-labor system
or grasp their intimate connection; and so the people died and this region was permanentl
impoverished.

  The best proof that the historians have been unjust to Hulagu Khan is to b
found in the sequel of the Spanish conquest of Peru. In literacy, in weaponry and in othe
ways, Spanish society belonged to a much later stage of development than Inca society
which was still chalcolithic. But the Spaniards of Pizarro's time had no understanding o
experience of vast water-management systems, such as the Incas used to ensure the fertilit
and to support the teeming population of their empire. Consequently, the Spaniards a
lowed the greatest works of the Incas to fall into ruin from sheer neglect. (The collaps
of the Bridge of San Luis Rey, which actually occurred, was a late incident in this process.
The failure of the water-management systems greatly reduced the former Inca Empire'
agricultural productivity, and it is now thought to have caused serious depopulation as wel
Good colonial husbandry ought to have dictated the opposite policy to Pizarro and his suc
cessors, but they simply did not know enough to understand this. Returning to Hulagu Kha
it must be noted that his massacre of a large part of the population of Baghdad was certain
intentional. This was standard Mongol treatment for cities that resisted or even half-resisted
and it has no bearing on the neglect of the Abbassid irrigation system. It should also b
noted that despite the fearful destruction caused by the arrival of the Mongols, enough o
the old Abbassid culture survived to infect and to transform the court of the Ilkhans withi
one generation. As the wise René Grousset has written, "there never was a conquest which
by contact with the vanquished, did not contaminate the victor."

But there have been other warrior-conquerors of advanced socie-ies who were less wasteful and more adaptable than the Dorians or Hulagu Khan. Roman history is generally supposed to end, and European history to begin, when the Ostrogoths and Visigoths broke into the West-ern Roman Empire. Yet these destroyers of the Western empire were in fact rather rapidly, though incompletely, Romanized; Latin, not Gothic, was the language of the chancery of Milan. For these and other related reasons, the great Henri Pirenne has argued that the real break with the Roman past should be placed not in the fifth century A.D. but in the seventh. In the same fashion, but on a small scale, Duke Rollo and his Vikings carved out a rich fief in Normandy in the tenth century A.D.; but although place names in Normandy contain reminders of the first occupation by these rough Northerners, the army that Duke William led into England in 1066 was purest Norman-French instead of Viking in its language and culture.* The partial transformation of the Norman-French who conquered Sicily we have already seen. In India, again, the Moghul conquerors, whom the British supplanted, were originally Turki-speakers; the memoirs of the great Babur were dictated in Turki and then translated into Persian. The Moghuls were not vastly less advanced in culture than the Indians they subjugated; indeed Babur owed his crucial victory on the plain of Panipat to the fact that his small forces possessed cannon. But these conquerors, like so many others, were none the less absorbed by their conquest. Earlier Muslim invaders had established Persian as the main administrative and court language of the Sultanate of Delhi. Under the Moghuls Persian

---

* By 1066, however, the Norman-French were more advanced than the rather backward English. Thus Norman technology and Norman administrative methods were in-troduced into England, and Norman-French became the administrative language. The period when Norman-French was the administrative language of England is still recalled by the formula that is used whenever the Queen signs an act of Parliament, and it is proclaimed as a law. "La Reyne le Veult" is the actual formula. But in Normandy, even in the eleventh century, no one used the Scandinavian Runic script.

213

continued to be the language of the court and government, and the late Moghul rulers were no longer able to speak Turki. Finally, if we look fo the most numerous and completely documented examples of this curiou process we have only to turn to the history of China, where the sam thing has often happened.

Most of North China first came under foreign rule in the earl fourth century A.D., in the troubled aftermath of the collapse of the Ha imperial system. Combinations of steppe peoples and other outliers wit troops of their own blood employed by the short-lived Chin dynasty, the established more than a dozen foreign kingdoms in North China. Th rulers of these kingdoms were probably Turkish, Mongol and Tibetan None the less, all these kingdoms were in part, and generally in larg part, Chinese in culture, organization and administrative language. Sinc many of these warlord-kingdoms' founders had no doubt been partl Sinified during their mercenary service, they are less revealing cases tha the next on the list. In the late fourth and early fifth century, Mongolian* invaders known to history as the Toba-Wei established the Northern Wei dynasty, with an initial heavy impact on Chinese culture. In some measure, the Toba-Wei were civilization smashers. To gain space for their herds they caused large areas of North Chinese arable land to be returned to pasture; and one of the more important consequences of their invasion was a massive flight to South China of Chinese of the educated and artisan classes—which in turn helped to promote the Sinification of the regions below the Yangtze River. At the outset, the Toba-Wei also kept their clan organization and their native aristocratic hierarchy; and although their Chinese subjects were largely governed by Chinese officials in the usual

---

*It is also argued that the Toba-wei were Tungusic (from Siberia) and Turkish—which only goes to show how completely they were Sinified before they left decipherable traces.*

manner, the invaders at first had enough attractive pull to cause fair numbers of the more ambitious Chinese who had not fled, to attach themselves to the Toba-Wei clans. (The founder of the great T'ang dynasty, substantially later in the story, was known to have an infusion of Toba-Wei blood.) But despite this independent start, the Toba-Wei finally succumbed to the power of the higher civilization they had conquered. The earliest Northern Wei rulers had been almost demonstratively un-Chinese, refusing even to learn the language of their subjects. But the Emperor Shao Wen not only spoke and wrote Chinese as his name indicates ("Wen" means "literary"); he was also the voluntary captive of the always-absorbent Chinese culture. Hence he commanded his people to become Chinese. He unified the administration by giving Chinese titles to the Toba-Wei tribal leaders, signifying their transformation into Chinese bureaucrats. And he ruled as a traditional Son of Heaven, as did his successors until the Northern Wei came to their appointed end.

Another group of barbarian rulers set up fiefs in China in the time of weakness in the late T'ang dynasty; but they may be rapidly passed over, since they closely resembled the rulers of the warlord-kingdoms of the fourth century. The next really interesting case is that of the Liao-Khitan invaders, probably of Mongol blood, whose tribal name, Khitan, has given China one of its world-names, Cathay. When they established the Liao dynasty in North China in the tenth century, they made what looks like a conscious effort to defend their national identity. Their main capital was north of the Great Wall, and their administration was divided, in effect, into Northern and Southern departments. The Southern department was Chinese in method, language and personnel; but in the Northern department, the Liao-Khitan tribes were still governed through their tribal chieftains; and a new script was invented to express the Liao-Khitan language, for use in this Northern department. But in the Liao case, too, these defenses soon crumbled—and this although the actual Chinese area under

Liao rule was never very large, and the Liao rulers themselves long continued to be tent-dwellers. The new Liao script rather rapidly went out of use, and was then completely forgotten. The administration relapsed into the normal Chinese pattern. The Liao-Khitan became Chinese in all but blood. In short, the Liao dynasty, like the Northern Wei, was thoroughly Sinified before it ended. Much the same curve was followed by another smaller foreign dynasty, the Western Hsia, established in Northwest China during the reign of the Liao. The Liao dynasty then fell before the onslaught of the Jurchens or "Gold Tartars." This people, whom the later Manchus claimed as ancestors, had been extremely primitive at the outset; but they had already been partly Sinified before their conquest, by infection from the Liao. They were proud of being Sinified, too. Almost from the moment of the conquest, therefore, their Chin dynasty was Chinese in everything except the blood of the emperors and of some members of the ruling class; and by the dynasty's close the capital had been moved deep into North China, to Kaifeng.

There followed China's solitary failure to digest a foreign conqueror. In the time of Genghis Khan, the Mongols had adapted their own script from the script of Islamic origin which was used by the Central Asian Uighurs. After the Mongol conquest of China, the higher administration of their Yuan dynasty was conducted in this script; and the administrators were largely foreigners, including Marco Polo. After the death of Kublai Khan, however, the Yuan administrators did not do a very successful job. The Yuan was one of the most short-lived of the greater Chinese dynasties; and the complete restoration of China's Chinese-ness was the first plank in the platform of the succeeding Ming dynasty.

Finally we have the last and perhaps the most striking case in point—the Manchu conquest of China in the first half of the seventeenth century A.D. The true conqueror, Nurhachi, was born a pastoral nomad, but long before the Ming dynasty fell, Nurhachi had already united Manchuria under his rule and had established his own administration there. The Manchus, furthermore, did not need to invent a script for administrative purposes; they had long possessed one, modeled on the Mongol script. Yet when Nurhachi's heir entered the Forbidden City (Nurhachi himself having died too soon) the establishment of the new Ch'ing dynasty was by no means the signal for the substitution of Manchu for Chinese administrative methods or the replacement of Chinese characters by the Manchu script. Initially, an experiment was made with a double system, at any rate at the top of the governmental pyramid. In others words, each ministry had both Chinese and Manchu ministers and vice-ministers, and all memorials to the throne were required to be presented in both languages. It is extreme doubtful, however, if the Manchu memorials were ever read by any emperor of the Ch'ing dynasty after the first one, Shun Chi. The Emperor Shun Chi's successor, the great K'ang Hsi, was already much more Chinese than Manchu. Within a couple of generations the Manchus had even begun to forget their own language; and the Manchu versions of the memorials to the throne, although still required as a formality, became scamped, unreliable and often half-illiterate. The Manchu bannermen retained their perquisites, but Chinese became the sole road to serious official advancement; the famous system of recruiting new officials by literary examinations based on the Chinese classics was even tightened and improved. In the eighteenth century Sinification was so complete that the Emperor Ch'ien Lung angrily defended orthodox Confucianism by a harsh system of thought control, severely harassing the Chinese scholars of that time who inaugurated the higher criticism of the books of the Confucian canon.*

These cases of conquests of more advanced societies by warrior

---

* But Ch'ien Lung also expurgated Chinese literature of discourteous references to Manchus and other northern peoples.

minorities have not been cited, I must again emphasize, to prove the existence of any historic law. There are none such, with the possible exception of the law that nothing succeeds like success and nothing fails like failure. But when the same political situation has produced much the same results in close to a score of cases, it seems to me reasonable to conclude that such results are at least highly probable when such situations arise. For our purposes, the Yuan dynasty is not indicative, since China, at the time of her subjection by the Mongols, was only one province of a much vaster empire with a well-established machinery of imperial administration. If we make a statistical compilation of all the other cases listed, we find that the kind of post-conquest script invention that is so widely assumed in Crete, occurred in only two cases of the long series. But the new kinds of writing that the Liao and Western Hsia rulers caused to be devised for use by their governments, not only fell out of use very soon in the subsequent competition with Chinese; both of these invented scripts would have vanished almost without trace if the only surviving Chinese archives were those written on clay and baked in palace burnings. We further find that *in all cases* the conquerors ended by learning the language and carrying on the administration in the writing of the conquered higher civilization.* And we find, finally, that this happened because, *in all cases,* the conquerors were more or less rapidly absorbed by the higher civilization they had conquered, partly or completely losing their own culture and often losing their own language, and adopting the culture, customs and administrative methods of the subjugated peoples. This should be enough, surely, to prove rather clearly why conquests of more advanced societies by warrior minorities must be considered as historical episodes of a special sort, with their own inherent tendencies and probabilities. I have already tried to suggest the strictly

---

* *The Norman-French in Sicily used three administrative languages, Greek, Latin and Arabic.*

practical, non-Toynbean reasons why this should hold true. All these reasons must have operated at Knossos, moreover, if the Greek conquest of Crete was an early episode of this special sort, as seems 90 per cent certain. And if we therefore assume that the Greeks entered Minoan Crete as a minority of warrior-conquerors of a more advanced society, we then find ourselves confronted with a number of fairly unsettling possibilities and/or probabilities as follows:

First, the Greek conquerors were probably quite rapidly re-molded in the Minoan image, whereas the subjugated Minoan society continued with few changes except in the composition of its ruling class.

Second, there was probably nothing resembling an archaeologically perceptible "break," although the changed composition of the ruling class may have caused a significant change in taste and creative outlook, as happened in China in the Manchu case.*

Third, the Greek conquerors probably continued the administration in the Minoan language, at least for a while; and they are much more likely to have gained full control of the administration by learning Minoan themselves than by demanding the invention of a new script that would permit the state's books to be kept in Greek.

It may not have happened like this, of course, even if the Greeks who first won Knossos were rough, unlettered and in every way rude folk compared to the defeated Minoans. It may even be denied that historical experience can teach us what is *likely* to have happened in such circum-

---

* *The Manchus, like the Victorian English businessmen who collected Royal Academy pictures, liked things that "showed a lot of work." The Ming dynasty was less creative than the Sung dynasty; and its products have therefore until recently been under-rated. But if you look at the best Ming furniture or porcelain or decorative objects, you find a remarkable purity and sobriety of form, showing great subtlety of taste instead of a liking for "a lot of work." The subsequent shift in taste under the Manchus is revealed, in extreme form, by the familiar Chinese objects of the "curio" class.*

stances. But as I have already remarked, no one can deny that historical experience as a minimum teaches what may have happened and what cannot be ruled out as having happened. That being so, we find that the outlines of a wide range of problems of Greek Bronze Age history are more or less drastically altered by new kinds of possibility/probability. Let us first have a look at the changed aspect of the problem of Linear B. Here the hard facts are relatively simple.

According to Ventris and Chadwick, "of the 87 known syllabic signs [on the Linear B] tablets . . . 45 have close equivalents in 'Linear A,' while 10 have more doubtful parallels; leaving 29 [Linear B] signs, or exactly a third, as apparent innovations." It seems pretty clear, therefore, that Greek Linear B was an adaptation of Minoan Linear A rather than a mere imitation of it. In other words, the inventor or inventors of Linear B did not just say, "That meaningless Minoan sign pleases me; let it stand for syllable X, in Greek." He or they said, instead, "Let us begin with

220

*Two Linear A tablets from Haghia Triada, and a Linear B tablet* (RIGHT) *from Knossos.*

syllable X, in Greek. In Linear A, the hen-track with the nearest sound to syllable X is this one here. So we shall let it stand for syllable X in Greek." So much is evident, although one must not omit the possibility, considered strong by E. L. Bennett, Jr., that the adaptation was not purely phonetic. Such are the few facts at our disposal. The vast majority of students of the Bronze Age give these facts the interpretation derived from the wrong kind of conquest, namely, that Linear A continued in use in Crete while the Minoans ruled there; but was replaced by Linear B after the coming of the Greeks, the new script being quickly invented in Crete to serve the conquerors' purposes.

Let us start with the first half of this interpretation, and let us have a brief further look at it, in simple terms of political process. To begin with, one can hardly doubt that the members of the invading Greek noble class thought of themselves as warriors, first, last and foremost. As the history of the European Middle Ages indicates, such men do not

221

take lightly to clerical pursuits. We have seen how one eminent scholar initially interpreted the discovery of the Pylos tablets as meaning that the Greek king of Pylos had hired Minoan scribes to keep his books for him, as medieval barons used to hire the church's clerks. In the Pylos case, the theory was disproved; but just this sort of thing may have happened at Knossos after the Greek conquest of Crete. Indeed, this sort of thing *must* have happened at Knossos, at least for a while, if the Greeks were still unlettered but carried on the Knossian state administration as before—as they rather plainly did. If this did happen, furthermore, the Minoan palace administrators must have had a strong vested interest in guarding their monopoly of literacy and the attendant, partly under-the-table perquisites which they no doubt derived from this monopoly. They must therefore have tried to go on using Linear A just as long as they could persuade their Greek masters to tolerate the monopoly. Nor is that the end of the matter, if we may judge by the Manchu case and the great majority of other cases already cited. Judging by these cases, the monopoly of the Linear A-using palace administrators is most likely to have been broken by the Greeks themselves learning Minoan. A commanded and enduring change in the administrative language and script cannot, of course, be absolutely ruled out; but if the change was both commanded *and* enduring, it was a unique incident in the history of this type of conquest, as far as I can discover.

That leaves us with the question, where and how Linear B was invented. Did this occur in Crete, perhaps after a massive further influx of Greek-speakers had Grecianized the island's population? Or did it occur on the mainland? Among the experts with whom I have discussed the problem, the proposition that Linear B may have originated on the mainland has caused every bit as much surprise as the parallel proposition, that Linear A may well have continued in use in Crete after the first Greek conquest. Among the script specialists, to be sure, E. L. Bennett, Jr., feels there are reasons to suspect a mainland origin of Linear B*; but he has not published his suspicion since he has no Bronze Age evidence to back it up. Yet if we look beyond the Bronze Age, we find that script inventions outside the area of main racial use of the language thus written down are just about as rare as hen's teeth. And when Linear B was invented, whenever that may have been, the mainland was certainly the area of main racial use of the Greek language.

Virtually all scripts whose origins can be traced fall into two well-defined categories—scripts devised to meet the needs of an increasingly complex society and scripts invented by missionaries or priests to record sacred books. The pictographic scripts of the Lolo and Mosu tribes of China were priest-invented, for example, whereas missionaries were responsible for the Pali-based, Brahmin-devised scripts of the kingdom of Champa and the Khmer Empire, for the Gothic uncial, for the unsuccessful alphabetic form of Chinese that early Buddhists tried to introduce for convenient translation of the *Tripitaka,* for the alphabetic Vietnamese which is now in use in both North and South Vietnam, and so on and on. For our purposes, however, we can ignore the missionary scripts, except to note that with a tiny number of exceptions belonging to the post-Bible Society era, even the scripts of missionary origin have always been devised in the area of main racial use of the language. In most cases, the origins of scripts in the non-missionary category are more difficult to trace with absolute certainty. But no one I know of imagines that the later Greek script was really invented in Tyre or Sidon, rather than in some newly flourishing Greek city where a growing trade had implanted some knowledge of the Phoenician alphabet†; and although the Etruscan script is based on a form

---

* *Professor Rhys Carpenter of Bryn Mawr has made the same suggestion, on the basis of the legend of Cadmus.*

† *In* Local Scripts of Archaic Greece *L. H. Jeffery has suggested that the invention was made in a half-Greek half-Phoenician city in North Syria, such as Sir Leonard Woolley has found in Al-Mina.*

223

of Greek in use in Italy, it is generally supposed that Etruria was the scene of the adaptation. In the same fashion, there are no documents which absolutely prove that the earliest Japanese adaptation of the Chinese script was not made in China or Korea; yet it is all but certain that the work was done in Japan, to which Chinese writing filtered from the Korean peninsula. Finally, it is absolutely certain that the first version of alphabetic Korean was invented in Korea; that the Vietnamese demotic adaptation of the Chinese script was made in Vietnam in about the sixth century A.D.; and that the Libyan-Numidian script, which is the great-grandfather of the writing still used by the Touaregs, was adapted from the Carthaginian Punic script at the court of King Massinissa, *after* the Romans had sowed salt in the ruins of Carthage.

I am no more an expert on script inventions than on the Bronze Age; but the foregoing is only a partial list of the cases I have inquired into; and all the cases in the list tell the same story. I should add that inquiry into this question of scripts and their origins shows that more advanced societies have a particularly powerful bullying effect, in this particular area of social custom. For example, the invention of the Libyan-Numidian script had no effect whatever on the administrative habits of Massinissa's kingdom; Punic remained the administrative language despite the new script's invention and the prior destruction of Carthage. In Korea, again, Chinese remained the administrative language for centuries after the invention of alphabetic Korean, although Korea was effectively independent of China for most of its history. And in Vietnam, too, the administrative language was always Chinese, from the posterior Han dynasty, when Chinese was implanted in Vietnam, down to the time of the last Annamite emperor, the French puppet Bao Dai. Vietnamese demotic was used for poetry and other literature. Alphabetic Vietnamese was used first by the Catholic Church and then by the French administration. But all the Vietnamese dynasties remained faithful to Chinese until the end, despite their long, recurrent periods of substantive independence of China. The father of President Ngo Dinh Diem, who was a great Vietnamese Mandarin, had to pass his classical examinations in Peking in order to gain admission to the Mandarinate; and the last memorial to the throne in Chinese was written at the end of the Japanese occupation in 1945.

Picking up once again the argument's main thread, I do not maintain for a moment that the evidence I have cited rules out the invention of Linear B in Crete; I merely maintain that this evidence makes it impossible to rule out the alternative solution, that Linear B was invented, like so many other scripts of comparable origins, in its main area of racial use. If later discoveries prove that Linear B originated on the mainland, we certainly ought not to be astonished. And even now we are justified in asking the further question: if Linear B was in fact invented in mainland Greece, in what circumstances is this likely to have happened?

The point here is that illiterate people, who keep almost no records at all, do not suddenly say: "Well, it would be nice to begin bookkeeping; and we need a script for that purpose." Priests or missionaries may confer a script on a people in this stage of development. But otherwise there has to be a long preparatory stage of more and more elaborate social-political organization, and therefore of more and more elaborate bookkeeping; in this stage, the records perhaps take the form of wooden tallies, or of the *quipus* string bundles used by the Inca administrators with such bewildering success.*

---

* *Although preliterate, the Inca Empire appears to have been one of the most elaborately controlled and one of the most successful planned societies in history. The Inca administrators carried their planning to the point of directing the marriages of the peasants in the villages, as they directed the matings of their great flocks of llamas and vicuñas on the Andean slopes. Even the Ptolemies in Egypt did not go so far as this; and in China today the Communists' exhortations to marry late and produce fewer children are reportedly falling on deaf ears.*

In several cases, we have clear evidence of more and more elaborate social-political organization just before a new script appeared. In their last preliterate phase, for instance, the Japanese buried their dead grandees in the tumuli that were decorated with the charming *hanewa* figures; and the later imperial tumuli, by their mere size, imply a very high degree of organization, necessarily attended by fairly elaborate record-keeping.* In sum, if rather elaborate records are already being kept, and if the example of writing somewhere else points the way, a new script will then be invented to make bookkeeping easier. On this rule, if Linear B was indeed invented in Greece, the invention is likely to have been made rather late in the Bronze Age story, when more pompous archaeological remains attest more elaborate social organization of the Greek mainland states.

As can be seen, many permutations and combinations of the Linear B problem are shown to be possible, if not probable, by historical experience outside the Greek Bronze Age. There is only one solution of the problem that I think must be excluded, although it has been suggested by more than one eminent archaeologist. In any society, a change of script and administrative language is the biggest, most unsettling political development that one can imagine. Hence this development, whenever and however it occurred in Crete, cannot conceivably have occurred for light and trifling causes. Unchallengeable authority must have been behind it. It therefore seems to me really wildly improbable that Linear B replaced Linear A merely because a Mycenaean prince came to the throne of Minos by marrying the heiress of the Knossian kingdom. Scripts and administrative languages are simply not replaced because of royal marriages, unless

---

* By the early fifth century, the time of the Emperor Nintoku, whose mound is the largest of all, writing had probably just reached the Imperial Clan's center in Kansai, having filtered across from Kyushu, nearest Korea, where writing began somewhat earlier.

the bride is won by force of arms. I do not think political human nature has altered very greatly since the Bronze Age; so it is a good test of the theory of script change owing to a peaceful royal marriage, if you try to imagine the consequences in modern Greece if Queen Frederika launched a campaign to win over Greek officialdom to record-keeping in German. But even if this particular solution is omitted from the list, the Linear B problem can be theoretically solved in at least three ways. I should list the possible solutions and quote the odds on each of them as follows:

First, Linear B is downright unlikely to have been invented in Crete as a direct sequel of a Greek conquest, at any rate if the Greek conquest occurred when the Greeks were in the stage of development that is generally supposed. But, although unlikely, this is imaginable.

Second, Linear B may well have been invented in Crete at a period later than the Greek conquest—but probably considerably later— when heavy immigration from the mainland had begun to Grecianize the island population.

Third, Linear B may equally well have been invented on the mainland; but it must then have been carried back into Crete by the kind of Greek influx above suggested, or even by another Greek invasion.

Unfortunately, this range of possibilities and probabilities is too wide to permit the Linear B problem to be used, as it has been rather commonly begun to be used, as a key to unlock the mystery of the Cretan-mainland relationship. The most widely assumed circumstances of Linear B's appearance are called into serious question; but that, at best, is a negative gain. We are left with the facts that Linear B was in use on the Greek mainland at the moment when Mycenaean civilization was destroyed; and was also in use at Knossos when the Knossos palace was finally destroyed—which is a date now being hotly debated. Let us turn, therefore, from the specialized problem of the two scripts to the larger, more basic problem of the character and consequences of the Greek con-

227

quest of the Minoans. As I have already pointed out, everything depends upon the stage of Greek development when Greeks first stormed up the approaches to the palace of Minos. But let us make the same assumption that has been made hitherto. Let us assume that the experts are right in thinking the Greek conquerors were unlettered warriors coming from a society markedly less advanced than the rich Minoan civilization. Let us assume further that much the same factors operated to produce much the same results which we have already seen after other conquests of this type. What, then, must have happened?

At a date not yet determined a strong Greek raiding party was organized on the mainland, in Mycenae or elsewhere, perhaps with no higher initial purpose than hit-and-run piracy. Whatever their first aim, the Greek raiders then broke through the Minoan sea defenses, effected a landing somewhere on the coasts of Crete, conquered Knossos, placed their leader on the ancient throne of Minos, and perhaps proceeded to subjugate most of the rest of the island. These first Greeks who were led into Crete by the new occupant of the throne of Minos, and the others who came in after the conquest, cannot have been immensely numerous. At any rate, they must have been vastly outnumbered by the native Cretans. Hence the Greek invaders must have been a ruling minority, taking the places of the former Minoan upper class, maybe intermarrying with the remnants of it, but not displacing the great mass of the people who had done the day-to-day work of the old Minoan society.

The character of this Minoan society before the Greeks conquered it (whenever that may have been) is rather clearly indicated by a large body of evidence. The great palaces that began being built in Crete about 1900 B.C. bespeak a centralized economic system producing large surpluses. (Or one might better say they bespeak palace-centered economies; as we have seen, there were probably at least three Minoan kingdoms in Crete in the period of the first palaces.) The identical sealings found at several different places in Crete again bespeak a unified economy; for they mean that the same person who used this seal was sending letters or documents to several different places. For the late period when Linear A was still in use, the road net further suggests an economy controlled from Knossos. Finally, the Linear A texts themselves strongly suggest the kind of highly centralized social organization revealed by the later Linear B tablets. For, although Linear A remains undeciphered, it is clear that most of the tablets in this script are the *same sort* of documents* as the Linear B tablets. Their form tells the scholars that much, as does the frequent recurrence of numerals and other telltale signs. For all these reasons, it seems highly probable that the economic-administrative machine existing in Crete at the time when the Greeks stormed and seized the palace of Minos was the forerunner, at least in broad outline, of the economic-administrative machine existing in Pylos at the time when the Dorians stormed and burned the palace of Nestor. But, unlike the Dorians, the invading Greeks did not smash the machine they found in Crete; otherwise Cretan society could not have continued until the much-disputed later moment when the archives of the Knossos palace began to be kept in Linear B.

But if the machine was not smashed, what, then, must have happened? Clearly, the new Greek occupant of the throne of Minos must have done a good many of the same things that were done, about three millennia later, by the new Manchu occupants of the Forbidden City. In particular, since we know the machinery of society continued to operate, the new Greek Minos must have been wise enough not merely to refrain from destroying the former administrative apparatus, but also to go on using it for his own benefit and the benefit of his court. At the outset this

* *This does not hold true for the religious or votive inscriptions, some of which survive in Linear A but not in Linear B.*

can hardly have been easy. Indeed, if we suppose that the Greek conquerors of Crete were not far evolved from the rough fighters of the early Indo-European warbands, the chances are that the first period of mutual accommodation was extremely painful, as well as comical on occasion. But the social and human scale was tiny by our standards—*that* must always be borne in mind—and when social groups are small enough to dissolve, so to say, into individual human faces, accommodation is always less difficult. On both sides, self-interest must have encouraged accommodation, too. The Greeks will have had much to gain by repairing the administrative machinery as soon as possible. The more ambitious Minoan palace administrators will have had much to gain by picking up pidgin Greek, and in other ways learning to get on with their new masters. Loving novelty like all Greeks, moreover, the new Greek ruling class will have been quick to borrow whatever pleased them among the Minoan fashions, sports and entertainments. If they followed the same course as other warrior-conquerors, they will have learned Minoan before long. And if the new Greek Minos thought it politically prudent to assume his predecessor's role as a priest-king, the Greeks may thus have absorbed more than a smattering of Minoan religious ideas as well.

The result of the Greek conquest, in other words, must have been the rapid emergence of a Greco-Minoan synthesis. This *must* have been the result, whenever the conquest happened and whenever Linear A gave way to Linear B. For this was not a machine-smashing conquest, as has been repeatedly noted; yet there is always a synthesis after a conquest or a revolution, even if the conquerors are smashers, like the Dorians, and even if the stated aim is to smash everything in sight and start anew. (The most curious recent example of the unforeseeable character of such syntheses is the Russian revolution, aimed to smash everything bourgeois, which has none the less enshrined the worst, dingiest, most second-rate Victorian-Russian bourgeois taste and ideas about the arts, as the aesthetic ark of the Communist ideological covenant.) As to the character and phases of the Greco-Minoan synthesis which must have taken place at Knossos after the Greek invasion, these aspects must have been controlled by the date of the conquest—which we do not know. The more advanced the Greeks were when they gained control of Crete the more Greek elements they will have been able to contribute to the synthesis. Whereas if Greek society had not developed very far when the successful Greek raid on Crete occurred, Minoan elements must have predominated very heavily, just as Chinese elements heavily predominated in the synthesis formed at Peking after the Manchu conquest.

Even at this distance in time, one must add that what probably happened to the Greek invaders is a thought to provoke mild, moralistic headshaking. For it is a reasonable—all too reasonable—guess that hardly a generation was needed to transmute rough warrior-conquerors into pleasure-loving, luxurious and refined Greco-Minoan aristocrats. In this connection, one cannot help but remember the tragicomic failure of the great Yoritomo. It was Yoritomo who brought to a decisive close the second phase of Japan's strange history. The power of the Kyoto nobility, already in grave decline because of the rise of a new class of provincial soldiers and frontier fighters remote from the Imperial Court, was broken for good by Yoritomo and his country samurai. Yoritomo then established the headquarters of his Regency-Shogunate at the small and remote town of Kamakura, for the specific purpose of protecting his hard, serious, war-seasoned followers from the softening, corrupting influence of the ancient, fantastically overrefined and luxurious, but wholly impotent Japanese Imperial Court at Kyoto. "Fear of the seductions of an aristocratic society," Sir George Sansom tells us rather primly, "had moved Yoritomo to forbid social intercourse between [his warriors] and the Court nobility. . . . But even as soon as A.D. 1210, not a dozen years after the death of Yoritomo, the favorites of [his son] Sanetomo were not earnest soldiers but young

231

*Fresco from Knossos, nicknamed the "Camp Stool Fresco."*
*The supposed gloves are hanging from the stool's*
*legs in the fragment at left.*

courtiers interested in elegance rather than the more sober virtues." Luxury
and refinement, in truth, have their own insidious power, slower no doubt
but sometimes greater than the naked power of the sword. The archaeological finds of objects in precious metals, indications of overseas trade and
eventually of massive fortifications, combine to suggest that Mycenae
began to grow in raw power and crude wealth at some time in the seventeenth century B.C. and was overtaking Knossos by the middle of the
second millennium; but the structures and surviving decorations of the
Cretan palaces also indicate that Knossos always held the palm for refined luxury, at least as long as Knossos lasted. Some of the highlights in
the picture are almost too vivid. In the supposed picnic attended by the

232

"Parisienne," for instance, Professor Marinatos believes the handsome young men have scarlet gloves—which he points out are the first gloves anywhere depicted. If the young men in the fresco were Greeks (and if the gloves were not tassels on a stool, as most experts argue), then the evolution of the conquerors of Crete must have gone very far and almost frighteningly fast. And if this fresco belongs to the Minoan era of Knossos, as is of course generally supposed, one can at least see the sort of thing the Greek conquerors were exposed to when they landed.

Those "ifs" just above lead me on to a vastly bigger "if," which I hardly dare to state, since it trenches directly upon the territory of the experts. Yet the fact has to be faced, and it would be cowardly not to face it: *if* the broad characteristics of the Greek conquest of Crete have been correctly summarized, the door is wide open for a third historical scheme, quite different from the two schemes given in the preceding chapter, which the experts have been arguing about since the Linear B decipherment. The door is wide open for the following reasons: first, there is no reason to suppose that the Greek conquest necessarily produced a radical, archaeologically perceptible break with the Minoan past. If Peking were to be destroyed and dug up again, for instance, the archaeologist who found the smallest trace of the Manchu conquest would be quite exceptionally lucky; and if he chanced to run across a Manchu inscription in the ruins of the lama-temple, he would almost certainly dismiss the inscription as mere evidence of an "intrusive foreign cult," because he would inevitably argue that there were no other signs of a "break." Secondly, for the similar reasons already given, there is no safety in the assumption that Linear A went out of use in Crete as soon as the Greek invaders put in their appearance; on the contrary, as we have seen, there are good reasons to suppose that Linear A may have long continued as the administrative script of a Greco-Minoan state. Hence there is no way of ruling out a Greek conquest of Crete *at any time* after the Greeks were strong enough

233

to dare to attack the temptingly rich and unwarlike Minoan society. For reasons that will be seen later, I am not a partisan of the quite novel historical scheme that results from assuming a rather early Greek conquest of Crete. But since a fundamental reappraisal of all the facts is now so obviously in order, the scheme needs to be outlined, and the arguments in its favor deserve to be weighed. Let us begin with the underlying power factors, which make the seventeenth century B.C. the time of doubt.

In that century, as may be recalled, Minoan civilization entered a kind of trough or low period after the destruction of the first palaces. As already noted, Professor Graham has written that it is "not an unlikely hypothesis" that the first palaces were destroyed by "a piratical, sea-borne raid by the Mycenaean Greeks of the mainland or, since Crete was subject to devastating earthquakes, that the Greek raiders followed in the track of a severe quake which had left the Cretan cities temporarily defenseless."

*Fresco fragments from Knossos, Minoan leading Negro troops.*

f this kind of successful raid cannot be ruled out, an actual conquest ob-
iously cannot be ruled out either. In addition, however the first palaces
1 Crete were destroyed toward the beginning of the seventeenth century,
is also noteworthy that this century was the period of the first surge of
Greek strength and wealth. So much may be deduced from the formation
f the first grave circle at Mycenae, about 1650 B.C. Hence a successful
Greek raid on Crete is an obvious possibility at some time during this
entury, even if not at the exact moment suggested by J. W. Graham.
Assuming there was such a raid, we get the following scheme:

AT SOME TIME IN THE SEVENTEENTH CENTURY B.C. Greeks invade Crete,
conquer most of the island, and make the palace of Minos at
Knossos the center of their new kingdom.

THE PERIOD OF THE SECOND PALACES THEREFORE OPENS IN 1600 B.C.
with Minoan Crete under the control of a new Greek ruling class.
The period of the second palaces is marked by a brilliant Greco-
Minoan synthesis; and the emergence of this synthesis explains
both the observable continuities with the Minoan past and the
great innovations which also take place. Linear A remains the
administrative script of the new Greco-Minoan state.

THE DEVELOPMENT OF THE NEW GRECO-MINOAN STATE is subject to history's usual hazards and misfortunes. It is, indeed, more vulnerable than a uni-racial state; and the relative smallness of the
Greek warrior class at the top requires the employment of foreign troops in the armed forces, as shown by the fresco of a
Knossian captain and his Negro company. But the Minos who
organized the thalassocracy—which seems to have been rather
late in date if it existed at all—was in fact a Greek.

PERHAPS IN THE WAKE OF THE GREAT NATURAL CATASTROPHE IN 1520
B.C. or perhaps at some later date and even as the result of

235

another Greek invasion, there is another major influx of Greek into Crete. This influx explains the Grecianization of the population suggested by Homer's account of Idomeneus' kingdom. It also explains the remains dated to the period between 1400 and 1200 B.C., which show a strongly Mycenaean style, though with the usual local overtones. As a result of this new Greek influx, Linear A is finally replaced by Linear B, at some time before 1400 B.C. if Evans' date for the destruction of the Knossos palace proves to be correct, or even at a later time if Evans is proved wrong.

Rule I in any serious reappraisal of puzzling historical facts is the rule that forbids the flat assumption that what can have happened none the less did not happen. Once the probable characteristics of the initial Greek conquest of Crete are understood, it becomes clear that the conquest could have happened in the way I have outlined. It is difficult to give the arguments for any historic scheme without seeming to be its active advocate, which I do not want to appear in this case. Yet the arguments are also interesting, and deserve consideration. To begin with, I think the new scheme provides a possible and much-needed explanation of two otherwise unexplained developments in the Cretan record.

The first of these developments is a bit hazy, but it is too significant to be passed over. In brief, there are good though not decisive reasons for thinking that most of Crete was unified under the palace of Minos at Knossos, from the beginning of the period of the second palace in 1600 B.C. As already noted, Henri van Effenterre, now in charge of the excavations at Mallia, does not believe in this unification, whereas Doro Levi, in charge of Phaistos, holds the opposite view that Knossos gained some sort of authority over the other palaces. Another who believes in the predominance of Knossos is Professor Spyridon Marinatos. In his *Crete nd Mycenae* he has written: "It looks as though the rulers of Knossos book the initiative" in the "renaissance of Cretan prosperity" which began n 1600 B.C. He further states that the other Cretan palaces, themselves in process of reconstruction, also "contributed to the construction of the New Second] Palace of Knossos." This is the proof, concludes Marinatos, "of the unification of Crete under the sole rule of Knossian Minos." Here, in short, is a very considerable political development—all the more so if the Phaistos palace was actually more rich and powerful than the palace of Minos in the earlier period, as the recent discoveries seem to indicate. The development (if it occurred) can be explained by the good fortune of Knossos, in having particularly energetic rulers able to lead Crete out of an empty transitional" trough of history into a new era of unity and creativeness. But it must be noted that the development can also be explained by the misfortune of Knossos—its occupation, in fact, by foreign conquerors, whose military superiority over the native Minoans also enabled them to bring the other major centers under their rule.

As to the second Cretan development that seems to me to call for explanation, it is the novel direction that Cretan civilization rather abruptly took when the period of the second palaces opened. Maybe I am overimpressed by the new departures of this remarkable period described by Sir Arthur Evans himself as a "New Era," which was marked by widespread and magnificent building activity and a general rise in prosperity, as well as the disputed indications of the unification of Crete under Knossian rule. Of the new departures found at Knossos itself, one of Evans' most faithful disciples, J. D. S. Pendlebury, also wrote: "Several architectural innovations were introduced, such as the low gypsum or limestone column-base . . . and the smooth, polygonal [paving] slabs of 'almond-stone,' the interstices of which were filled with red or white plaster [in place of the earlier] thick, irregular limestone paving slabs. Compact courses of regular masonry replaced the older clay-embedded blocks. These

237

*Kamares ware from the first palaces:*
(BELOW) *a spouted jar from Phaistos;*
(RIGHT) *vase with palm trees in the latest Kamares style, Knossos.*

new features . . . argue, if not a change of dynasty, at least a change o
spirit." There were other innovations, too, that Pendlebury did not note
It is now generally agreed that all the famous fresco decorations of th
Cretan palaces date from after 1600 B.C. In addition, the Kamares wan
of the first palaces was replaced, in the second palaces, by dark-on-ligh
painted pottery gloriously decorated in a much more naturalistic manner
and this delightful naturalism in pottery decoration then endured until th
beginning of the more grandiose "palace style" dated by Evans aroun
1450 B.C. Finally, and most important of all, the period of the secon
palaces produced all the incomparable objects like the vessels from Haghi
Triada and the two rhytons from Knossos, which I have already discussec

Despite the impressive range and unprecedented character o
the innovations in the period of the second palaces, the experts tend t

Pottery from the second palaces:
(UPPER LEFT) *vase with octopus from
Knossos;* (RIGHT) *jug with leaf decoration
from Phaistos;* (LOWER LEFT) *a later "palace
style" vase with stylized papyrus decorations,
Knossos.*

*Evidence of the transformation in the Cretan creative outloo*
*votive figures from Chamaizi, age of the first palaces, c. 1900–1800 B*
*Figures from the age of the second palac*

stress the continuities rather than the changes. Friedrich Matz, for instanc
not only holds that all the best things from the mainland as well as Cre
are Minoan; he also holds that all of Minoan art, from beginning to en
is unified by what he calls the "torsion principle," by which he seems
mean a fondness for spiraling forms. Most of his colleagues are le
abstruse than Matz; but the majority still support the view of Sir Arth
Evans, that there "was no break." It all depends, I take it, on how y
define "break." As we have seen, Greeks may well have gained contr
of Crete without producing the kind of "break" that the archaeologi

240

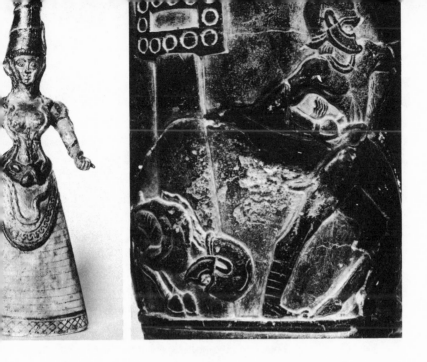

(LEFT) *snake goddess from Knossos, c. 1600* B.C.;
(RIGHT) *boxer detail, sports rhyton from Haghia Triada, c. 1550–1500* B.C.
*In comparing these first and second palace figures, allowances must be made for
the conservatism customary in the design of religious ex-votos.*

ere have in mind. But there were at least changes enough to make Pendle-
ury think of the possibility of some sort of change of rule at the begin-
ing of the period of the second palaces; and I would further say that
ne physical changes, such as the architectural innovations noted by Pendle-
ury, were less striking than the underlying change of style. This change
f style is especially noticeable in the finest objects, and it implies the
ccurrence of an equally sharp change in the Cretan artists' and craftsmen's
ray of looking at the world around them.

    To be sure, the evidence for the Minoan artists' style in the

241

earlier period of the first palaces is fragmentary at best. We have the Kamares ware, plus a good many crude but lively pottery figurines, plus what remains of the first palaces themselves, plus a considerable number of seals and some jewelry. Naturalistic tendencies are perhaps suggested by certain seals and by some of the pieces of jewelry. But if you look at these objects, and then look at the objects from the period of the second palaces, like the sports rhyton, for instance, you cannot resist the conclusion that the style and, above all, the creative outlook that the style implies were both magically transformed. Both style and outlook became more life celebrating, more joyous, more natural, more centered on human beings their sports and delights on this earth and the pleasures their eyes afford them. The objects in the new style are things with few parallels. Nothing really resembling an important Cretan object of this type was ever produced in any contemporary Asian center that is now known to us. One may argue for an Egyptian link, since the Egyptian artists also were life-celebrating, although they so often used tomb walls for the purpose. But the closest kinship, amounting to stylistic identity, is with numerous objects that have been found in mainland Greece.

The change of style I have been trying to describe and the implied accompanying shift in the angle of creative vision are certainly quite sharp enough to be equated with the Gothic-into-Renaissance shift in Europe. So far as I am aware, no convincing explanation of this shift has yet been offered; none has ever been attempted except by L. R. Palmer, with his Luvians. As the example of the Gothic-into-Renaissance shift indicates, this wonderful shift in the Cretans' angle of creative vision may well have sprung entirely from the soil of Crete, beginning one might say, with the birth of a Minoan Giotto. But the appearance of a new kind of object, revealing a new kind of taste and a different outlook on the world, certainly raises questions about the simultaneous appearance on the scene of a new people. These questions are automatically nswered, if a Greco-Minoan state was established considerably earlier han the experts have as yet suggested. In this kind of mixed state, more->ver, creative continuities would naturally coexist with creative innovations. :ross-fertilization would in fact occur. The Minoan craftsmen would re-pond to the novel taste of a new ruling class, and the taste of the Greek onquerors would also be altered by the Minoan *ambiance*. To this one nust add one further fact. It is a good deal easier to explain the unitary haracter of Greco-Minoan art as a whole, including the finest things ound in Greece as well as the finest from Crete, if we suppose that one >f the two interacting centers of the style was a Greco-Minoan state in :rete, whose Greek aspect ensured easy and natural links with the other enter on the Greek mainland.

Finally, a successful Greek attack on Crete, organized in My-enae toward the middle of the seventeenth century B.C., is also a much nore natural explanation of the treasures deposited in the two Mycenaean ;rave circles than the explanation that this gold was earned by mercenaries erving in Egypt. Egyptian influence is hardly deniable; very possibly some ;old was won in Egypt. But it is easier to suppose that most of the My-enaean gold was won in Crete. We may then guess that the formation of he earlier grave circle, about 1650 B.C., reflects a local social-political hange which also led to the organization of a raid on Crete. And we may ;uess, too, with J. W. Graham, that Crete was the main source of the reasures of both the grave circles. Nor is it needful to make the additional ssumption that Crete was actually subject to Mycenae; the pillage of Crete n the first onslaught, plus profits from subsequent trade with an independ-nt Greco-Minoan kingdom in Crete, should have provided quite enough reasure for the Mycenaean royal graves.

Such, then, are the positive arguments in favor of an early ;reek invasion of Crete. In the present state of our knowledge, it is at :ast a possibility that deserves exploration and testing. It will not be

243

staggeringly surprising if the wonderful things that have so long been called Minoan in the end turn out instead to be Greco-Minoan—with emphasis on the second contributing element. In the present stage of reappraisal, open-mindedness should be the rule; closed-mindedness invites the kind of error that was made by the nineteenth-century scholars who explained Mycenae as a Phoenician trading post. Although I do not say they are bound to be proved wrong, I think those experts are rather unwise who now say in effect, "Give me for my admired Minoans everything I've always credited them with; but I'll grant you Linear B for the Greeks." That just could turn out to be like declaiming, in a wrong context, the line from the quarrel scene in *Ruy Blas:*

"Donnez-moi l'arsenic; je vous cède les nègres."

While convinced that all possibilities must now be tested, I myself am not fully persuaded by the alternative historical scheme which we have been examining, because I am not sure how well it meshes with the other great political process which is so plainly discernible in the Greek story in the Bronze Age. Although this second process must have been even more crucial and all-controlling than the Greek conquest of Crete and its aftermath, the archaeologists and prehistorians have not had much to say about it. Yet something must have happened—some complicated and very powerful political process must have been at work—to transform the tribal, warlike, Indo-European form of society that the Greeks undoubtedly brought into Greece into the tightly centralized, bureaucratically controlled, palace-directed and palace-planned form of society that is revealed by the Linear B tablets. How did this unlikely transformation occur? What caused it? What were its stages? These seem to me the basic questions (or the basic riddles, if you like) in the whole story of the Mycenaean Greeks. After all, social and political forms are not catching, like pottery

244

yles and influenza. The established social and political forms in any
ciety are always guarded by strong vested interests. Hence the members
a tribal warband, for instance, do not amiably say to one another, "Well,
ow that we know how they manage things in Crete (or Egypt—you can
oose your own model), let's do it the same way here at home." Voluntary,
dical self-transformation, by conscious imitation of a foreign model, is
e rarest sort of episode in human history, except when a religious or
iasi-religious movement like Christianity or Communism is winning con-
erts to a salvationist doctrine. The Japanese are the only people I can
ink of who have the habit of conscious self-transformation, without hot-
spelers to spur them on. And in the earlier instance, when Chinese
lministrative forms were imported, and Buddhism was introduced, there
as an urgent need to strengthen the authority of the Imperial Clan. In
e most recent instance, too, the primary aim of the leaders of the Meiji
storation was not to reform Japanese society but to protect Japan against
e threat of Western imperialism, by importing the industrial methods
at gave the Westerners their technological advantage. And this again was
1 urgent need.

The transformation of Bronze Age Greek society, moreover, was
early very radical and very profound. To be sure, our evidence of the
tact form of the society that the first Greeks brought into Greece is ex-
emely sparse, to say the least. But it is at any rate certain that the Greeks
gan as semi-nomads—else they would not have reached Greece at all.
rom this it may be deduced with confidence that their original social
ganization was tribal in character—indeed, the Greeks of all the dif-
rent dialect groups, including those presumably descended from the
lycenaean Greeks, retained a ghostly sort of tribal organization into the
assical period. If their organization was tribal when they entered Greece
1900 B.C., it was therefore a rather loose organization at that time; for
story contains no record of a tightly planned and closely administered

245

tribal and semi-nomadic economy. Furthermore, every fairly loose, tribal semi-tribal society is always full of strong, competing vested interests—w chiefs of lesser kindreds, for instance, who think they did every bit as we as the king himself on the last raid, and maybe a bit better, who may als gain a following in the tribe among admirers of their prowess. In such society, the king or leader is always no more than the first among equal he is never "the one man, the unique man." Among the Indo-Europea Hittites, as we have seen, the kingship was originally elective; the princip of hereditary kingship was only adopted perforce, when the Hittite Empi threatened to founder because of the multiplicity of pretenders to th throne backed by powerful competing interests. Politics having been pol tics since the Stone Age, squashing all the competing interests in Gree society cannot have been easy; yet they must have been largely squashe before the Greek Bronze Age kingdoms took the final form we find in th clay tablet-records.

This is only the beginning of the mystery, moreover. The fir highly centralized and bureaucratically directed societies of the remote pa did not, after all, spring up like mushrooms. They were exceedingl elaborate and ingenious *social inventions,* which had to be perfected ov long periods. In all known cases of the actual origination of this kind c society, the invention was made in response to a specific, urgent nee The need was always the same—an agriculture increasingly dependent o big irrigation and water-control works, which could not be built withou disciplined mass-labor, or kept in efficient operation without strong centr administration. In response to this need, the same social invention wa made several times in history, at several different places. There may b some link between the early Mesopotamian society of the Sumerians an the society of predynastic Egypt. But roughly the same kind of societ was also developed independently, by the people of the Indus Valle civilization, in ancient China, and in the Americas.

246

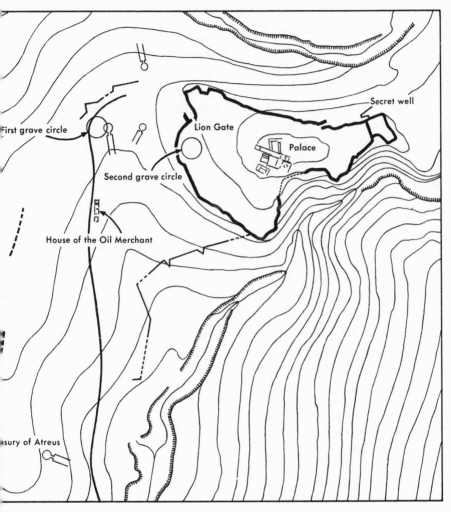

*The citadel of Mycenae (after Mylonas).*

There are two points to this long digression. In the first place the Bronze Age Greeks were certainly not driven to centralize their social system by the need to build and maintain huge water-management systems. There are remains of major Mycenaean drainage works at Lake Copais near Gla, but in general Bronze Age Greek farming did not depend on large-scale irrigation or water control. For this and other reasons, in the second place, it is as certain as anything can be that the centralized planned form of society revealed by the Linear B tablets was an import or acquisition. In other words, the system was taken over more or less bodily from another people, as the Chinese today have taken over the system of the Russian Communists of the Stalin era. Yet we may not imagine that in the Greek Bronze Age a dedicated, planning-minded minority worked underground for decades on end to bring about a new era, until their great day came at last. It cannot have happened like that.

The problem, then, is to find out how Greek Bronze Age society may have evolved from its first loose, tribal form into its final, Linear B form—which was a series of *oikos*-type royal economies closely resembling the royal economies of the Near East and Egypt, but without the water-management requirements which originally caused this kind of economy to come into being in Mesopotamia and on the Nile. At all stages in this remarkable process, the evidence is grossly inadequate. Almost everything has to be deduced, except the end product which the Linear B tablets reveal. Yet up to a certain point, I think that deductions may be made with a fairly high degree of confidence.

What must have happened in the early period—let us say, between the nineteenth century B.C. and the end of the second Mycenaean grave circle about 1500 B.C.—is pretty clear in very broad outlines from the existing archaeological record. Let us simply recapitulate that record. At Mycenae, until the formation of the first grave circle about 1650, the graves are simple; the grave goods are sparse; and there are no stone ircles to set royal graves apart from the common run. The later graves of the first circle show wealth; almost all graves of the second circle show great wealth. And the experts are at least more unanimous than usual that the persons buried in the grave circles belonged to the royal kindred.*

The course of development up to this point can therefore be traced with considerable certainty, provided we are careful to stick to very broad outlines. It is clear, to begin with, that the first tribally organized, village-sized community at Mycenae must have grown and prospered in the early centuries. Otherwise the rulers could not have begun to lay away

* Or kindreds. There is a complex theory about the presence at Mycenae of more than one ruling family.

Gold jewelry, c. 1400 B.C.,
found in a chamber tomb
outside Mycenae.

(RIGHT) *Gold cup found by Schliemann,*
*which he dubbed "Nestor's Cup."*
(UPPER LEFT) *Gold goblet also found*
*in second grave circle.*
(LOWER LEFT) *Silver cup with inlaid heads*
*from a chamber tomb at Mycenae.*

heir dead with the rich grave goods that the grave circles have yielded. n addition, the members of the royal house must have been progressively differentiated—more and more set apart, as the grave circles symbolically indicate—from the other members of Mycenae's warrior class. This is a development familiar in history. At the outset the king, or chief, or war eader, is hardly higher than the warriors he leads. As leader, his share of he spoil is larger when a raid is successful. As leader, his hall is likely o be larger too; for it must accommodate the other warriors at feasts on great occasions. But he is only the leader; he is merely, as I have said, "the irst among equals" at this early stage. Then a particularly shrewd leader uses the advantages of his position with exceptional astuteness, either in trade, or in piracy, or in war, or in all three. His greater wealth perhaps permits him to arm additional warriors from his own resources, and so he acquires a personal bodyguard. His success in his enterprises increases his authority, which his guard also supports against malcontents. Thus true kingship begins, in the sense that the leader rules as well as leads.

In the world of the sagas, this initial social transformation can be rather exactly pin-pointed. In Norway, Harald Fairhair was the first true king in the sense given to the phrase just above. Iceland was quite largely settled, in fact, by men from Norway who preferred the old ways of the time before Harald Fairhair, and were ready to strike out as pioneers in another, harsher land, rather than bow their necks before a king. For Mycenaean Greek society, our evidence begins and ends with the contrast between the grave circles and the earlier burials, and plus the fact that these were circles set apart for royal graves. But if you study, however briefly, the treasures from the second grave circle, that Schliemann found,* you can hardly doubt that Mycenaean kings, by that time, were very

---

* It is usual to speak of "Grave Circle A"—Schliemann's—and "B"—the latest discovered. I use "first" and "second" as simple indications of date.

kingly indeed. And there is nothing to suggest, at any rate in the existing archaeological record, that the rulers of Mycenae were at all kingly before the first grave circle was laid out.

In the first chapter, we have already noted how Professor Blegen poked a little friendly fun at the great Martin Nilsson's picture of the Mycenaean Greeks "as a body of illiterate adventurers who imposed their domination by a series of Viking raids." For the late period of the Pylian kingdom, the Linear B tablets show that Nilsson's comparison with the Vikings was decidedly misleading. But it usefully (though not certainly) suggests what Mycenae may have been like at the time of the second grave circle, in the sixteenth century B.C. The society was extremely war-like—the numerous weapons among the grave goods leave little room for doubt about that. The kings were already very rich, as the grave goods also show; and this wealth—derived from trade, or piracy, or war, or hiring out mercenaries, or the Cirrhan tin workings, or all these combined sources of profit—had already aggrandized the institution of kingship in a most important way. But, although the argument from absence is always dangerous, it must also be noted that these rich kings of Mycenae ruled over a quite primitive community, if we may judge from the lack of other architectural remains except for the graves.

In Mycenae's case, the argument from absence has extra dangers, since the place of the citadel is rocky, so remains cannot go deep in most areas. But against this one must balance the kind of meticulous inch-by-inch excavation to which Mycenae has been subjected, most recently and with notable success by Professor Mylonas. When one sees how little is needed to provide sure proof of the existence and design of later structures which have also vanished, it is difficult to believe that the Mycenaean kings of the sixteenth century B.C. reigned in a grand stone-built palace or provided their citadel with even the most modest stone-built walls. If such structures had existed in the sixteenth century one cannot help but feel that a fragment of a wall, or a deep-laid corner-stone, or some other trace would have been found by Mylonas or one of his co-workers or predecessors. Lacking such traces, it seems to be reasonable to picture this earlier Mycenae as architecturally rude, with a stockade for its only fortification, if it had any, and with habits of life not vastly more evolved than its architecture, despite the warlikeness of the people and the wealth of the king. It must also be noted that the evidence from Mycenae is confirmed by other sites. Except for tombs, no grandiose architectural remains from the early period survive anywhere in Greece.

Because historical parochialism is so deep-rooted in most of us, this contrast between the richness of the grave goods and the probable rudeness of Mycenae's daily life may seem extremely troubling at first glance. A linked difficulty arises from the huge yield of gold objects from the earlier Greek periods whose architectural remains are so unimpressive, and the sparse yield of objects in precious metals from the period in Crete when the second palaces were in full glory. Once again, it is helpful to remember the Vikings in this connection. Before its tomb-chamber was pillaged, the Oseberg ship burial no doubt contained a greater treasure than came from Sutton Hoo; the astonishing richness of the ship itself, and of the carts and other objects neglected by the robbers, at least indicates that much. There is ample other evidence that objects in precious metals were commonplace in Scandinavia from the early Viking period onward. But for most of this period, the most impressive evidence is provided by the graves and treasure hoards. There are no traces of contemporary domestic architecture to compare in any way with the Oseberg ship burial and the others like it. Even the trading towns were meanly built. In fact, there is hardly anything that is impressive that was inhabited by living men, until we come to the Trelleborg camp, which was probably laid out toward the end of the Viking age for the standing army created by the grandfather of King Canute the Great, Harald Bluetooth of Denmark. In a warlike people, just emerging onto the stage of history from a primitive and provincial way of life, there is nothing unprecedented in this combination, which seems so odd to us, of grand graves for the dead and rude living conditions for their survivors. In the same way, think of the circumstances of life of the great landowners and churchmen who suffered from the Vikings after the Norsemen took to raiding southward. Precious objects were not the main form of wealth of the Vikings' victims—although they had them—but their dwellings and churches were certainly far grander and more civilized than the rough wooden halls to which the Viking chiefs took home their loot if they were lucky. If this contrast is remembered, the Knossos-Mycenae contrast that seems to be implied by the surviving objects becomes much less difficult to comprehend and credit. The truth is that when success comes to a warlike people in a stage of development that is relatively not very advanced, the accumulation of precious objects always tends to precede the change in ways of life. The steppe peoples whose incursions plagued and sometimes ravaged China for close to four millennia often accumulated great treasures in the tents of their chiefs when their raids were successful; but they did not change their way of life, unless they abandoned the steppe. For a more modern case, we need only think of Ibn-Saud, who died, as he was born, a desert Arab, yet loved to accumulate costly portable objects which could be fitted into the old way of life; whereas his son, King Saud, briskly took to the new, Cadillac-and-air-conditioning way of life as soon as his father died.

Thus far the development of Greek Bronze Age society has been easy enough to deduce from the archaeological evidence, with the aid of the experience of other peoples and simple political logic. But at this point —say about 1500 B.C., when the last burial was made in the second grave circle—the real mystery begins. From a hill village led by a war chief or king, it is a long step to a stockaded king's-town ruled over, rather than led, by a king whose table and person glitter with gold. But if the people

254

*Bronze body armor belonging to a Mycen*
*warrior-noble who lived c.1450–1400 B.C., fro*
*chamber tomb at Dendra, not far from Myce*

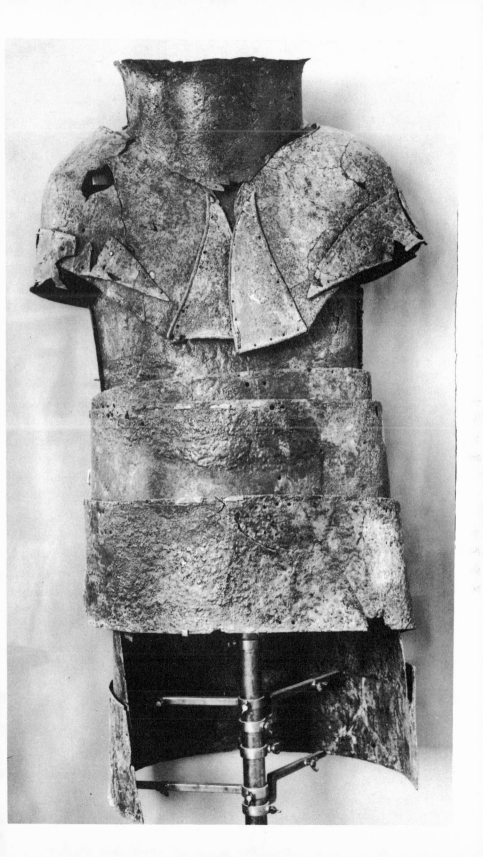

of the hill village were brave, enterprising, and hard-working, and had good land, and used their other opportunities to the utmost, and if the leaders were also shrewd and tough, this first step is neither improbable nor mysterious. What is improbable to the point of being mysterious is the second step taken by Greek Bronze Age society, from the stage we may picture at Mycenae in 1500 B.C. to the final stage of the head-counted, herd-counted, palace-centered and palace-planned royal economies revealed by the Linear B archives from Pylos and Knossos. Remember the men listed in the *Landnamabok,* most of whom went to Iceland because they objected to the kind of royal authority asserted by King Harald Fairhair. Think, too, about the probable reaction of the average Mycenaean warrior-noble when the first scribes appeared on the scene, and head-counting and herd-counting were first introduced. Then you will see, I believe, why this further transformation seems to me the central mystery in the Greek Bronze Age story.

As to the correct explanation of the mystery, we have no scholarly guidance to date. If a political reporter's instinct has any value in judging such remote and abstruse matters, I can only say that it seems clear to me that the explanation of this mystery must lie in Knossos. Furthermore, I am convinced that it most probably lies in a Knossos already under Greek rule. Here the reasoning is simple—and exclusively political. In brief, it is abundantly clear that the kind of social system revealed by the Linear B tablets was a Greek import or acquisition from overseas. It was also an import which was not required by conditions in Greece. As already noted, Greek Bronze Age society did not depend for its prosperity on large water-management and other public works. So far as one can judge, there was no other compelling need for a high degree of centralized authority. Finally, the new social system was an import which was advantageous only to the rulers of the Greek Bronze Age states, and was quite clearly dis-advantageous to everyone else—for no one likes to have his freedom and

*The Queen's bath, Knossos, built c. 1400* B.C.

his relative status diminished, even if his material prosperity somewhat increases. Add to these considerable difficulties the Indo-European origins and warrior traditions of the Bronze Age Greeks. The sum of all this, I think, at least greatly weakens the possibility that the mainland Greek kingdoms were remodeled on the pattern of Ugarit or some other entirely foreign state, even including Minoan Knossos. Given the Minoan influence on the Greek beginnings, the thing is imaginable, of course. If a truly foreign model was followed, one can be pretty certain that the model was Minoan. Yet it is very much easier to picture the mainland kingdoms being successively remodeled on the pattern of a Greek state overseas, which was quite different in organization, but was also impressive, glamorous, and not too foreign to be excluded as a pattern of imitation. When the Greeks invaded Crete and captured Knossos (whenever that may have been) just this new kind of Greek state must have been formed from a combination of Greek and Minoan raw materials. Behind the political process we are now considering—the final transformation of the Greek mainland kingdoms—we may thus discern the other political process already considered—the Greek conquest of Knossos and the creation of a Greco-Minoan synthesis in Crete.

If this conjecture is correct (and though politically logical, it is purest conjecture), we may regard our two processes as so closely linked together that they all but form a single, continuous process. The probable stages are clear. First came the Greek conquest of Crete. Second, the aftermath of this conquest soon produced, in Crete, a quite new kind of Greek society, with many Minoan elements and all sorts of novel features and ways. Third, this Greco-Minoan synthesis fed back, as it were, into mainland Greece, because the mainland rulers observed with envy how promptly the corps of bureaucrats in the palace of Minos got in the taxes, how well they managed the flocks and herds, how admirably they organized other forms of production, for the Greek ruler of Knossos and his luxurious

*Copper ingot
from Cyprus, found
at Haghia Triada.*

court. But it is by no means enough to imagine the mainland Greek kings being persuaded by the example of Knossos of the great advantages of the *oikos*-type of royal economy. If the rulers alone had been persuaded, the split would have been too deep between them and their people. It is also necessary to imagine Greco-Minoan Knossos as a kind of fashion center, with a deep impact upon all the more impressionable members of the Greek warrior class on the mainland. Only thus can ideas and administrative methods have been easily imported, along with art styles and craft secrets and fashions of the lighter sort. It is not exaggerating, in fact, to suggest that the first scribes may have put in their appearance at Mycenae at the same moment when the more extravagant young nobles were outraging their elders, and even their more sturdily conventional contemporaries, by flaunting scarlet gloves—always assuming Professor Marinatos is right about those controversial gloves.

    If the Bronze Age Greeks were like other people, the older, more conservative members of the upper class must have growled horribly in their beards about newfangled ways. One can all but hear the elders

condemning all the latest fashions, in both ornament and state administration, as subversive, immoral, and menacing to the true, ancient Greek
spirit. When the first palace chanceries were established, and the first head-
counting and herd-counting began in mainland Greece, there may well
have been strong passive or even active opposition. But the young men
who were most exposed to the fascination of the Greco-Minoan synthesis
we have assumed at Knossos, and the ambitious elders who were chiefly
interested in which side their bread was buttered on, must have formed
an opposing party favoring innovation; and the innovating ruler or rulers
must have relied upon and rewarded this support. Furthermore, both the
Pylos and Knossos tablets contain ample proofs that the Bronze Age Greek
rulers did not accomplish the transition to a highly centralized state organization without making important compromises. The object of this great
change, it must be remembered, was to increase the state's wealth by increasing all forms of production, as well as the state's profits from trade.
Larger surpluses were therefore earned; and the more serious potential
opponents of the change in state organization were rather obviously con-
ciliated by being given a generous share of the larger surpluses. Neither
the bronze-armed upper class nor the sanctuaries of the gods appear to
have been skimped or scanted.

By the end of the process, to be sure, the lion's share of state
surpluses evidently found its way into the storerooms and treasure chambers of the royal palaces. But we may not suppose that this was the state
of affairs from the outset. The transformation of Bronze Age Greek society
is most likely to have been accomplished by gradual stages, perhaps beginning when one of the mainland rulers first employed specialized persons
to administer the royal domains and trading ventures; thence widening into
orderly recording of tax receipts; and then expanding, bit by bit, until the
final stage of close approximation to the *oikos* economic pattern of the
ancient Oriental monarchies. It must have been a complex and sometimes

touchy business—this aggrandizement of the rulers of the larger, more successful Greek Bronze Age kingdoms, until they at length reached the status of "the one man, the unique man," at any rate in the economic and administrative sense.

When I was a young reporter in New York, an older man who was rightly much imitated by his juniors used to ponder a new political development; then he would say, "If it did not happen exactly like that, it must have happened pretty much like that"; and then, guided by his own knowledgeable reconstruction of what had probably happened, he would go out and learn what really had happened. Most often, his reconstruction would turn out to be correct; and the fact that he generally knew what to look for also greatly eased and speeded his inquiries. As we are dealing in this instance with the Bronze Age, there is no way to go out and check the reconstruction that has been offered above with the best current sources of information. Except for the archaeological record that has been used as the basis of the reconstruction, no sources of information exist; and the reconstruction can only be proved, or disproved, or made to seem less probable or more probable, when further excavation amplifies the archaeological record. But if you think about how the late Greek Bronze Age kingdoms finally approximated the ancient Oriental economic pattern, you are all but driven to conclude that "if it did not happen exactly like that, it must have happened pretty much like that."

Moreover, I think we can go even further than this reconstruction of the probable stages of Greek society's transformation in the Bronze Age. At first glance, the archaeological record looks sparse and naked— a mere heap of bare bones of the past, as it were. But if the record is carefully tested for political implications, I believe it can be made to show not only how Greek Bronze Age society was probably transformed but also about when the final transformation probably took place. For this purpose, appropriately enough, it is best to start with the story of

Pylos, where the secret of the tablets began to be unlocked. Briefly recapitulating, Messenia, though rich and fertile, seems to have been a politically backward area of small hill baronies and petty kingdoms until Nestor's father, Thessalian Neleus, descended on the land and unified it by force. Large numbers of tombs, some of them very handsome, like the tholoi that led Blegen to Pylos, attest the wealth of the land. The grave goods not only prove the prosperity of the region; they also point to a wide-ranging trade. Yet the scale of these Messenian states or baronies must have been minuscule by our standards; for there were certainly several of them in the narrow area—less than 50 by 100 miles—which Neleus later subjugated. None the less, the fragment of defense wall and the gate towers on the

*Carved limestone ceiling*
*of the side chamber of*
*the "Treasury of Minyas,"*
*Orchomenos.*

hilltop at Epano Englianos, which belong to the time before Neleus, are the earliest Mycenaean stone fortifications in Greece. They hardly compare with the great defensive works of the later period, but they are unique all the same, for they date from the fifteenth century B.C., whereas the first Cyclopean wall of Mycenae is dated in the middle of the fourteenth century, as has been seen. Perhaps all the special features of pre-Neleid Messenia—the smallness of its subdivisions, the earliness of the fortifications above-noted, and the vulnerability of the region when Neleus attacked it—are to be explained by the existence of endemic feuds among the region's barons and petty kinglets. At any rate, Messenia had some sort of weakness which made it vulnerable, and since the region was naturally rich, we must assume it was a political weakness. Otherwise, the enterprise of Neleus would not have succeeded. Even after Neleus had established his kingdom, moreover, what are best described as frontier conditions must have prevailed for a while. This much may be judged from Nestor's account in the *Iliad* of the cattle raids of his youth—the same account that has led to so many arguments about Pylian geography. But when Nestor built his own palace, on a much larger, grander scale than his father had attempted, the strength and wealth of the kingdom must have increased very greatly. For the last stage of Pylos, the story is the same. In the clay tablet archive there is no hint of frontier conditions, despite the preparations to repel invasion. The inventories instead suggest conspicuous, even showy luxury. And the herds in the scribes' cattle censuses altogether dwarf the herds that Nestor boasted about recapturing from border raiders—although we may safely assume that the old man did not diminish this feat of his youth.

From the Pylian story, two strikingly interesting points emerge. In the first place, almost the whole development took place in only a century, between 1300 B.C., when Neleus built his first palace, and 1200 B.C., when the palace of Nestor went up in flames. Unification and organization evidently led to rapid economic progress. Nestor's high place on the *Iliad* ship list confirms the evidence of his building activities; the enrichment of the Pylian kingdom must therefore have gone forward at a truly remarkable rate in the first decades after Messenia was brought under one rule. This is noteworthy in itself. Yet I think the rather late date of Neleus' palace is even more noteworthy. Messenia, after all, was a distinctly tempting target, being greener and more fertile than the Eastern Peloponnese. It was also a fairly easy target, as its conquest by Neleus proved. Once again, the dangers of the argument from absence need to be remembered; yet it still strikes me as pretty remarkable that someone else—the king of Mycenae, for instance—did not think of doing what Neleus did and at a much earlier date. If Greece had been crowded, and the larger states had been land-hungry, someone else surely would have thought of doing what Neleus did. From this, it seems to me a fair guess that the period of the Greek mainland kingdoms' greatest power and highest organization must be placed quite late on the time-scale. Otherwise, the odds on Neleus' being forestalled would have been very high indeed.

That conclusion is also strongly confirmed by the evidence of the general archaeological record. Barring tombs, the greatest structures in the greatest Greek kingdoms of the Bronze Age are all quite late in date —as has been noted, the first Cyclopean walls of Mycenae itself were built only about 1350 B.C., and this is also the approximate date of the first true palace that can be shown to have been built there. Beginning in the fourteenth century, however, there was an extraordinary surge of grandiose building activity in all the more important kingdoms. Semi-competitively, as it seems, the Greek states then began encircling their citadels with huge walls, providing their living kings with splendid frescoed halls, and laying away their dead kings in tholos-tombs that steadily increased in size and grandeur. Furthermore, the structures of the thirteenth century B.C. are generally much more ambitious than the structures of the fourteenth century. At Mycenae, as we have seen, the largest

*View from the door*
*of the "Treasury of Atre*

and most imposing of all the royal tombs, the Treasury of Atreus, is dated about 1250 B.C. by Professor Mylonas. The new Cyclopean walls, with their great Lion Gate, are also dated about 1250; and the new walls take in a much larger circumference and are in all ways far more impressive than the fortifications that were built a hundred years earlier. In general, the rule seems to have held true for about a century, that each new structure exceeded its predecessors; at Tiryns, for instance, the parts of the fortifications in which the stones of most staggering size appear are also the parts that are latest in date.

From all these facts, it is reasonable to draw the obvious political and economic conclusions. More than one expert has written about the late Bronze Age in Greece as a time of fear and impoverishment. But it runs counter to human experience for states to undertake greater and greater public works while their wealth declines. If there was impoverishment, it must have begun toward the end of the thirteenth century, when trade was disrupted by the new folk movements that are indicated by the attack on Egypt of the "peoples of the sea." If there was fear among the Greek states, too, it is most likely to have been fear of one another, at any rate until the time after the Trojan War. After all, Greek states of the classical period were seldom good neighbors; and Bronze Age Greek kings with more and more treasure in their storerooms must have wanted stronger and stronger walls to discourage neighborly acquisitiveness. From the early fourteenth century down to the second half of the thirteenth century B.C., in fact, the archaeological record in reality indicates a major, rapid and continuous increase in the wealth of the major Greek states. Without such an increase in wealth, these states—only relatively major and very small in land area—could not have met the calls on their resources that were inevitably made by all their tomb-building and palace-building and wall-building.

It further seems to me that we must suppose that the population also increased in this period, and that the people were better organized as well for the service of the state. Consider, for instance, what was built at Mycenae in the mid-thirteenth century. The Lion Gate, the new Cyclopean walls, the Treasury of Atreus, the enlarged palace within the citadel, the improved stone-built roads radiating out to all parts of the kingdom, and the other great tombs that are close in date to the Treasury of Atreus must have required really enormous levies of corvée laborers, as has already been pointed out. This is because all the earth was moved, and all the stone was quarried and dressed and dragged into place by manpower alone. That is proof enough that Agamemnon inherited an extremely populous kingdom, as well as a kingdom great in wealth and power; for nothing is more dangerous or debilitating than imposing heavy, continuous labor-corvées on too small a population. (In ancient Chinese history, the comment that the corvées were light and were ordered only after the harvests had been gathered, regularly recurs in accounts of prosperous and beneficent imperial reigns.) Furthermore, the ability to command labor-service on such a big scale, and to direct it with such success, has another most important implication. It points, in fact, to precisely the kind of state organization that we find in the Pylos archive of Linear B tablets.

Indeed, we can go still further than we have gone above, and with fair confidence. The phenomena we have been discussing—the widespread, grandiose surge of building, the evidence of the use of labor service on a big scale, and so on—not only point to a particular kind of state organization. They also suggest, as they are new phenomena, that this particular kind of state organization was a recent introduction. On the sole topic of the political significance of bouts of architectural construction, a whole essay might be written, but for our purposes a few examples will suffice. The Emperor Augustus did not find Rome brick and leave it marble, solely because he preferred marble to brick. His prior organization of the Empire both made possible his reconstruction of the capital city, and demanded this glorification of the imperial center. In the same fashion, a modest hunting lodge became the palace of Versailles by order of Louis XIV, but the social-political foundations of Versailles were laid before Louis himself took over the reins of power, by Richelieu and Mazarin. Or if we seek a case closer in character to the Greek case we have been examining, there is the highly apposite story of the beginning of large scale public construction in Japan. In brief, as we have seen, writing probably reached the Kansai center of the Imperial clan during the reign of the Emperor Nintoku, in the fifth century A.D. But for some time thereafter, there was no radical change in the organization of Japanese society, which was more conservative than Greek society and also much more remote from the models it imitated. During this period, there was no fixed capital, the death of each emperor being the signal for a move to a new site, and the construction of a new palace. During this period, too, the palaces were almost certainly in the extremely simple, almost farmhouse-like style of which the Grand Shrine at Ise preserves the beautiful model. The great change in Japan dates from the seventh century, when the famous regent, Prince Shotoku, carried out his "constitutional reform." This partially successful attempt at wholesale borrowing of Chinese methods may be reasonably equated with the transformation of Greek society, by adoption of the methods of the Oriental *oikos*-type economy. And from Prince Shotoku onwards, the grandiose architecture which had never before been attempted, became more and more commonplace in Japan. The first great surviving structure, the Horyuji temple, was begun, according to tradition, by Shotoku himself, and it still conserves his portrait statue which was first brought to light once more by Ernest Fenollosa after being hidden in linen wrappings for something like a millennium. The next stage, after Prince Shotoku, was the adoption of a fixed and permanent capital city. Then came the marvels of Nara. From all this, it is logical to draw the probable (though of course not certain) inference that a social-political change of the kind we have been exploring was the immediate prelude to the near-orgy of palace- and wall- and tomb-building in late Mycenaean Greece.

There is another "join" that can be made here, too, as the students of the clay tablets might put it. In brief, the character of all this burdensome and costly building activity fits very neatly with its other implications. Its character means that the kings were now taking the lion's share and more than the lion's share; for every one of the more imposing structures of the late Greek Bronze Age was designed to provide a palace setting for a living king, or a place of honor for the last remains of a dead king, or to ensure the impregnability of a royal citadel. The king was now the center, the mainspring, the all-controlling, all-directing head of the society, just as the Linear B tablets indicate that he was.

So much, then, for the points and conclusions that can be wrung from the still-inadequate evidence at our disposal. Review them all. Then ask, about when did the major Greek Bronze Age states enter the last stage of the astonishing transformation revealed by the Linear B tablets? To this question, it seems to me that the most probable answer is that the last stage of the transformation began about 1400 B.C. or a little later. The aim of the stricter, more centralized organization of the state was to increase the state's resources. It is reasonable to allow about a generation for resources to accumulate, as a result of tighter state organization, before the real surge of building activity started. This happened, just as might be expected, in the mid-fourteenth century. And I think it is also reasonable to guess that by this date—say by the date of Mycenae's first Cyclopean walls in 1350 B.C.—the organization of the larger Greek states had at least reached a form foretelling the final form found in the Linear B archives. Some such organization was needed for such construction works.

But if this kind of organization had existed earlier, we ought to have more remains of earlier buildings to give evidence that it had come into being.

These considerations in turn dictate my own hunch concerning the competing answers to the problem of the Minoan-Mainland Greek relationship. The two historic schemes outlined in the previous chapter and the additional scheme proposed in this chapter are all theoretically feasible. Curiously enough, however, the scheme putting the Greeks into Crete at an early date seems to me to fit the facts of the Minoan story rather better than it fits the facts of the Greek story. To my eye, for instance, there is more than a hint of the Greek genius in the humanistic, life-celebrating masterworks of the second palace period; and there is nothing Asian in these wonderful objects, although the Minoans were presumably of Asian origin. It is easy to imagine these things being produced by the infusion of a new Greek spirit into the old Minoan civilization. But if you look at the archaeological record on the Greek mainland, the theory of an early Greek invasion of Crete seems less persuasive. The point is that the model for the final transformation of Greek Bronze Age society is provided rather too soon, if a Greco-Minoan state is assumed to have existed in Crete as early as the sixteenth century B.C. In that event, the feedback into mainland Greece ought also to have begun earlier than the mainland evidence suggests. Hence the times work better, so to say, if you assume a somewhat later Greek landing in Crete, and therefore a later series of social-political borrowings and transforming changes on the mainland.

Perhaps the turning point was the catastrophe in Crete, which Professor Marinatos dates to about 1520 B.C. and explains as volcanic in origin. The devastation of Crete would have provided the mainland Greeks with an opportunity hard to resist; and in that event, the Greco-Minoan state in Crete would date from the very late sixteenth century. But there is a clear possibility that in the sixteenth century Greek mainland

ociety was not as yet far enough evolved to respond rapidly to the impact
if a newly formed Greco-Minoan state across the water. And there is also
clear possibility that the correct chronology will turn out to be the one first
>roposed by Professor Blegen.

The truth is that the needed data are now lacking, on which to
>ase a firm choice between the alternative solutions of the problem. Cer-
ain ground rules are indeed suggested by historical experience outside the
Aegean Bronze Age. It is wrong, for instance (as the Linear B decipher-
nent has already proved), to base an argument for continuity of rule
>n the absence of a "break" in the archaeological record. It is wrong,
again, to assume that Linear B must have rapidly replaced Linear A, im-
nediately after a Greek conquest of Knossos; indeed, the opposite assump-
ion ought to be made, if it is also assumed that the Greeks were illiterate
it the time of their conquest. Finally, it is also wrong to exclude the possi-
>ility that Linear B originated on the mainland, and was then carried
>ack into Crete. But these ground rules are all negative. On the positive
ide, meanwhile, there are all sorts of combinations of untested possibilities.
t is possible, for instance, that the Linear B script was devised on the
nainland much earlier than anyone now supposes, and that it went on
>eing written in exactly the same way for a very long time, like the
uneiform scripts noticed by Professor Blegen, or the English "lawyer's
1and," which is only now going out of use. In that event, the Greek conquerors of Knossos may have been accompanied by their own scribes.
Their arrival may in fact be reflected by the signs of trouble* in the palace
>f Minos in the mid-fifteenth century; and the Linear B archive of the
Knossos palace may then commemorate a Greek occupation perhaps en-
luring only a little more than half a century, and ending about 1400 B.C.,

---

* For a conquest of course can leave such traces. The error is assuming that it
must do so.

271

when Evans said the great palace was abandoned forever, except for those squatters. This is close to the scheme impressively advocated by Dr. Emily Townsend Vermeule in her study of the problem. One prime objection to the scheme of course lies in the lack of any indications, in the fifteenth century archaeological record on the Greek mainland, of the kind of social advance that ought to have preceded the invention of a script—and especially a script employed mainly for administration, which has left no trace whatever of any priestly use. But this in turn merely suggests, I think, where we must look for the final solution of this problem that lies at the very center of the story of our own beginnings. Concerning the course of Greek development between 1700 and 1400 B.C., our main evidence now comes from graves. We may guess, we may deduce, we may reconstruct, as I have boldly done. When the detailed course of Greek development in these centuries is known, the guesses may even be justified. Yet experience teaches that even the best guesses, even guesses that are true in themselves, never reach more than halfway to the complete truth about the remote past. Fortunately, the Greek archaeological record for this crucial period will surely be enriched and amplified by the field archaeologists' spades before very long. Much is to be hoped from the excavation of Iolkos, which is just about the only known major Mycenaean Greek site that is undisturbed and fully stratified. Much is probably to be hoped, too, from the excavation of subsidiary sites, such as the centers of the baronies or petty kingdoms that existed in Messenia before Neleus. Eventually, in sum, hard answers will surely be given, first by new findings of the field archaeologists, and then by the unending dialogue of the brilliant company of learned men and women of many nations, who have given their lives to interpreting the new data that the field archaeologists unearth. Meanwhile, this essay's aim is neither to give any answer, nor to argue any case, except the case for a more careful re-appraisal of the facts already known; and its other aims are only to lay out those facts in an intelligible manner, and to suggest the kind of political processes that may be dimly discerned behind the facts.

As we approach this essay's end, the temptation is all but irresistible to speculate on the different course that history might have taken if the Mycenaean Greek society had not been so suddenly and completely destroyed. Would the main Greek states have gone on growing richer and more populous, until they were seriously crowding one another and the stronger began to gobble up the weaker? Would the late form of state organization have gone on growing more palace-centered, more palace-directed, until the last vestiges of the Greeks' Indo-European origins were finally forgotten? Should we then have inherited, from our own earliest beginnings, a rather different tradition resulting from the survival of Mycenaean ways into the Iron Age? Here, after all, was where the story of Western civilization began, and all of us would have been affected somehow if Mycenaean Greek society had continued into the fully historical era. But such speculation is always fruitless. The truth is that time and history always give the verdict, from which there is no appeal.

As so often before and since, the verdict of time and history on the Greek Bronze Age civilization was both cruel and final. This first civilization inspired by the Greek genius had started from rude beginnings; it had achieved great things; it had gone through a course of evolution as remarkable as it was strange. These first Greeks, together with the creative Minoans, had in fact reached one of the early peaks of human accomplishment. But all of history is no more than a remorseless cycle of decline and resurgence, of destruction and reconstruction, of death and rebirth; and so time's passage brought the civilization of the Mycenaean Greeks to its term at last. Dust and ashes not only covered the hilltop of Epano Englianos where this essay began; dust and ashes not only covered every other major Bronze Age site in Greece except the Athenian Acropolis; dust and ashes also covered many another famous center of the other Bronze Age civilizations of the Mediterranean and the Near East. For the

273

end of the second millennium B.C., like the end of the third, was another time of troubles marked by great, convulsive folk movements and sudden emergences of new peoples upon the stage of history. Priam's Troy fell in 1260 B.C. if Professor Blegen is correct. A few decades later, Egypt suffered the first onslaught of the "peoples of the sea." Then came the Dorian invasion of Greece. Then once again the peoples of the sea were at Egypt's throat. The sea peoples were beaten off, but Egypt none the less entered her final decline. Meanwhile all Anatolia and Syria-Palestine were already in upheaval. Mitanni fell very early; Assyria rose; the Hittites went under; and the nations that had once been rude and humble, like the twelve tribes of Israel, seized places in the sun amid the general ruin. The world men had known for so long came to its close, only to be renewed again in another form. The Bronze Age ended, and the Age of Iron then began.

# ILLUSTRATIONS

*The present locations of objects appear in italics.*

276

277

# ENGLISH READING LIST

BENNETT, E. L., JR. *Olive Oil Tablets of Pylos*, Salamanca, 1958.

———. *Pylos Tablets, Preliminary Transcription*, Princeton, 1955.

BLEGEN, C. W. *Troy and the Trojans*, New York, 1963.

BLEGEN, C. W. *et al. Troy* (4 vols.), Princeton, 1950-58.

BOARDMAN, J. (with L.'R. Palmer). *On the Knossos Tablets*, Oxford, 1963.

BOWRA, C. M. *Heroic Poetry*, London, 1952.

———. *Tradition and Design in the Iliad*, Oxford, 1930.

CHADWICK, J. *The Decipherment of Linear B*, Cambridge and New York, 1958.

DOW, S. "The Greeks of the Bronze Age" (first published in the proceedings of the XIe Congrès International des Sciences Historiques at Stockholm, 1960, 1-34, reprinted in *The Language and Background of Homer*, ed. by G. S. Kirk, Cambridge, 1964).

EVANS, A. J. *The Palace of Minos at Knossos*, Vols. I-IV, London and New York, 1921-36.

FURUMARK, A. *The Chronology of Mycenaean Pottery*, Stockholm, 1941.

———. *The Mycenaean Pottery: Analysis and Classification*, Stockholm, 1941.

GRAHAM, J. W. *The Palaces of Crete*, Princeton, 1962.

GRUMACH, ERNST (ed.). *Minoica* (*Festschrift* for Johannes Sundwall on his eightieth birthday), Berlin, 1958.

GUTHRIE, W. K. C. *The Greeks and Their Gods*, London, 1950, and Boston, 1955.

HEICHELHEIM, F. *An Ancient Economic History*, Leiden, 1958, and New York, in prep.

279

HUTCHINSON, R. W. *Prehistoric Crete,* Harmondsworth and Boston, 1962.

HUXLEY, G. L. *Achaeans and Hittites,* Oxford, 1960.

JEFFERY, L. H. *The Local Scripts of Archaic Greece,* Oxford, 1961.

KENNA, V. E. G. *Cretan Seals,* Oxford, 1960.

LORIMER, H. *Homer and the Monuments,* London, 1950.

MARINATOS, S. *Crete and Mycenae,* London and New York, 1960.

MATZ, F. *The Art of Crete and Early Greece,* New York, 1962.

MYLONAS, GEORGE. *Ancient Mycenae,* London and Princeton, 1957.

NILSSON, M. P. *The Minoan-Mycenaean Religion,* Ed. 2., Lund, 1950.

————. *The Mycenaean Origin of Greek Mythology,* Cambridge and Berkeley, 1932.

————. *Homer and Mycenae,* London, 1933.

PAGE, D. L. *History and the Homeric Iliad,* Berkeley and Los Angeles, 1959.

PALMER, L. R. *Interpretation of Mycenaean Greek Texts,* Oxford, 1963.

————. *Mycenaeans and Minoans,* London, 1961, and New York, 1962.

————. (with J. Boardman). *On the Knossos Tablets,* Oxford, 1963.

PENDLEBURY, J. D. S. *The Archeology of Crete,* London and New York, 1939.

SINGER, C.; HOLMYARD, E.; HALL, A.; WILLIAMS, T. (eds.). *A History of Technology,* Vols. 1-5, Oxford, 1954-58.

STARR, C. G. *The Origins of Greek Civilization,* New York, 1961.

STUBBINGS, F. H. *Mycenaean Pottery from the Levant,* Cambridge, 1951.

TAYLOUR, LORD WILLIAM. *Mycenaean Pottery in Italy and Adjacent Areas,* Cambridge, 1958.

VENTRIS, M. G. F., and CHADWICK, J. (eds.). *Documents in Mycenaean Greek,* Cambridge, 1956.

VERMEULE, E. *Greece and the Bronze Age,* Chicago, 1964. (Worth special notice as the most recent and most comprehensive scholarly treatment of the problem which is also readable.)

WACE, A. J. B. *Mycenae,* London and Princeton, 1949.

WACE, A. J. B., and STUBBINGS, F. H. (eds.). *A Companion to Homer,* London, 1962, and New York, 1963.

WEBSTER, T. B. L. *From Mycenae to Homer,* London, 1958, and New York, 1959.

and the following fascicles of *The Cambridge Ancient History:*

Vol. I, Chap. VI, STUBBINGS, F. H., "Chronology—The Aegean Bronze Age"

Vol. I, Chap. XXVI(a), CASKEY, J., "Greece, Crete, and the Aegean Islands in the Early Bronze Age"

Vol. II, Chap. IV(b) and XII, MATZ, F., "Minoan Civilization Maturity and Zenith"

Vol. II, Chap. XIV, STUBBINGS, F. H., "The Rise of Mycenaean Civilization"

Vol. II, Chap. XXXVI, DESBOROUGH, V., and HAMMOND, N., "The End of Mycenaean Civilization and the Dark Age"

281

# INDEX

Hera, 70
Herodotus, 129
Hieroglyphic script (Crete), 166, 166n, 167-68
Historians, 3
Historical analogies, 206
Historical experience, 219-20, 271
Historical parochialism, 206, 253
Historic scale, problem of, 83-85, 88
History: argument from absence, 252, 264; cycle of, 273; in Homer, 5-6; laws, 205; reappraising, 236, 244; self-transformation, rarity of, 245; truth vs. error, 38; Usher's chronology, 4; verdict of, 273
Hittites, 83-85, 168, 274; archives, 84; Asia Minor, 89; culture, 5; -Greeks, 91, 95; kingship, 246
Holy Roman Empire, coronation cape, 204-5
Homer: Achaeans, 130; archaeologists' confirmations of, 73, 81; birthplace, 156; Blegen, 23; Bronze Age kings, 69; *corps d'élite*, xii; communications, 104-5; epics, 126, 128, 154-55, Achaean civilization, 130, composition theory, 80-81; heroes, and Linear B tablets, 124; historical context, 79; historical reliability, 23; history in, 5-6; Idomeneus, 236; Knossos, 184; Mycenae, 11; Nestor, 46-47; omissions, 83, 156; Pylos, 1, 82, 149; reliability of, 82; Schliemann, xiii, 4, 6; ship lists, 96 (*see also under Iliad*); Tiryns, 96; wines, 72
"Horn of consecration," 70, *ill.* 71
Horses: Cortes, 42, 90; Greeks, 42, 90; Troy, 42-43
Hsu Cho-yun, xvii
Hulagu Khan, 212-13
Hyksos kings, 173

Ibn-Saud, 254
Idomeneus, King, 98, 186
*Iliad*, 2, 5-6, 8, 82, 263; bases, 81-82; composition: date, 155, locale, 155; Greek

social unity, 104; Knossos, 184; Nestor's drinking cup, 56; *Odyssey*, relation to, 80; Pylos location, 24; ship list, 23, 120, 263-64
Illiteracy, 153-54
Illyria, 135n
Immerwahr, Sara, 95
Incas, 212, 225n
India: Aryans, 4, 89; British in, 213; earliest civilization, 79; Moghul conquerors, 213
Indo-European folk wanderings, 88-89, 108
Indonesia, 5
Indus Valley, 4, 5
Inouye, Mitsusada, xviii
Iolkos, 91, 98; excavation, 272
Ionian Greece, 155
Ionic dialect, 130
Iran, 89
Iraq, 41, 211-12
Iron Age, 273, 274
Iron weapons, xii, 154
Ischia, Mycenaean pottery, 94
Israel: Children of, 90; salt studies, 85
Italy: Greek trade with, 120; Mycenaean pottery, 94; Phaistos excavation, 14, 16, 157
Ithaca, Schliemann and, 7
Ivories, Mycenaean Greek, 122

Japan: architecture, 268; Meiji restoration, 245; Nara, 268; self-transformation, 245; script, 224, 226; Yoritomo, 231, 232
Jeffery, L. H., 223n
Jordan, 86
*Journal of Hellenic Studies,* 173

Kadesh, battle of, 84
Kalamata, 39, 43, 47
Kamares ware, 161, *ill.* 161; first palaces, *ill.* 288
K'ang Hsi, Emperor, 217
Karnak, temple of, 84
Karouzos, Christos, xviii

Linear B tablets, 13, 21, 28, 29, 53, 167, *ill.*
17, 28, 31, 140, 141, 221; accuracy of
evidence, 74-75; class differences, 110;
decipherment: problems posed by, 93,
significance of, 79; Evans, 18; Homer,
89; illiteracy, 153-54; interpretation of,
75; invasion preparations (Pylos), 138,
140-48; labor-service, 115; land-owner-
ship, 110; Mycenaean Greek monarchy,
93; Myres' publication, 29; origin, 36,
222-27; number, 138-40; palace treasures, 123; pottery-sequence, 41; ration
scales, 116-17; religious sanctuaries,
147; "rower," 142, 143-44; salt, 84n;
scribes- disproportion, 139; society
revealed by, 105ff., 109, 244, 248, 256,
269-70; users, 125; Ventris' decipherment, 30-35, *ill.* 31
Lion-Gate (Mycenae), 23, 24, 175, 266,
267, *ill.* 25
Lion Kingdom, 19
Literacy, 125-26
Lloyd, Seton, 168n
*Local Scripts of Archaic Greece,* 223n
Louis XIV, King of France, 268
Luvians, 168-69, 183, 242; Palmer theory,
169-70, 171n
Luxury, power of, 232

McDonald, W.A., 28
Mackenzie, Duncan, 182
Mallia, 16, 166; art objects, *ill.* 159; ex-
cavations, 236; palaces, 158, 160;
second palaces, 163-64; Sarpedon, 160
Manchuria, 216
Manchus, 216-17, 218n
Maoris, 90
Marco Polo, 216
Marcus Agrippa, 100
Marinatos, Spyridon, 76, 172, 174, 198-99,
233, 270; Cretan catastrophe, 166;
*Crete and Mycenae,* 159, 162, 236-37;
Knossos predominance, 236; scarlet
gloves, 233, 259, *ill.* 232
Marriage, control of, 225n

"Mask of Agamemnon," 7, *ill.* 7
Massinissa, King, 224
Matz, Friedrich, 198, 199, 240; Crete-Greek
art objects similarity, 193
Mazarin, 268
*Megaron,* 57, 91-92
Megiddo, 122
Mellaart, James, 168n
Menelaus, King, 83, 98, 105
Mercenary soldiers, 173, 174, 179
Mesopotamia, 5; copper weapons, 87;
ration scales, 117
Messara plain, 16, 160
Messenia, 26, 43, 262ff.; centralized rule,
45; Neleus, 67; Nestor, 50; royal
tombs, 46; subsidiary sides, excavation,
272; taxes, 52; unification, 45
Mexico, 52, 90
Middle Ages, Homer's heroes, 5-6
Middle East, petroleum and, 85, 86
Middle Minoan, 157
Military matters: bronze, 50, 87; conserva-
tism, xii; mercenary soldiers, 173,
174, 179. *See* Weaponry
Mimnermus, 150, 155
Minoans: art: creative vision shift, 241-43,
"torsion principle," 240; bull-games,
163; chronology, 74; civilization, 14,
17; decline, 180; end of, 167; Evans,
35, 74; first palaces period, 158, 160-
161, 162, 234-35; gold votive double
axes, *ill.* 13; Grecianization, 236;
-Greeks relationship, 176, 178ff.,
186ff., 209-10, prior to conquest, 228-
229; history, 157ff.; "horn of consecration," 70, *ill.* 71; imperialism, 18-19,
35; Mycenae, x-xi, 178; navy, 177-78;
neolithic culture, 158, 159; origin,
18-19, 74, 167-69, 170; outpost/colon-
ies, 177, 178, 180; political organization, 164, 166; priest-king, 107;
prosperity, 85; second palaces period,
158, 160-61, 163-64, 166, 168, 235;
thalassocracy, 176-77; unification, 236

Minos, King, 160; historical-mythological, 14; navy, 177; palace of, 12-13, 18, 19, 166, 235; thalassocracy, 14
Minyas, *see* Treasury of Minyas
Missionary scripts, 223
Mitanni, 274; Asia Minor, 89
Mochlos, art objects, *ill.* 159
Moghuls, 213-14
Mohenjo-Daro, 4, 5, 79
Monarch, authority of, 124
Mongkut, King, 5
Mongols, 212
Moses, 90
Mount Aigaleon, 47
Mubarrak the Great, Sheikh, 146
Mühlestein, H., 148
Mursilis, King, 95
Muwatallis, King, 84
Mycenae: Agamemnon, 55; archaeological history, 170; Argos rule, 24n; argument from absence, 252; art, x; bronze body armor, *ill.* 255; bronze dagger blade from grave circle, *ill.* 81; building activity, 266-69; bull's-head rhyton, 189, *ill.* 189; centers, 91; citadel, 252, *ill.* 247; civilization, x-xi, xii, 36, 82; Crete, conquest of, xii-xiii; Cyclopean walls, 174, 263, 264, 266, 267, 269-70; dagger with Nile scene, 172, *ill.* 172; destruction levels, 135; -Egypt, 21, 172-73, 174; end of, xii, 129-34, 148, 151-52, 153, 176; Evans, 12, 18-20, 29; excavation, 252; fresco fragment, *ill.* 122; "fire-scar," 134; gold, 56; gold diadem, 61-62; gold necklace, *ill.* 103; grave circles, 152, 171, 174, 251, *ill.* 8-9, death mask, *ill.* 171, diadem, *ill.* 105, first, 179, 235, 248, ornaments, 7, *ill.* 6, second, 248, 252; Greece-overseas, 95; Greek-speakers, 91; history, 170-76; "horn of consecration," 70, *ill.* 71; independence, 24n; iron rings, 88; kings, 251-52; late mon-archies-Oriental economies, 108-9; Lion-Gate, 23, 24, 175, 266, 267, *ill.*

25; lion's head rhyton, 188, *ill.* 187; location, 23-24, 45; mercenary soldiers, 173; origin, 19, 88ff.; palace, 50, 81, bureaucracies, 151; Phoenician trading post, 82, 244; population, xii, 99; pottery, 94, 169; raw materials, 87; road systems, 105; ruling family, 249; Schliemann, viii, 7, 18, 23; scribes, 52; secret cistern, *ill.* 175; silver pitcher, 194, *ill.* 194; society: heroic, 128, and history, 74, Pylos tablets, 82-83, transformation, 248ff.; tombs, 10, 56, 100, 102, 122, jewelry, *ill.* 249, 250; trade, 94-95, 96; treasure trove, 10-11; Treasury of Atreus, 175, 197, 198, 266, 267, *ill.* 265; Ventris, xiii; Wace, 19-22, 36; walls, 46, 84, 146, 174, 263, 264, 266, 267, 269-70; warriors: aristocracy, 108, grave circle, *ill.* 136, vase, *ill.* 80, 127; wealth, 85, 102, 104, 172, 173-74, 252; weaponry, 145
*Mycenaeans and Minoans,* 74, 117, 138
Mylonas, George, 152, 169, 252-53; on Cirrha findings, 174n; Mycenae, 153, 170-76; Treasury of Atreus, 266
Myres, John, 29, 34, 75
Myths, 96

Nabataeans, 86
Navarino Bay, 1, 47, *ill.* 3
Near East, royal economies, 248
Nehru, Jawaharlal, 4
Neleids, 72, 150
Neleus, 45-46, 73, 146; descendants, 150; palace, 46-47, 51, 69, 100, 152, construction date, 46, site, 69; rule of Messenia, 67
Nestor, King of Pylos, 1-2, 50, 83, 96, 110, 143; birth, 46; Blegen theory, 53-54; court, appearance of, 62; divinity, 108; drinking cup, 56; father, 45; historical context, 79; kingdom, 26, 53, 83; merchant theory, 53-54; oil trade, 55; palace, viii, 1-2, 45, 48-50, 152, *ill.* 46, 48, 49, 51, bath, 65-66, *ill.* 65,

292

Pizarro, Francisco, 208, 209, 212
Place names, 82, 88; military units, 142; Normandy, 213
Poetry: oral, tradition of, 80-81; survival from Bronze Age, 154-55
Poland, World War II, xii, 135, 137
Political processes, 202ff.: conquest, 208-218, 228ff., 234ff.; Linear B script, 222-27; objects, 203; power factors, 234-35; Pylos development, 261-64; ruins, 203; script change theory, 223-226; strata, 203; transformation of Bronze Age Greek society, 244ff., 258. *See also* Greco-Minoan synthesis
Population, 83, 85; 1800 B.C., 92; Knossos, 99; late Bronze Age, 266-67
Poseidon, 70
*Potnia,* 70; temple of, 147
Pottery, 118; Bronze Age remains, 54; Crete, second palaces period, *ill.* 239; Dark Ages, 154; geometric style, 154; Mycenaean, 94, 169; naturalism, 238; Nestor's palace, 53-54; periods, xvii; Pylos, 118, *ill.* 119; stirrup jar, 54-55, *ill.* 55; as time-indicator, 40-41
Power: relativity of, 85; wars, 84
Pre-Columbian civilizations, 5
Priam, King, 83; Schliemann, 10; Troy, 42, 43, 169
Priest-king theory, 107-8
Proto-Greeks, Mycenaean art, x
Ptolemies, 123, 225n
Pylos: administration, 110-17; airport, 39, 43; armed forces, 144; beauty, 39; Blegen rediscovery of, 23, 24, 26-30, 38; bronze weaponry, 136-37; censuses, 112, 115; confusion of experts, 3; Crown Prince-Queen Dowager theory, 69; cult of Clan Hero, 70, 72; destruction of, 82, 119, 129, 132, 148-49, 152; deities, 70; discoverer, ix; discovery, significance of, 79; Dorian invasion, 135, 148-49; Dorian trade contacts, 134, 136; economic organization, 106; excavation plan, 74; fleet,

120, 142, 143; fortifications, 46; frescoes, 62, 73, 77; frieze from propylon, *ill.* 76; geography, 134-35, 263; gold seal from tomb, *ill.* 44; Greek civilization, proof of, 3; "horn of consecration," 70; inlaid dagger from tomb, *ill.* 156; invasion (*see* Dorian invasion); inventory, 121, 122-23, 263; landholdings register, 139-40; *Lawagetas,* 64; location, mystery of, 23-24, 26; lyre-player fresco, *ill.* 61; museum for Pylos finds, 75-76; noble class, 62; palace, 41, 45, archive room, 52, burning of, 148-49, stirrup jars, 54-55, storerooms, 53, tax collector's office, 52, throne room, 124 (*see also under* Nestor); plumbing, 70; political development, 261-64; pottery, 118, *ill.* 119; refugees, 150; royal tomb, 56; ruins, xii; sanctuary, 70; size, 99; state organization, 156; tablets, 28, 29, 35, 53, 62-63, 67, 72, 256, *ill.* 28, 140, 141, Bronze Age society transformation, 260, confirmation of Homer, 82, invasion preparations, 133, 138, 140-48, Mycenaean age, picture of, 83, number of, 52, 138-40, records, 52-53, religious sanctuaries, 147, "rower," 142, 143-44, scribes, disproportionate number of, 139; votive shield, *ill.* 136; walls, 146; warrior aristocracy, 108; wealth, 134-135; wine cups, 73, *ill.* 118. *See also* Nestor
*Pylos Tablets, The,* 29, 30, 32, 34

Queen's bath (Knossos), *ill.* 257

Ramses II, 84
Ras Shamra, cuneiform records, 33
Rations, 146
Ration scales, 115-17
Raw materials, influence of, 85-87
Rawson, Marion, 73
Reischauer, Edwin, xvii
Religious sanctuaries, 147